AF560010

ENV BOOKS SERIES

SEED TECHNOLOGY PLANT GROWTH AND CROPPING SYSTEM

Editors

Dr. Pawan Kumar Tyagi
Managing Director
ECON Laboratory & Consultancy
Inderpur, Nawada Road, Dehradun - 248 005 (UK), India
Email: *econlab.consultancy@yahoo.in*

Dr. Pawan Kumar 'Bharti'
Vice President (Executive)
Society for Environment, Health, Awareness of Nutrition & Toxicology (SEHAT)
1775, Sohan Ganj, Near Clock Tower, Delhi - 7, India
E-mail: *gurupawanbharti@rediffmail.com*

Associate Editor
Dr. Mahadev Semwal
ECON Laboratory & Consultancy
Inderpur, Near Defense Colony Police Chawki
Nawada Road, Dehradun - 248 005 (UK), India

DISCOVERY PUBLISHING HOUSE PVT. LTD.
NEW DELHI-110 002

Published by:

Tilak Wasan

DISCOVERY PUBLISHING HOUSE PVT. LTD.

4383/4B, Ansari Road, Darya Ganj

New Delhi-110 002 (India)

Phone : +91-11-23279245, 43596064-65

Fax : +91-11-23253475

E-mail : discoverypublishinghouse@gmail.com

sales@discoverypublishinggroup.com

web : www.discoverypublishinggroup.com

***First Edition:* 2015**

ISBN: 978-93-5056-738-8

Seed Technology, Plant Growth and Cropping System

Printed at:

Infinity Imaging Systems

Delhi

ENV Books Series, India

Calls lengthy and error free chapters for further volumes of books on various environmental issues. (Send your manuscripts to envbooks@gmail.com)

Founding Editor (Editor-in-Chief)

Dr. Pawan Kumar 'Bharti'
Society for Environment, Health, Awareness of nutrition & Toxicology (SEHAT-India)
1775, Sohanganj, Near Clock Tower, Delhi-7, India
E-mail: gurupawanbharti@rediffmail.com

Other titles by Editor-in-Chief:

1. **Advances in Agriculture and Ecology (2013)**
Bharti, P.K.; Chauhan, A. and Ezeaku Peter Ikemefuna (eds.)
(ISBN: 978-93-5056-362-5).

2. **Advances in Biotechnology and Ecological Sciences (2013)**
Bharti, P.K., Chauhan, A. and Ray, J. (eds.)
(ISBN: 978-93-5056-358-8).

3. **Agriculture and Environmental Biotechnology (2014)**
Bharti, P.K. and Chauhan, A. (eds.)
(ISBN: 978-93-5056-479-0).

4. **Agriculture Ecology and Environment (2014)**
Bharti, P.K. and Olubukola O. Babalola (eds.)
(ISBN: 978-93-5056-480-6).

5. **Agro-forestry and Climate Change (2014)**
Bharti, Pawan K. and Singh, Narayan (eds.)
(ISBN: 978-93-5056-514-8).

6. **Aquaculture and Fisheries Environment (2014)**
Gupta, S.K. and Pawan K. Bharti (eds.)
(ISBN: 978-93-5056-408-0).

7. **Aquatic Biodiversity and Pollution (2013)**
Bharti, P.K.; Chauhan, A. and Kaoud, H.A.H. (eds.)
(ISBN: 978-93-5056-359-5).

8. **Aquatic Ecology and Biotechnology (2014)**
   Bharti, P.K. and Zaki, M.S.A. (eds.)
   (ISBN: 978-93-5056-451-6).

9. **Aquatic Environment and Toxicology (2013)**
   Bharti, Pawan K. (ed.)
   (ISBN: 978-93-5056-236-9).

10. **Biodiversity of Aquatic Ecosystem:**
    Significance, Threat and Conservation **(2013)**
    Bharti, P.K. and Kaoud, H.A.H. (eds.)
    (ISBN: 978-93-5056-297-0).

11. **Clean Technologies and Environmental Protection (2015)**
    Chauhan, A.; Sharma, S. and Bharti, P.K. (eds.)
    (ISBN: 978-93-5056-731-9).

12. **Climate Change and Agriculture (2012)**
    Bharti, P.K. and Chauhan, Avnish (eds.)
    (ISBN: 978-93-5056-148-5).

13. **Climate Change and Biodiversity (2013)**
    Bharti, P.K. and Chauhan, Avnish (eds.)
    (ISBN: 978-93-5056-360-1).

14. **Conservation and Cultivation of Medicinal Plants (2015)**
    Bharti, P.K. and Narayan Singh (eds.)
    (ISBN: 978-93-5056-740-1).

15. **Eco-toxicology and Eco-technology (2013)**
    Bharti, P.K. and Zaki, M. (eds.)
    (ISBN: 978-93-5056-313-7).

16. **Environmental Biotechnology and Application (2013)**
    Bharti, P.K. and Chauhan, Avnish (eds.)
    (ISBN: 978-93-5056-262-8).

17. **Environmental Conservation and Biotechnology (2014)**
    Chauhan, A. and P. K. Bharti (eds.)
    (ISBN: 978-93-5056-512-4).

18. **Environmental Health and Problems (2013)**
    Bharti, P.K. and Gajananda, Kh. (eds.)
    (ISBN: 978-93-5056-263-5).

19. **Environmental Pollution and Biodiversity (2012)**
    Bharti, P.K.; Chauhan, Avnish and Kumar, P. (eds.)
    (ISBN: 978-93-5056-149-2).

20. **Fisheries and Toxicology (2014)**
    Zaki, M.S.A.; Bharti, P.K. and Chauhan, A. (eds.)
    (ISBN: 978-93-5056-452-3).

21. **Freshwater Ecosystem and Xenobiotics (2013)**
Bharti, P.K.; Zaki, M. and Chauhan, A. (eds.)
(ISBN: 978-93-5056-299-4).

22. **Limnology and Aquatic Science (2015)**
Sharma, S. and Bharti, P.K. (eds.)
(ISBN: 978-93-5056-735-7).

23. **Medicinal Plants:**
Distribution, Utilization and Significance **(2015)**
Sharma, P.; Bharti, P. K. and Narayan Singh (eds.)
(ISBN: 978-93-5056-734-0).

24. **Microbial Applications and Environment (2014)**
Bharti, Pawan K. (ed.)
(ISBN: 978-93-5056-515-5).

25. **Microbial Ecology and Habitat (2014)**
Bharti, Pawan K. (ed.)
(ISBN: 978-93-5056-514-8).

26. **Prakriti me Aushadhi (*in Hindi*) (2012)**
Singh, J.R.; Bharti, P.K. and Bharti, B.
(ISBN: 978-93-5056-200-0).

27. **Soil Contamination and Conservation (2015)**
Bharti, P.K. and Ezeaku, P.I. (eds.)
(ISBN: 978-93-5056-737-1).

28. **Soil Quality and Contamination (2013)**
Bharti, P.K. and Chauhan, Avnish (eds.)
(ISBN: 978-93-5056-361-8).

29. **Waste Disposal and Management (2015)**
Bharti, P.K.; Tabassum, B. and Bajaj, P. (eds.)
(ISBN: 978-93-5056-729-6).

30. **Water Resources and Agriculture (2014)**
Bharti, P.K. and Ezeaku Peter Ikemefuna (eds.)
(ISBN: 978-93-5056-481-3).

Preface

Quality seed is an integral component of great relevance in tree improvement programme. In agriculture and forestry efforts are now on for production and use of superior and quality seeds to ensure better survival and growth of plantations undertaken under various programmes. Seed quality depends on factors like source, time and techniques of harvest, processing and storage practices. Unlike agriculture, the forestry seeds have great variation in size, shape, dormancy, viability, moisture content, etc. It needs special techniques for collection, handling, processing and storage of the seeds of the large number of forest species. The information available is scattered in diverse literature and publications. There was an urgent need to assemble some of this basic information in a comprehensive manner to be of use readily by agriculture technologists, foresters and others interested in growing trees and crops.

Feistritzer (1975): Defined seed technology as the method through which the genetic and physical characteristic of seeds could be improved.

It involves such activities as variety development, evaluation and release seed production, seed processing, seed storage, seed testing, seed certification, seed quality control, seed marketing, etc.

Seed technology includes the development of superior crop plant varieties, their evaluation and release, seed production, processing, seed storage, seed testing, seed quality control, seed certification, seed marketing, distribution and research on seed these aspects. Seed production, seed handling based on modern botanical and agricultural sciences. The role of seed technology is to protect the biological entity of seed and look after its welfare.

The three major functions that are basic to plant growth and development are:

Photosynthesis – The process of capturing light energy and converting it to sugar energy, in the presence of chlorophyll using carbon dioxide and water.

Respiration – The process of metabolizing (burning) sugars to yield energy for growth, reproduction, and other life processes.

Transpiration – The loss of water vapor through the stomata of leaves.

Plant growth is also determined by environmental factors, such as temperature, available water, available light, carbon dioxide and available nutrients in the soil. Any change in the availability of these external conditions will be reflected in the plant's growth.

Biotic factors are also capable of affecting plant growth. Plants compete with other plants for space, water, light and nutrients. Plants can be so crowded that no single individual produces normal growth, causing etiolation and chlorosis. Optimal plant growth can be hampered by grazing animals, suboptimal soil composition, lack of mycorrhizal fungi, and attacks by insects or plant diseases, including those caused by bacteria, fungi, viruses, and nematodes.

The term cropping system refers to the crops and crop sequences and the management techniques used on a particular field over a period of years.

The term cropping system refers to the crops and crop sequences and the management techniques used on a particular field over a period of years. This term is not a new one, but it has been used more often in recent years in discussions about sustainability of our agricultural production systems.

The present book provides comprehensive coverage of the fundamental principles and current practices and trends in the field of seed technology, factor responsible for plant growth, plant biotechnology, conservation and cultivation of rare plants, cropping system and agriculture management. This book updates the subject matter, illustrations and problems to incorporate new concepts and issues related to seed technology, plant biotechnology and crop system.

Thanks are due to contributors and publisher of the book. I hope this book will provide a multi-disciplinary forum to explore emerging areas in the field of seed technology, plant growth, plant biotechnology, cropping system and agriculture management.

–Editors
(envbooks@gmail.com)

Contents

Pages: 1-12

SEED TECHNOLOGY, PLANT GROWTH AND CROPPING SYSTEM
Edited by: Dr. Pawan Kumar Tyagi; Dr. Pawan Kumar 'Bharti'
ISBN: 978-93-5056-738-8
Edition: 2015
Published by: Discovery Publishing House Pvt. Ltd., New Delhi (India)

1

Community Based Seed Production
Panacea for Seed Security of Endangered Species

Chukwudi, U.P., and C.U. Agbo

INTRODUCTION

Agricultural sector employs about two-thirds of the Nigeria's total labour force, provides a livelihood for about 90% of the rural population and accounts for about 41% of the nation's Gross Domestic Product, 85% of which is from crop sub-sector (Liverpool *et al.*, 2009). Nigeria is the world's largest producer of cassava, yam and cowpea – all staple foods in sub-Saharan Africa (FAO, 2008), also a major producer of fish. Yet it is a food-deficit nation and imports large amounts of grain, livestock products and fish.

Despite Nigeria's plentiful agricultural resources and oil wealth, poverty is widespread in the country and has increased since the late 1990s. Over 50% and 70% of its general and rural population, respectively are now classified as poor, living on less than US $1 a day (Liverpool *et al.*, 2009).

Department of Crop Science, University of Nigeria, Nsukka, Nigeria.

Poverty is especially severe in rural areas, where up to 80% of the population lives below the poverty line and social services and infrastructure are limited. The country's poor rural women and men depend on agriculture for food and income. About 90% of Nigeria's food is produced by small-scale farmers who practice rain-fed rather than irrigated agriculture.

The successes of agricultural development in relation to agrobiodiversity have been variable and much disputed. While achievements in crop improvement in the last decades are undeniable, the needs of many poor farmer households have remained unaddressed and valuable genetic resources have been lost (Almekinders, 2001). Agrobiodiversity is the part of biodiversity that is directly relevant for agricultural production. It includes the genetic diversity within and between crops and animals used for agricultural production. Farmers and community access to the genetic resources embodied in seed is affected by the extent to which it is traded on markets or through other social institutions, as well as by related norms and legal frameworks, national and international agreements (Nagarajan and Smale, 2005). Due to bureaucratic bottleneck and poor enforcement of seed rules and harmonization of different nations' seed laws in developing agriculture, farmers' access to quality seeds is often limited.

There is an urgent need for more private companies to bridge this growing demand gap by farmers for better quality seeds. One promising strategy is the launch of Community Based Seed Production schemes to improve both seed production and marketing (Badu-Apraku, 2011). Nigeria is among the nations recognized by FAO (Food and Agriculture Organization) as technically unable to meet its food needs (CBN, 2007).

FOOD SECURITY

United States Agency for International Development (USAID) recognized three key elements as important in the definition of food security and these include: food availability, food access, and food utilization (World Bank, 1986).

Availability, access and utilization are hierarchical in nature. Food availability is necessary but not sufficient for food accessibility and access is necessary but not sufficient for utilization. In a larger sense, two broad groups of factors determine food security. These are supply side factors and demand side factors (Omonona and Agoi, 2007). The supply-side factors are those that determine food supply or food availability. In other words, they are determinants of physical access to food at national, household and intra-household levels. The demand side factors on the other hand are factors that determine the degree of access of countries, households and individuals to available food.

Food insecurity is generally accounted within fluctuations in household own food production and food prices (Siamwalla and Valdes, 1994). Gurkan

(1995) suggested that to improve food production element of the food security matrix alone requires consistent improvement in yield and labour productivity. The availability and access to seeds is of particular importance to farmers in developing countries or areas frequently subjected to droughts or other natural or human disasters.

SEED SECURITY

Seed is an important catalyst for the development of agriculture. More importantly, quality seeds of any preferred varieties are basis of improved agricultural productivity since they respond to farmers needs for both their increasing productivity and crop uses (Pelmer, 2005). The availability of quality seed is the foundation for food production and productivity and a precursor to crop and food diversification. Efforts to improve the performance of the agricultural sector should include seed production and delivery systems. Seeds, which embody the genetic potential of plants, determine the upper limits on plant yield and therefore the productivity of other agricultural inputs (Jaffee and Srivastava, 1994; Usman, 1994; Louwaars and Marrewijk, 1999). It is the repository of the genetic potential of crop species and their varieties resulting from the continuous improvement and selection over time. The potential benefits of seed to crop productivity and food security can be enormous. In addition, production increases brought about by the use of adapted varieties increases farmers' income when market linkages exist.

Food security, therefore, is heavily dependent on the seed security of the farming community. Seed security is defined as ready access by rural households, particularly farmers and farming communities, to adequate quantities of quality seed and planting materials of crop varieties, adapted to their agro-ecological conditions and socioeconomic needs, at planting time, under normal and abnormal weather conditions (FAO, 2012).

SEED SYSTEMS

Thiele (1999) defined seed system as an interrelated set of components including breeding, management, replacement and distribution of seed. Seed systems are complex and dynamic. One system is usually not necessarily better or more effective than the other; they meet different kinds of needs, sometimes for different environmental niches, and for different types of farmers.

The informal sector is the main provider of seed in much of the developing world as regards main food crops. In order to improve farmers' access to quality seed, it is crucial to strengthen linkages between the formal and the informal seed systems (FAO, 2009).

A well-functioning seed system is defined as one that uses the appropriate combination of formal and informal supply channels, market and non-market transactions to stimulate and meet efficiently the evolving demand of farmers for quality seeds (Maredia *et al.*, 1999)

Two broad types are recognized: formal seed systems and local or informal seed systems.

- **Formal seed system** refers to a framework of institutions deliberately constructed and linked together, including research institutions (breeding varieties), government seed companies or parastatals, and private commercial companies dealing with clearly defined products-certified seed (Louwaars, 1994).
- **Informal or local seed systems**, on the other hand, comprised of individual farmers retention of seeds from a previous harvest as well as farmer-to-farmer seed exchanges which enabled farmers to meet their seed requirements (Cromwell, 1996).

The formal seed system derives its strength from mechanisms and resources that ensure uninterrupted supply of good quality seeds and planting materials to farmers. But its major flaw is its inability to deliver the required quantities of seeds and planting materials to the doorsteps of farmers at affordable prices (Asiedu *et al.*, 2006). The seed system used in most traditional farming systems is based on the local production of seeds by the farmers themselves. Farmers consistently retain seed as a security measure to provide a back-up in case of crop failures. They always store seeds for three main purposes: consumption, sale, and seed stock (for sowing in the next season).

Farmers practice seed selection, production, and saving for informal distribution of planting materials within and among the farming communities. Variety use and development, seed production and storage by farmers under local conditions, and seed exchange mechanisms still remain the important components of the dynamic system that forms the most important source of food crops for smallholder farmers (Melaku *et al.*, 2000). The complementarities in the formal and informal systems will, therefore, enhance effective distribution of quality seeds to increase production and incomes of farmers (Almekinders and Louwaars, 1999).

A sustainable seed system will ensure that high quality seeds of a wide range of crop varieties are produced and fully available in time and affordable to farmers and other stakeholders. However, in many developing countries farmers have not yet been able to fully benefit from the advantages of using quality seed due to a combination of factors, including inefficient seed production, distribution and quality assurance systems, as well as bottlenecks caused by a lack of good seed policy on key issues such as access to credit for inputs (FAO, 2012). Furthermore, the pressure from the fluctuating food prices and climate change creates additional challenges.

The objective of the formal seed system in most cases remains at odds with the needs of smallholder farmers, who require multiple varieties of seed for all crops, and in small amounts, at the right time and at a reasonable cost (Regassa, 2000). Similarly, most public and private seed enterprises do not produce and distribute seeds to meet the subsistence needs of rural households or for farmers living in economically marginal and environmentally challenging areas.

Not only are farmers having difficulty in obtaining the necessary inputs on time and in good quality, but also they are paying very high prices (IFDC/IITA/WARDA/FGN, 2001). In Ghana and Nigeria, only 5 to 10% of total seeds and planting materials of the major cereals and legumes planted annually come from the formal seed sector (Asiedu, 2002; Oresajo, 2002).

Farmers in many communities are yet to have access to improved seeds. Most seeds planted by farmers come from local sources including farmers' own crop, neighbors, and relatives, or from local markets (Cromwell *et al.*, 1992; Jaffee and Srivastava, 1994; Louwaars and Marrewijk, 1999).

Many of the improved seed varieties reportedly have been in use for between one and two decades. As a result their potential yield is no longer attainable especially under the poor seed management system adopted by the farmers. Farmers have continued to use these varieties in the absence of replacement stock of improved varieties. Improved seeds often take a very long time to get to farmers, and adulteration has been reported in many communities (Kormawa *et al.*, 2002). Consequently, many farmers have resorted to the use of local seed varieties that are readily available and relatively cheap. The informal seed sector often adopted by local farmers has a comparative advantage in the production of seeds of vegetatively propagated crops as well as open pollinated varieties.

There still exist problems associated with non-availability of adequate quantities of certified seeds to the farmers due to low production of breeder and foundation seeds as well as poor seed distribution and information dissemination networks; slow release of improved varieties which encourages the dominance of the local low-yielding crop varieties; and the existence of adulterated, unviable and infested seeds due to poor implementation of seed quality regulatory mechanisms

Dugje *et al.*, (2008) reported that about 90% of farmer's seed are sourced from the informal seed sector. Consequently, there would be very large gains if seeds from the informal seed system are improved as it may be the most appropriate in: remote areas, where seed distributors find access difficult and farmers cannot easily reach seed markets; a narrow agro-ecological zone, where the seed market is limited and widely marketed varieties may not be suitable; or areas where the major crops have very high seeding rates, implying high transport costs to move large quantities of seed over considerable distances.

In spite of massive investments in plant breeding research, the rate of adoption of improved seeds in sub-Saharan Africa remains low, partly due to the inefficiency of local seed systems. The quality of seeds from the local seed system can be improved in any of these ways:

- Train farmers in selection, treatment, and storage of seed from their own farms. Own-saved seed is often the most appropriate, certainly for farmers who cannot afford to purchase seed. The training will help them increase production through better use of their own saved seeds.
- Encourage farmers to make their own selection of traditional varieties, to multiply and store seed of such varieties, and to sell this quality seed of traditional varieties to other farmers. This strategy is best suited to farmers that are capable to do some experiments and who are potential users of modern varieties. Initially they should be encouraged to stabilize varieties that they have selected.
- Develop new varieties at research stations, and produce good quality seeds of these varieties through either formal or informal channels-whichever that provides good or acceptable quality seed at affordable prices. This strategy will work best for farmers who can be persuaded to buy inputs, provided seed is available at prices considered worth the risk by those farmers.

COMMUNITY BASED SEED PRODUCTION

A community is a group of farm households with strong socio-economic relations, although there can be significant differentiation of interests between and within households, depending on gender, economic status, age, ethnicity, etc. (Almekinders, 2001).

Community based seed production (CBSP) is an informal mechanism of seed production which basically entails the production of seed of the varieties preferred by the farmers by themselves in their own locality by organizing themselves into small groups. These groups cultivate the same variety avoiding cross pollination and follow the recommended cultivation practices particularly seed selection procedures. CBSP is an approach of producing and distributing seeds with the participatory involvement of farmers' groups.

Seed production can be a profitable activity, especially for food crops with market potential. There is a need to adopt an integrated approach to support the emergence of small-scale seed enterprises through organization of producers, linkage to markets and value adding (FAO, 2009).

Activities should be integrated with community development in order to increase the capacity of farmer-communities to manage crop genetic diversity in a sustainable way. Market and product development is a very important area of activities which can increase the attractiveness for farmers to continue growing products from endangered genetic resources, and ensuring benefits for the rural communities rather than commercial external agents or companies.

This entails Participatory Plant Breeding (PPB), which aims to combine farmers' knowledge and capacity to select under local conditions with the breeders' expertise and access to exotic germplasm. Whereas a breeder may not select a particular line or population because it is not among the best yielding in all testing sites, farmers may pick up such material on the basis of other criteria like taste or colour preferences when it performs well in their fields. Basically, PPB aims to involve farmers both in setting criteria and in selection in a much earlier phase of the breeding process than conventional breeding (Almekinders, 2001). Instead of on-farm testing in the final phase and releasing finished varieties, breeders could distribute a wide range of advanced populations and lines to farmers. Farmers can then select among and within these materials, enhancing location-specific adaptation and exploiting Genotype-Environment interaction (G x E). Such approaches also have important implications for the organization of seed distribution, and for variety and seed regulations.

In this approach, seed producer farmer associations are formed to multiply the seed of farmer-preferred varieties using a cost-effective approach having several unique features. It is market-oriented with an unusual characteristic of placing greater emphasis on developing skills in marketing than in production. It takes account of the entire seed innovation system from initial identification of new varieties through participatory varietal selection to commercial seed production. It involves all stakeholders, and develops strong linkages between the private sector and the community-based groups.

The group members are the primary users of this output while the farming communities across the country are the secondary users. Each member participates in the decision making on planning, production and marketing and shares in the benefits. This allows groups to be more cohesive and committed to maximising profits.

Most community-based seed production schemes are initiated because farmers are concerned about lack of seed at planting time. Acute seed shortages may be attributed to unavailability, environmental stresses (e.g. drought), civil disturbances, high unaffordable prices, etc.

The community seed and planting material scheme complements the formal seed delivery system rather than competing with it. Understanding systems for planting material is crucial for managing crop biodiversity on farms in locations where it is believed to be of both private value to farmers and social significance for future crop improvement and the resilience of the farming system. Though the physical unit of seed that reproduces a crop is a private good, the diversity of the genetic resources embodied in it is a public good (Morris *et al.*, 1998). Seed systems convey incentives for farmers to grow one crop variety rather than another, or to grow a number of crops and varieties CBSP can produce the following types of seed: Certified seed, Quality-declared or standard seed and Informal seed.

For certified seed and quality-declared or standard seed, the producer needs to follow National Seeds Authority regulations normally monitored by government-appointed inspectors. In a small scheme, where the seeds will only be sold within the community, it may not be necessary to register the seed crops with the National Seeds Authority. However, it will still be necessary to follow basic seed quality assurance methods to ensure that farmers will receive good quality seed.

The quality of seeds produced informally is guaranteed only by its seller. The incentive for paying a higher price for seed than grain usually comes from having confidence in the seller or having seen their seed production field, otherwise there is little quality guarantee. Most countries have special regulations to permit trade on informally produced seed within a community.

BENEFITS

The CBSP system provides benefits to the seed-producer farmers and their groups and also provides benefits to the grower who use quality improved seed. Thus, there is a two-fold benefits; direct and indirect.

Direct benefits: These groups have a clear organizational structure and the members have defined roles and responsibilities. It is assumed that this will help in the development of human capital and the empowerment of the members of the groups. It adds to the capability of the community to produce seeds of improved varieties.

Indirect benefits: The seed produced and sold is sufficient to sow several thousands of hectares and can give very high yield advantages. The seeds from the CBSP outputs contribute to the improved livelihoods of those that grow them; they include the resource poor, socially excluded, marginal and vulnerable farming communities.

OTHER BENEFITS

Relative advantage: Farmers of CBSP groups have considerably increased incomes and also perceive that the technology embodied in the new seed has considerable benefits.

Reliability: The CBSP groups can be established for a relatively short period of time but are known to be delivering profits.

Compatibility: Farmers are used to growing the crops for which they are producing quality seed. It does not require significant departures from their customary agricultural practices.

Visibility: Farmers can directly experience the benefits of belonging to a CBSP group and the purchasers of the seed can readily observe the higher yields and other beneficial traits of the new varieties.

Independence: Farmers need to adopt this approach with others although there is a possibility of individuals also being entrepreneurial with additional land for crops not covered by the group.

Profitability of the enterprise is the most important factor that motivates others to participate. Table 1.1 showed the usefulness of CBSP in the quality of life of rural farmers while Table 1.2 highlights the incremental effect of the project on land area under seed production activities.

Table 1.1: Response of Farmers to the Usefulness of Community-based Seed and Planting Material System to Their Production

Practice	Ghana (%)	Togo (%)	Nigeria (%)
Have easy access to improved varieties	100	100	83
Save time in purchasing seeds	100	100	75
Select good seeds	100	83	75
Where to get seed	92	75	75
Type of improved seeds	73	100	83
Receive extension advice	92	88	92
Improve interaction with farmers	100	75	83
Provides cheaper seeds	100	100	92
Type of pre-flowering insecticides	NA	NA	92
Type of post-flowering insecticides	NA	NA	92
Helped to expand farm	55	40	75
Facilitated credit acquisition	18	33	–
Increased credit worthiness	64	71	33
Obtain extra income	82	88	100

Source: Asiedu *et al.* (2006) NA= Not Available.

Table 1.2: Impact of Community Seed Production on Farmers' Productivity

Year	Ghana (kg/acre)	Nigeria (kg/acre)
Previous years	315.6	255.6
Current year	600.0	495.6
Difference	284.4	240.0
Current over previous yields	90.1%	93.9%

Source: Asiedu *et al.* (2006)

Table 1.3: Impact of Community Seed Production on Farmers' Welfare

Item	Ghana (%)	Togo (%)	Nigeria (%)
Goats/sheep/cow	45.5	25.0	100.0
Mattress	10.0	5.0	47.7
Bicycle	9.1	5.0	50.0
Furniture	–	–	47.7
Sound system	–	–	50.0
Poultry	–	–	50.0
Motor cycle	–	–	25.0
Vehicle	–	–	8.3
Built house	10.0	5.0	25.0
Television set	–	–	16.7

Source: Asiedu *et al.* (2006)

CHANLLENGES

Essentially, the concept of seed production as a business rather than a development activity is a constraint to its adoption because of over emphasis on the technical aspects of seed production which often lead to less attention being paid to the strengthening of groups by helping to establish good cooperative arrangements among their members.

Lack of demand for seed may be an issue in the case of new varieties because of an inadequate supply of information on their advantages.

New groups tend to be limited by capital to invest in seed and infrastructure. Start-up funds in the form of soft loans can greatly facilitate the process of forming and strengthening CBSP groups.

Marketing is a vital issue for the seed business to succeed.

CONCLUSION

Closing the hunger gap for the growing population of developing nations that practice underdeveloped agriculture had remained a major concern to both national governments and international organizations. The dependence on agriculture to provide income for majority of the people and raw materials for industries further puts pressure on the produce meant for consumption.

Hence, increased agricultural production through production and adoption of high yielding quality seeds will impact positively on the nation's food security. As an integral aspect of seed security, sustainable seed system will help to ensure seed security for food security in areas where the formal seed system is ineffective. The capacity of the informal seed sector should be improved for a reliable supply of locally adapted varieties through community based seed production.

REFERENCES

Almekinders, C. and N. Louwaars (1999). Improving Local Seed Systems In *Farmers' Seed Production: New Approaches and Practices* (ed. C. Almekinders and N. Louwaars), pp. 33-58. Intermediate Technology Publications, London.

Almekinders, C. (2001). Management of Crop Genetic Diversity at Community Level. Deutsche Gesellschaft für Technische Zusammenarbeit (GTZ) GmbH. Eschborn, Germany.

Asiedu, E.A., A.A. Dankyi, k.O. Marfo, S.S. Denwar, B.B. Singh, N. Maroya and A.G.J. Van Gastel (2006). Enhancing Crop Productivity Through Community-based Seed Multiplication System. *Ghana Jnl. Agric. Sci.* 39: 181-187.

Asiedu, E.A. (2002). *An Assessment of Fertilizer and Seed Sector in Ghana: Policy Reforms to Enhance Trade of Agricultural Inputs in West Africa*. The African Trade and Investment Programme. USDA, IFDC, AFSTA. pp 33.

Badu-Apraku B. (2011). It All Starts with Seeds. *SPORE*. No. 154, pp. 12.

CBN-Central Bank of Nigeria (2007). *Annual Report and Statement of Accounts*. Abuja.

Cromwell, E. (1996). Governments, Farmers and Seeds in a Changing Africa. Overseas Development Institute Wallingford, UK: *CAB International.*

Cromwell, E., E. Friss-Hansen and M. Turner (1992). The Seed Sector in Developing Countries: A Framework for Performance Analysis. Working Paper 65, Overseas Development Institute, London.

Dugje, I.Y., J.E. Onyibe, F. Ekeleme A.Y. Kamara, A. Tegbaru, L.O. Omoigui and S.A. Bassi (2008). Guide to Certified Seeds Production in Borno State, Nigeria. IITA, Ibadan, Nigeria. 20 pp.

FAO (2009). Seed Security for Food Security in the Light of Climate Change and Soaring Food Prices: Challenges and Opportunities. *Committee on Agriculture* Twenty-first Session Rome, 22-25 April 2009.

FAO (2012). Seed systems. http://www.fao.org/agriculture/crops/core-themes/theme/seeds-pgr/seed sys/en/ accessed 7th March, 2012.

FAO (2008). Accessed at http://faostat.fao.org/default.aspx. Accessed April 5th, 2009.

Gurkan, A.A (1995). "The Mathematics of Hunger." *CERES* 27(2): 31-33.

IFDC/IITA/WARDA/FGN (2001). Agriculture Input Markets in Nigeria: An Assessment and a Strategy for Development.

Jaffee, S. and J. Srivastava (1994). The Roles of the Private and Public Sectors in Enhancing the Performance of Seed Systems. The World Bank Development. The World Bank for the Construction and Development. *The World Bank.* 9(1): pp. 97-117.

Kormawa, P., E. Okorji, and R. Okechukwu (2002). Assessment of Seed-Sub Sector Policy in Nigeria. International Institute of Tropical Agriculture PMB 5320, Ibadan, Nigeria.

Liverpool L.S.O., Gbolagade B.A. and R.O. Oyeleke (2009) Enhancing the Competitiveness of Agricultural Commodity Chains in Nigeria: Identifying Opportunities with Cassava, Rice, and Maize using a Policy Analysis Matrix (PAM) Framework. Nigeria Strategy Support Programme (NSSP) Background Paper No. NSSP 013 December 2009.

Louwaars, M.P. and G.A.M. Marrewijk (1999). Seed Supply Systems in Developing Countries, CTA.

Louwaars, N (1994). Seed Supply Systems in the Tropics: International Course on Seed Production and Seed Technology. Wageningen The Netherlands: International Agriculture Centre.

Maredia, M., J. Howard, D. Boughton, A. Naseem, M. Wanyala, and K. Kajisa (1999). *Increasing Seed System Efficiency in Africa: Concepts, Strategies and Issues.* MSU International Development Working Paper No. 77, Department of Agricultural Economics. East Lansing, Michigan: Michigan State University.

Melaku W., T. Tesfaye and F. Regassa (2000). Keeping Diversity Alive: An Ethiopian Perspective. *In* S.B. Brush (ed), *Genes in the Field, on Farm Conservation of Crop Diversity*. pp. 143-161. IPGRI (International Plant Genetic Resources Institute), Rome, IDRC (International Development Research Centre), Ottawa, Lewis Publishers, London, New York, Washington D.C.

Morris, M.L., J. Rusike and M. Smale (1998). Maize Seed Industries: A Conceptual Framework. In *Maize Seed Industries in Developing Countries*, ed. M. Morris Lynne Rienner and CIMMYT, Boulder and Mexico, D.F.

Nagarajan, L. and M. Smale (2005). Local Seed Systems and Village-Level Determinants of Millet Crop Diversity in Marginal Environments of India. EPT Discussion Paper 135. www.ifpri.org Accessed 2-05-2012.

Omonona, B.T. and G.A. Agoi (2007). An Analysis of Food Security Situation Among Nigerian Urban Households: Evidence from Lagos State, Nigeria. *J. Cent. Eur. Agric.* 8(3): 397-406.

Oresajo, F. A. (2002). *An Assessment of Fertilizer and Seed Sector in Nigeria: Policy Reforms to Enhance Trade of Agricultural Inputs in West Africa.* The African Trade and Investment Programme. USDA, IFDC, AFSTA. 37 pp.

Pelmer, D.P. (2005) Agriculture in the Developing World: Connecting Innovation in Plant Breeding Research to Downstream Applications. *PNAS* 102 (44) 15739-15746.

Regassa, F. (2000). Community Seed Banks and Seed Exchange in Ethiopia: A Farmer Led Approach. *In* E. Friis-Hansen and B. Sthapit (eds), *Participatory Approaches to the Conservation and Use of Plant Genetic Resources*. pp. 142-148. IPGRI, Rome.

Siamwalla A., and A. Valdes (1994). Food Security in Developing Countries: International Issues. IFPRI Washington D C.

Thiele G. (1999). Informal Potato Seed Systems in the Andes: Why are They Important.

Usman, I.A. (1994). Welcome Address. Evolving the Nigerian Seed Development Plans. (eds.) Adedipe, N.O., I.A. Usman and N.S. Maini. Federal Department of Agriculture, Abuja. pp.1-3. What Should we do with them? *World Development* 27(1): 83-99.

World Bank (1986): Poverty and Hunger; Issues and Option for Food Security in Developing Countries. A World Bank Policy Study, Washington.

Pages: 13-23

SEED TECHNOLOGY, PLANT GROWTH AND CROPPING SYSTEM

Edited by: **Dr. Pawan Kumar Tyagi; Dr. Pawan Kumar 'Bharti'**

ISBN: 978-93-5056-738-8

Edition: **2015**

Published by: **Discovery Publishing House Pvt. Ltd., New Delhi (India)**

Effect of Pre-sowing Treatments on Seed Germination of *Dendrocalamus strictus* (Roxb.) Nees

Sajad Razvi, Samaresh Biswal, Rahul Bhandri, Tshering, Tengrimchi Sangma, Lisa Dimchi, Simchi Horik, Monica, Imliyanger Norkey, Vishaka and **Lechenmit Lepcha**

ABSTRACT

The object of the study was to explore the effects of pre-sowing treatments on germination behaviour and to assess the possibility of increasing the germination rate of *Dendrocalamus strictus*. Seeds of *D. strictus* obtained were subjected to eight pre-sowing treatments viz., control (T_1) unsoaked seeds directly sown in the plastic trays and apply water upto saturation, (T_2 to T_4) seeds soaked in hot water (100 °C) for three different time periods and (T_5 to T_8) seeds soaked in tap water for four different time periods. From all the treatments maximum 72.25% germination was recorded in the seeds soaked in tap water for 60 minutes (T60) followed by 67.00% in seeds soaked in tap water for 120 minutes (T_8) and 65.75% germination also in the seeds soaked in tap water for 90 minutes (T_7) and minimum 47.75% germination was recorded in the seeds soaked in hot water (100 °C) for 30 minutes (T_4).

Department of Forestry, Dolphin P.G. Institute of Biomedical and Natural Sciences, Manduwala, Dehradun, (UK) - 248 007, India.

As regards germination energy and germination value percentage, maximum 18.39 and 15.72 was recorded in the seeds soaked in tap water for 60 minutes (T_6) followed by 17.94 and 13.67 in the seeds soaked in tap water for 120 minutes while minimum 11.75 and 7.14 was recorded in the seeds soaked for 30 minutes in hot water (T_5) respectively. Seed weight was also recorded (mean of 10 replicates of 100 seeds each) which was 2.37 gms/100 seeds. Overall maximum seed germination was observed in the seeds soaked in tap water.

Key words: Germination percentage, germination energy, germination value, germination index, *Dendrocalamus strictus.*

INTRODUCTION

Bamboo is of vital importance from ecological, commercial and socio-economic points of view. Bamboo occupies an unparalleled position in plant kingdom in terms of its distribution, diversity, flowering and uses in the tropics and subtropics (Rai and Chauhan, 1998; Rawat and Kahduri, 1999; Ansari *et al.*, 2002). Bamboo is a group of fast growing woody plant growing almost all over in India, except the Kashmir Valley. Bamboo forest constitutes about 13% of the total forest area of the country. Deogun (1937) has summarized all available knowledge regarding the flowering habit of *Dendrocalamus strictus.* He called it an "Irregularly flowering bamboo", based on his visit to bamboo forests in Uttar Pradesh, Orissa, Panjab and Madhya Pradesh. He reported that the physiological cycle of gregarious flowering of *Dendrocalamus strictus* in some localities was more than 65 years and might possibly be over a century. Chaturvedi (1988) reported the physiological cycle of *Dendrocalamus strictus* at long intervals of 20-65 years.

Tatwawadi and Kali (1983) reported 35 years physiological cycle of *Dendrocalamus strictus* in Jarida range of East Melghat division of Maharashtra state. The average periodicity of physiological cycle of *D. strictus* in Allapalli, Chandrapur and Central Chanda division of Maharashtra was reported to be 43 years, 40.5 years and 40.5 years, respectively (Prabhu and Dabral, 1989).

In Garhwal region, its gregarious flowering was reported by Gamble (1896) and Troup (1921). From Kalagarh, the gregarious flowering reported by Mathuda (1952) and Shah (1968) and from New Forest, Dehradun by Naithani (1993). The events of flowering were also recorded in seedlings of bamboo (Pathak, 1899; Birbal, 1899; Lauris, 1937; Ahmed, 1969). As per Troup (1921), the physiological cycle of *Dendrocalamus strictus* may be influenced to a slight extent by climatic and other causes, but primarily it is determined by physiological reasons. The bamboo resources in the country are shrinking day by day due to various reasons particularly gregarious flowering/seeding and subsequent dying. The flowering in bamboo is a rare phenomenon. Generally it occurs at long intervals. The period of physiological cycle (the period between two consecutive flowerings) is species-specific. The demand of bamboo has risen tremendously. For meeting the demand, it is therefore necessary to take steps to increase the yield of bamboo through developing rehabilitation techniques/guide lines for gregariously flowered bamboo areas (Chaubey *et al.*, 2013).

Dendrocalamus strictus also known as Male Bamboo or Solid Bamboo is a tropical and subtropical clumping species native to Southeast Asia. This bamboo is extensively used as raw material in paper mills and also for a variety of purposes such as light construction, furniture, musical instruments, bamboo board, mats, sticks, agricultural implements, rafts, baskets, woven wares and household utensils. Young shoots are edible and used as food. Considering the forgoing scenario, as well as the rapidly increasing demand of economically important bamboo species, many innovating techniques for rapid mass multiplication have been developed during the past few years. Tissue culture technique has been developed for a large number of species of bamboo for large scale production (Tikia, 1984; Chaturvedi and Sharma 1985: and Banik, 1987) but these techniques are yet to be commercialized.

Recently Adarsh Kumar (1991, 1992 and 1994) has developed a method called macroproliferation which is very easy and economically viable method, but this method also needs the separable propagules, which can be obtained from seedlings, but seeds are not always available due to long gestation period of most bamboo species. Hence, innovative methods to assess the possibility of increasing the germination rate are essentially required to fulfill heavy demands of planting material. In this context the present study was undertaken to explore the effect of presowing treatments on germination of *Dendrocalamus strictus* which was carried out in open laboratory conditions (30 °C ± 5°C temperature) at Department of Forestry, Dolphin P.G. Institute of Biomedical and Natural Sciences, Manduwala Dehradun India.

MATERIAL AND METHODOLOGY

The seed germination study of *Dendrocalamus strictus* (Roxb.) Nees were carried out in open laboratory conditions in Department of Forestry, Dolphin P.G. Institute of Biomedical and Natural Sciences, Manduwala Dehradun at 30°C ± 5°C temperature. Seeds of this species were collected and different treatments of hot and tap water were applied to those seeds to assess the posibility of increasing the germination rate (Table 2.1). For seed germination studies, 400 seeds per treatment (Table 2.1) were taken (4 replicate of 100 seeds each) and sown in plastic trays and were kept under room temperature 30°C±5°C in laboratory. Germination counts were taken daily and were analyzed for germination percentage, germination energy and germination value as shown in tables 2.2, 2.3 and 2.4.

Table 2.1: Different Treatments Given to the Seeds of *Dendrocalamus strictus*

T_1	Control (Seeds sown directly into trays)
T_2	Seeds soaked in hot water (100°C) for 10 minutes
T_3	Seeds soaked in hot water (100°C) for 20 minutes
T_4	Seeds soaked in hot water (100°C) for 30 minutes
T_5	Seeds soaked in tap water for 30 minutes
T_6	Seeds soaked in tap water for 60 minutes
T_7	Seeds soaked in tap water for 90 minutes
T_8	Seeds soaked in tap water for 120 minutes

The germination studies were carried out by considering following germination parameters.

1. **Germination per cent**: Germination per cent was calculated by following formula:

$$\text{Germination per cent} = \frac{\text{Total number of seeds germinated}}{\text{Total number of seeds sown}} \times 100$$

2. **Germination energy**: The germination energy were calculated by applying the following formula:

$$GE = \frac{A1}{N1} + \frac{A2}{N2} + \frac{A3}{N3} + \ldots \frac{An}{Nn}$$

Where $A_1+A_2+A_3$............. A_n are the number of seeds newly germinated on $N_1+N_2+N_3$.................. N_n days respectively.

3. **Germination value**: Daily germination counts were carried out and the germination value were calculated according to the method presicribed by Czabatar (1962) as follows

$$GV=PVxMDG$$

Where GV= germination value.

PV is the peak value of germination and is the highest value of the cumulative germination per cent divided by the number of days since the start of the experiment and MDG is the mean daily germination.

4. **Germination Index:** Germination index (GI) was calculated according to the method described by Kendrick and Frankland (1969) as follows:

$$GI = \frac{\text{Total percentage of germination}}{\text{Time taken for 50\% germination}}$$

5. **Seed weight:** Seed weight of the seeds was also done in quadruplicates using an electronic balance. The data shown is the mean value of 10 replicates of 100 seeds each. The mean seed weight was calculated according to the formula as follows:

$$\text{Mean seed weight} = \frac{\text{Total seed weight of all replicates}}{\text{Total number of replicates}}$$

RESULTS

The seed germination study of *Dendrocalamus strictus* (Roxb.) Nees were carried out in open laboratory conditions in Department of Forestry, Dolphin P.G. Institute of Biomedical and Natural Sciences, Manduwala Dehradun at 30ºC ± 5ºC temperature. For seed germination studies, 400 seeds per treatment were taken (4 replicate of 100 seeds each) and sown in plastic trays and were kept under room temperature 30ºC ± 5ºC in laboratory. Germination counts were taken daily and were analyzed for different germination parameters shown in Table 2.2, 2.3 and 2.4.

1. Germination percentage

Daily germination counts were carried out and the germination percentage was calculated. Maximum seed germination percentage 72.25 was recorded in the seeds soaked in tap water for 60 minutes treated (T_6) followed by 67.00% in seeds soaked in tap water for 120 minutes (T_8) and 65.75% germination also in the seeds soaked in tap water for 90 minutes (T_7) while, minimum 47.75% germination was recorded in (T_4) the seeds soaked in hot water (100 ºC) for 30 minutes (Table 2.2). Overall, maximum germination percentage was achieved in the seeds soaked in tapr water for different time durations than those soaked in hot water for different time durations and control (Seeds sown directly into trays)

Table 2.2: Seed Germination Percentage, Germination Energy and Germination Value of *Dendrocalamus strictus* Under Different Pre-sowing Treatments

Treatment	Germination Percentage	Germination Energy	Germination Value	Germination Index
T_1 (Seeds sown directly into trays)	55.25	14.13	7.90	2.30
T_2 (Seeds soaked in hot water for 10 min.)	56.75	14.21	9.65	2.58
T_3 (Seeds soaked in hot water for 20 min.)	57.75	15.50	10.21	2.75
T_4 (Seeds soaked in hot water for 30 min.)	47.75	11.75	7.14	1.71
$T5$ (Seeds soaked in hot water for 30 min.)	52.50	13.66	7.85	2.19
T_6 (Seeds soaked in hot water for 30 min.)	72.25	18.39	15.72	3.61
T_7 (Seeds soaked in hot water for 30 min.)	65.75	16.51	13.86	3.13
T_8 (Seeds soaked in hot water for 30 min.)	67.00	17.94	13.67	3.35
Average	59.37	15.26	10.75	2.70

Table 2.3: Germination Studies of *Dendrocalamus strictus* Under Open Room Temperature

T_1 Control (Seeds Sown Directly into Trays)				T_2 Seeds Soaked in Hot Water for 10 min.				T_3 Seeds Soaked in Hot Water for 20 min.				T_4 Seeds Soaked in Hot Water for 30 min.			
Days After Sowing	Daily Total	Cumulative Total	Cumulative Total As % of Total Seeds	Days After Sowing	Daily Total	Cumulative Total	Cumulative Total As % of Total Seeds	Days After Sowing	Daily Total	Cumulative Total	Cumulative Total As % of Total Seeds	Days After Sowing	Daily Total	Cumulative Total	Cumulative Total As % of Total Seeds
8	4	4	1	8	3	3	0.75	8	4	4	1	8	1	1	0.25
9	6	10	2.5	9	4	7	1.75	9	9	13	3.25	9	4	5	1.25
10	10	20	5	10	8	15	3.75	10	13	26	6.5	10	7	12	3
11	11	31	7.75	11	9	24	6	11	14	40	10	11	6	18	4.5
12	13	44	11	12	11	35	8.75	12	16	56	14	12	9	27	6.75
13	16	60	15	13	13	48	12	13	18	74	18.5	13	11	38	9.5
14	15	75	18.75	14	16	64	16	14	15	89	22.25	14	13	51	12.75
15	12	87	21.75	15	19	83	20.75	15	11	100	25	15	15	66	16.5
16	14	101	25.25	16	14	97	24.25	16	19	119	29.75	16	11	77	19.25
17	21	122	30.5	17	22	119	29.75	17	26	145	36.25	17	18	95	23.75
18	14	136	34	18	20	139	34.75	18	18	163	40.75	18	17	112	28
19	13	149	37.25	19	25	164	41	19	13	176	44	19	16	128	32
20	12	161	40.25	20	16	180	45	20	12	188	47	20	22	150	37.5
21	15	176	44	21	13	193	48.25	21	14	202	50.5	21	11	161	40.25
22	12	188	47	22	10	203	50.75	22	11	213	53.25	22	8	169	42.25
23	10	198	49.5	23	9	212	53	23	7	220	55	23	7	176	44
24	8	206	51.5	24	5	217	54.25	24	4	224	56	24	5	181	45.25
25	7	213	53.25	25	3	220	55	25	3	227	56.75	25	4	185	46.25
26	4	217	54.25	26	4	224	56	26	2	229	57.25	26	2	187	46.75
27	3	220	55	27	2	226	56.5	27	1	230	57.5	27	3	190	47.5
28	1	221	55.25	28	1	227	56.75	28	1	231	57.75	28	1	191	47.75
Total	221			Total	227			Total	231			Total	191		

Table 2.4: Germination Studies of *Dendrocalamus strictus* Under Open Room Temperature

T5 Seeds Soaked in Tap Water for 30 min.				T6 Seeds Soaked in Tap Water for 60 min.				T7 Seeds Soaked in Tap Water for 90 min.				T8 Seeds Soaked in Tap Water for 120 min.			
Days After Sowing	Daily Total	Cumulative Total	Cumulative Total As % of Total Seeds	Days After Sowing	Daily Total	Cumulative Total	Cumulative Total As % of Total Seeds	Days After Sowing	Daily Total	Cumulative Total	Cumulative Total As % of Total Seeds	Days After Sowing	Daily Total	Cumulative Total	Cumulative Total As % of Total Seeds
8	3	3	0.75	8	5	5	1.25	8	2	2	0.5	8	5	5	1.25
9	5	8	2	9	9	14	3.5	9	9	11	2.75	9	15	20	5
10	9	17	4.25	10	13	27	6.75	10	12	23	5.75	10	14	34	8.5
11	12	29	7.25	11	14	41	10.25	11	13	36	9	11	16	50	12.5
12	14	43	10.75	12	16	57	14.25	12	13	49	12.25	12	18	68	17
13	17	60	15	13	18	75	18.75	13	14	63	15.75	13	20	88	22
14	14	74	18.5	14	14	89	22.25	14	16	79	19.75	14	17	105	26.25
15	11	85	21.25	15	16	105	26.25	15	14	93	23.25	15	12	117	29.25
16	17	102	25.5	16	18	123	30.75	16	15	108	27	16	11	128	32
17	22	124	31	17	28	151	37.75	17	24	132	33	17	30	158	39.5
18	15	139	34.75	18	32	183	45.75	18	21	153	38.25	18	21	179	44.75
19	14	153	38.25	19	18	201	50.25	19	31	184	46	19	17	196	49
20	11	164	41	20	14	215	53.75	20	13	197	49.25	20	14	210	52.5
21	15	179	44.75	21	17	232	58	21	15	212	53	21	15	225	56.25
22	13	192	48	22	15	247	61.75	22	12	224	56	22	12	237	59.25
23	9	201	50.25	23	13	260	65	23	11	235	58.75	23	10	247	61.75
24	4	205	51.25	24	11	271	67.75	24	9	244	61	24	7	254	63.5
25	3	208	52	25	8	279	69.75	25	8	252	63	25	6	260	65
26	1	209	52.25	26	6	285	71.25	26	7	259	64.75	26	5	265	66.25
27	0	209	52.25	27	3	288	72	27	3	262	65.5	27	2	267	66.75
28	1	210	52.5	28	1	289	72.25	28	1	263	65.75	28	1	268	67
Total	210			Total	289			Total	263			Total	268		

2. Germination energy

Daily germination counts were carried out and the germination energy were calculated according to the method given in material and methods. As regards germination energy same trend was found as in germination percentage having maximum 18.39 germination energy percentage in the seeds soaked for 60 minutes in tap water followed by 17.94% in the seeds soaked in tap water for 120 minutes and 16.51% also achieved in the seeds soaked in tap water for 90 minutes. However, 11.75% germination energy was observed in the seeds soaked for 30 minutes in hot water.

3. Germination value

Germination value was calculated according to the method prescribed by Czabatar (1962). Maximum germination value of 15.72% was recorded in the seeds soaked in tap water for 60 minutes followed by followed by 13.86% in the seeds soaked in tap water for 90 minutes and 13.67% also achieved in the seeds soaked in tap water for 120 minutes while, 7.14% germination value was observed in the seeds soaked for 30 minutes in hot water.

4. Germination index

Germination index was calculated according to the method prescribed by Kendrick and Frankland (1969). Maximum 3.61 germination index was recorded in the seeds soaked in tap water for 60 minutes followed by followed by 3.15 in the seeds soaked in tap water for 120 minutes and 3.13 also achieved in the seeds soaked in tap water for 90 minutes while, 1.71 germination index was observed in the seeds soaked for 30 minutes in hot water.

DISCUSSION

Bamboo species, giant woody perennials belonging to the family Poaceae are of vital importance from ecological, commercial and socio-economic points of view and are mainly propagated by seeds. Even though huge quantities of seeds are produced, most of them cannot be utilized because of rapid loss of viability. The germination of seeds is strongly influenced by variation in temperature, water stress and light requirements. These factors often show significant interaction in their effect on germination (Thakur, 2002). The International Seed Testing Association (1993) has recommended temperature between 20 and 30°C as best suited for obtaining maximum germination in most of the forest tree species.

From our findings on effect of pre-sowing treatments on seed germination of *Dendrocalamus strictus* (Roxb.) Nees in natural conditions 30 °C ± 2 °C (room temperature) suggest that the seeds of this species can germinate under different pre-sowing treatments with a wide range of temperature, light and humidity conditions and maximum 72.25 germination percentage was recorded in the seeds soaked in tap water for 90 minutes followed by 67.00% in the seeds soaked in tap water for 120 minutes and minimum 47.75% germination was achieved in the seeds soaked in hot water for 30 minutes.

For germination energy and germination value percentage same trend was revealed from the results with maximum values observed in the seeds soaked in the tap water for 90 minutes and minimum in the seeds soaked in hot water for 30 minutes. Geetika and Chauhan 2013 also study the effects of a number of pre-sowing treatments in improving the germination of *Cassia tora* and observed highly significant differences between the different germination treatments. As regards germination energy and germination value percentage maximum was recorded in the seeds treated with T_6 followed by in control treated seeds and minimum. Meyer *et al.*, (1989) also documented correlation variation germination rate for *Artimisia tridantata* and *Chrysothamus nauseosus* and Uniyal, (1998) revealed that germination parameters of *Grewia optiva* may change from provenance to provenance and it may be due to the variation in seed size and weight among the seed source.

However, Mugasha and Msanga (1987) recorded highest germination per cent (77%) and germination value (0.82) on the germination of seed of Maesopsis eminii Engl. From the present study it was observed that the seeds soaked in tap for different time durations gave better results than the seeds soaked in hot water for different time durations which may be due to rupture of seed coat that allows water to permeate the seed tissues causing physiological changes, especially oxygen permeability and subsequent germination of embryo Sabongari, 2001. It may be concluded from the present study that for better germination of *Dendrocalmus strictus*, seeds should be soaked in simple tap water than boiling (hot) water.

REFERENCES

Adarsh Kumar (1991). Mass Production of Field Planting Stock of *Dendrocalamus strictus* Through Macro-proliferion- A Technology. *Indian Forester*, 117: 1046-1052.

Adarsh Kumar and Mohinder Pal (1994). Mass Production of *Bambusa tulda* Through Macroproliferation for Raising Industrial and Commercial Plantations. *Indian Forester*, 120(2): 152-157.

Adarsh Kumar; Mohinder Pal and Shiv Kumar, (1992). Mass Production of Field Planting Stock of *Dendrocalamus hamiltonii* Vegetatively Through Macro-proliferation. *Indian Forester*, 118: 638-646.

Ahmed, M. (1969). Flowering of Seedlings of *Dendrocalamus strictus, Indian Forester*, 95 pp. 214.

Ansari, A.A. O.P. Chaubey, A. Sharma and A. Pandey (2002). *Hand Book of Bamboos with Particular Reference to Madhya Pradesh"*, SFRI Bulletin, No. 45, pp. 1-53.

Banik, R.L. (1987). *Techniques of Bamboo Propagation with Special Reference to Prerooted and Prerhizomed Branch Cuttings and Tissue Culture*. In Rao, A.N.; Dhanarajan, G.; Sastry, C.*B.* ed., Recent Research on Bamboo. Proceedings of the International Bamboo Workshop, Hangzhou, China, 6-14 October 1985. Chinese Academy of Forestry, Beijing, China; International Development Research Centre, Ottawa, Canada. pp. 160-169.

Birbal, B. (1899). The Flowering of Seedlings of Dendrocalamus Strictus, *Indian Forester*, 25: 305-306.

Chaturvedi, A.N. (1988). Management of Bamboo Forests, *Indian Forester*, 114: 489-495.

Chaturvedi, H.C. and Menna, Sharma (1985). Micropropagation of *Denderocalamus strictus* Through in vitro Culture of Single Node Stem Cuttings. *Proc. 75th Ind. Sci. Cong*. Part III: Abstract.

Czabator, F.J. (1962). Germination Value: An Index Combining Speed and Completeness of Pine Seed Germination, *For. Sci.*, 8: 386-396.

Deogun, P.N. (1937). The Silviculture and Management of the Bamboo *Dendrocalamus strictus, Indian Forest Records* (NS) Silviculture, II, Vol. 4, pp. 1-173.

Gamble, J.S. (1896). Bambuseae of British India. *Annals of Royal Botanical Graden*, Calcutta, Vol. 7, pp. 1-133.

Geetika Pant and Ugam K. Chauhan (2013). Germination Behaviour of *Cassia tora* Seeds in Various Pre-sowing Treatment Methods. *International Journal of Pharma and Bio Sciences*, 4(3): 773-778.

Lauris, M.V. (1937). Two Years Old Bamboo Seedling, *Indian Forester*, Vol. 63, pp. 857.

Meyer, S.E., E.D. McArthus and S.B. Monsen (1989). Variation in Germination Response to Temperate in Rubber Rabbit Brush and its Ecological Implications. *American Journal of Botany*, 76: 981-991.

Mugasha, A.G. and H.P. Msanga (1987). *Maesopsis eminii* Seed Coat Impermeability is not the Cause of Sporadic and Prolonged Seed Germination. Forest Ecology and Management, 22(3): 301-305.

Naithani, H.B. (1993). *Contributions to the Taxonomic Studies of Indian Bamboos*. Ph.D. Thesis, Garhvwal University, Srinagar, Vol. 2, pp. 278.

Orlande, T., J. Laarman and, J. Mortimer (1996). Palmito Sustainability and Economic in Brazil Atlantic Coastal Forest. *Forest Ecology and Management*, 80: 257-265.

Pathak, P.L.S. (1899). Seedlings of *Dendrocalamus Strictus* in Flower, *Indian Forester*, Vol. 25, pp. 22.

Prabhu, V.R. and S.L. Dabral (1989). *A Status Paper on Bamboo in Maharashtra State*. Proc. Seminar on Silviculture and Management of Bamboos, held at Institute of Deciduous Forests, Jabalpur (M.P), (1989) December 13-15, pp. 59-77.

Rai, S.N. and K.V.S. Chauhan (1998). Distribution and Growing Stock of Bamboos in India, *Indian Forester*, 124: 89-98.

Rawat J.K. and, D.C. Kahduri (1999). *National Report on the Status of Bamboos and Rattan in India*. Submitted to, INBAR Sponsored Workshop on "Strategy 2005" Beijing (China), (1999) April 12-14.

Sabongari, S. (2001). Effect of Soaking Duration on Germination and Seedling Establishment of Selected Varieties of Tomato (*Lycopersicum esculentum* Mill). M.Sc.Thesis, Department of Biological Sciences, Usmanu Danfodiyo University, Sokoto, Nigeria, 2001.

Shah, N.C (1968). Flowering of Bamboos, *Dendrocalamus hookeri* and *Dendrocalamus strictus* in Assam and Bihar States, *Indian Forester*, Vol. 94, pp. 717.

Tatwawadi, H.N. and B.G. Kali (1983). Gregarious Flowering of Bamboo *Dendrocalamus strictus* in Jarida Range of East Melghat Division", Amravati Circle – Maharashtra State. *Indian Forester*, 109: 111-114.

Thakur, I.K., A. Gupta and V. Thakur (2002). Germination of Scarified Seeds of *Grewia optiva. Indian Journal of Forestry*, 25(2):158-160.

Tikia, Nirmal (1984). *In vitro* Propagation of Golden Bamboo. *M.Phil. Thesis*, University Delhi, India, pp. 89.

Troup, R.S. (1921). *The Silviculture of Indian Trees*, Oxford Publication, Vol. 3, (1921), pp. 977-1013.

Uniyal, A.K. (1998). *Provenance Variation in Seed and Seedlings of Grewia Optiva Drumm.* D. Phil Thesis, H.N.B. Garhwal University Srinagar.

Kendrick, R.E. and Frankland, B. (1969). Photocontrol of Germination in *Amaranthus caudatus, Planta*, 85: 326-329.

ISTA (1993). International Rules for Seed Testing. *Seed Science and Technology*, 21: 228.

Pages: 24-57

SEED TECHNOLOGY, PLANT GROWTH AND CROPPING SYSTEM
Edited by: Dr. Pawan Kumar Tyagi; Dr. Pawan Kumar 'Bharti'
ISBN: 978-93-5056-738-8
Edition: 2015
Published by: Discovery Publishing House Pvt. Ltd., New Delhi (India)

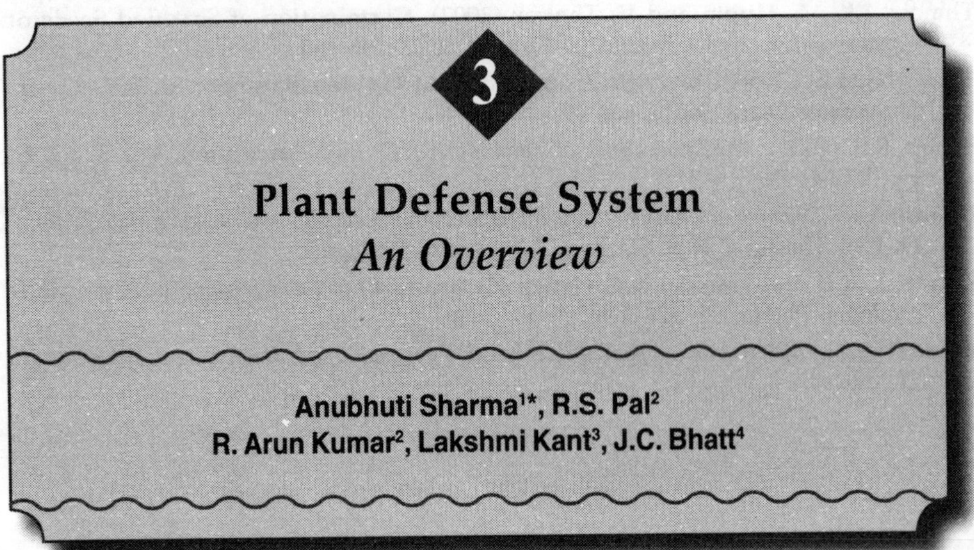

3

Plant Defense System
An Overview

Anubhuti Sharma[1*], R.S. Pal[2]
R. Arun Kumar[2], Lakshmi Kant[3], J.C. Bhatt[4]

INTRODUCTION

Plants have evolved sophisticated mechanisms to survive the stresses imposed on them by biotic and abiotic environments. Several kind of plant–pathogen interactions result in generation and emission of long distance signals from the site of infection to healthy uninfected parts of the plant where subsequent resistance is induced. Physiology of disease resistance is one of the most fascinating areas of research. The establishment of battling response by the plant against a pathogen is correlated with a number of phenomena. In 1902, Ward in England emphasized on the induction of defense response in plants against the fungal attack. Wingard (1928) observed symptoms of recovery in ring spot infected tobacco plants and presumed that infected plant has acquired immunity against the disease.

1 Senior Scientist, VPKAS, ICAR Institute, Almora, Uttarakhand, India.
2 Scientist, VPKAS, ICAR Institute, Almora, Uttarakhand, India.
3 In-Charge Head & Principle Scientist, CID, VPKAS, ICAR Institute, Almora, India.
4 Director, VPKAS, ICAR Institute, Almora, Uttarakhand , India.

The potential of plants to react against an invader by triggering local and systemic responses was first described by Carbone and Arnaudi (1930). They considered the possibility that plants react to bacterial or fungal infection in the same way as animals react to microorganisms or viral infection by producing specific antibodies. It was explained by the production of a signal released from the infected leaf and translocated to other parts of the plant where it induces defense reactions (Ross, 1966). At that time, scientists believed that they were investigating a phenomenon analogous to the immune response in mammals. Muller and Borger (1940) also explained that plants possess the similar mechanism comparable to antigen-antibody reactions in animals. They demonstrated the formation of an inhibitory compound in potato tubers infected with *Phytophthora infestans*, which ultimately leads to the development of resistance in plants. These active inhibitory compounds were termed as phytoalexins (Gr-phyton = warding off, alexin = compound).

However, the direct experimental evidence for the hypothesis came more than 20 years later with the isolation and characterization of *pisatin* from fungal infected pea pods (Perrin and Bottomley, 1962). Local accumulation of phytoalexins appeared to be the first, important, coordinate expression of antimicrobial response to the attack by various fungi, although they were also produced under abiotic stress. Later, it became apparent that phytoalexins represented only one of the many events responsible for successfully halting the pathogen invasion (Kuc, 1972). According to Ingham (1976) phytoalexins are "post inflectional metabolites whose formation involves either gene activation or depression of a latent enzyme system."

In the past 30 years, Localized acquired resistance (LAR) and Systemic acquired resistance (SAR) have been demonstrated in many plant species and the spectrum of resistance has been broadened to include not only viruses and bacteria, but also many agronomically important phytopathogenic fungi. The activation of LAR and SAR by a pathogen in host plant cell triggers a signal throughout the plant, which leads to activation of defense genes in uninfected tissues, and ultimately results in the plant showing enhanced resistance to subsequent infection by an array of pathogens (Glazebrook et al., 1997).

ELICITATION OF DEFENSE RESPONSE

When a plant and a pathogen come into contact, close communication between the two organisms carries out (Hammond-Kosack and Jones, 2000). Plant-pathogen communications rely on the interaction among a wide and heterogeneous world of molecules referred as "elicitors". They were first described in the early 1970 (Keen, 1975). Originally the term elicitor was used to describe molecules capable of inducing the production of phytoalexins (a class of defense molecules in plants) but it is now commonly used for compounds stimulating any type of plant defense (Ebel and Cosio, 1994; Hahn, 1996; Nurnberger, 1999) like activation of enzymes and generation of reactive oxygen species (ROS) (Chai and Doke, 1987; Legendre et al., 1993), production of defense proteins, induction of a hypersensitive response (HR), and a localized cell death around the site of infection which is able to stop the spread of the pathogen (Montesano et al., 2003). According to Radman et al. (2003) elicitors are classified biotic or abiotic depending on their origin and molecular structure.

ABIOTIC ELICITORS

The abiotic elicitors encloses environmental stress factors, like UV lights, heavy metals ions, air pollutants and chemical compounds acting as hormones or signalling molecules in the plant.

BIOTIC ELICITORS

The biotic elicitors include all molecules derived from living microorganisms. The first biotic elicitor was described in the early 1970 (Keen, 1975). Since then, numerous publications have accumulated evidence for pathogen-derived compounds that induce defense responses in intact plants or plant cell cultures which includes oligosaccharides or lipo- and glycoproteins (Angelova et al., 2006). Such biotic elicitors often originate from the pathogen (exogenous elicitors) but in some cases are liberated from the attacked plants by the action of enzymes of the pathogen (endogenous elicitors) (Ebel and Cosio, 1994; Boller, 1995). Their recognition occurs directly, via receptor ligand interaction, and indirectly, via host-encoded intermediates (Figure 3.1).

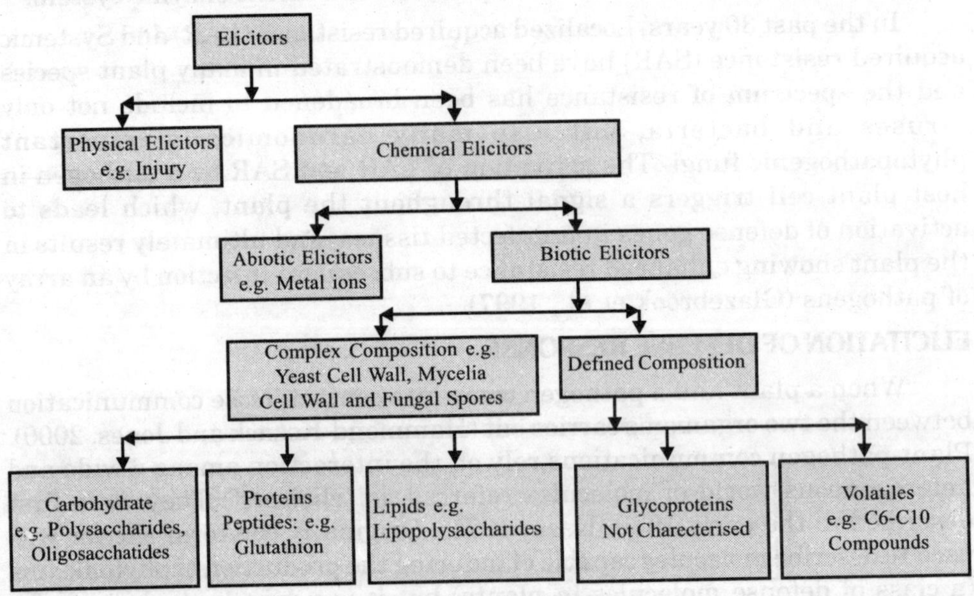

Fig. 3.1: Elicitors

MECHANISM OF DEFENSE RESPONSE

Plants responds to pathogen attack or elicitor treatments by activating a wide variety of protective mechanisms designed to prevent pathogen replication and spreading (Malolepsza and Rozalska, 2005). The local and systemic response is induced in plants in response to pathogen attack that can prevent the infection and provide enhanced resistance to subsequent infections by the same or even unrelated pathogens (Pozo *et al.*, 2002). The early local response includes the hypersensitive response (HR) which leads to a local programmed cell death (Kombrink and Schmelzer, 2001); as a result pathogen remains confined to necrotic lesions near the site of infection. This defense strategy, which is particularly successful towards biotrophic bacteria and fungi as well as towards viruses, is based on pathogen recognition and cell-to-cell communication in the tissue adjacent to the site of infection (Thomma et al., 2001).

During hypersensitive response plants employ general resistance mechanism to combat infection from pathogen or to prevent an existing infection from spreading further. One such general defense mechanism is known as localized acquired resistance (LAR). These are the localized acquired resistance which often triggers non specific resistance throughout the plant towards a broad spectrum of pathogens (Ryals et al., 1996; Sticher et al., 1997; Van Loon, 1997; Fritig et al., 1998), termed as, systemic acquired resistance (SAR). In case of SAR, the signal is transmitted from the infected tissue into the whole plant for induction of overall defense gene expression (Ryals et al., 1994). This demonstrates that signal perception in initial pathogen recognition and signal transduction to initiate further defense responses is essential for plants to counteract phytopathogens (Nurnberger and Scheel, 2001). Saikia et al. (2006) studied the activation of defense response in chickpea using a phytopathogenic fungi *Fusarium oxysporum* f. sp. *ciceri*. Further, the induction of resistance in banana against leaf blight pathogen, *Fusarium oxysporum* f. sp. *cubense* proves the active role of plant defense system against the pathogen attack (Thakker et al., 2007).

HYPERSENSITIVE RESPONSE (HR)

Strategies developed by plants to defend themselves against pathogens involve restriction of the pathogen to its site of penetration. This can be achieved with the help of hypersensitive response (HR) (Dorey et al., 1997; Heath, 1998; Kortekamp and Zyprian, 2003). The HR is a commonly activated resistance process characterized by the rapid induction of localized host cell death at the site of infection limiting further pathogen multiplication and spread (Gilchrist, 1997; Heath, 2000; Shirasu and Shulze-Lefert, 2000). During this response the plant sacrifices some of its cells to circumvent the invading pathogen with a layer or a ring composed of dead plant cells thus inhibiting the growth of the pathogen by killing of infected or non-infected cells and thus producing a physical barrier. Activation of the HR results in the formation of distinct lesions on leaves or stems, termed HR lesions, and the pathogen is generally restricted to these lesions (Iakimova et al., 2005).

The HR is characterized by other metabolic disturbances, such as ion influx (Ca^{2+} and K^{+}) and ion efflux (Cl^{-}) across the plasma membrane as well as changes in pH and membrane depolarization (Levine et al., 1996; Heath, 2000). The HR also involves the deposition of newly formed carbohydrate material in cell wall in response to penetration attempts by fungal hyphae (Aist, 1976), cell wall cross-linking and localized cell death (Bradley et al., 1992; Levine et al., 1994). Further, lignification of cell walls of infected higher plants may be involved in disease resistance mechanisms as the lignified cells apparently form a barrier to the invasion or spread of micro-organism (Friend, 1980). Lipid peroxidation and lipid damage may be partially responsible for some of these cell changes and probably affect membrane function (Firdous et al., 2007).

The cells undergoing the HR produce reactive oxygen species (ROS) (Gechev et al., 2006) including super oxide anions, hydrogen peroxide, and hydroxyl radicals (Baker et al., 1993; Hutcheson, 1998). These molecules are highly reactive and toxic and can lead to the oxidative destruction of cells (Asada and Takahashi, 1987). The oxidative burst is correlated with the HR in a number of plant-pathogen interactions and, therefore, may be an important element contributing to disease resistance (Mehdy, 1994). The HR leads to accumulation of antimicrobial compounds, such as phenolic compounds and phytoalexins (Ortega et al., 2005) along with increase in the activity of peroxidases (Kortekamp and Zyprian, 2003) and polyphenol oxidases enzymes (Agrios, 1997) in cells surrounding the lesion which are eventually involved in defense responses (Thipyapong et al., 2004).

The strength of HR-based resistance is the induction of multifactorial defense pathway (Hammond-Kosack and Jones, 1996). Rajab et al. (2009) showed the formation of ROS, lipid peroxidation, PAL activity and total phenolics as a part of hypersensitive response developed in *Sesamum prostratum* against *Fusarium oxysporum f. sesame* infection. Ehrenfeld et al. (2005) also documented the activation of HR response along with accumulation of phenolic compounds, such as antimicrobial phytoalexins in tobacco plants inoculated with tobaccovirus coat protein.

PHYTOALEXINS

Phytoalexins are antimicrobial compounds which accumulate in plants in response to fungal or bacterial challenge (Wilkens et al., 2010). They are also formed after plant exposure to non-biological stress factors, including irradiation with short-wavelength UV light and treatment with ions of heavy metals, such as copper or mercury (Grayer and Kokubun, 2001).

Phytoalexins have been well documented in the field of plant defense. Much research has been conducted on the elicitation process, and specific elicitors have been discovered (Dakora and Phillips, 1996). Phytoalexins are thought to be synthesized in cells adjacent to the infection site, in response to a signal produced either by the invading pathogen or by infected host cells. Consequently, the infected cell becomes a toxic micro-environment for the invading pathogen. Wharton et al. (2000) reported the specific induction of four phytolexins namely luteolinidin, 5-methoxy luteolinidin, apigeninidin and caffeic acid ester of arabinosyl-5-0-apigeninidin upon inoculation of sorghum seedlings with a non pathogenic fungus *Cochliobolus heterostrophus.*

The phytoalexins are generally lipophillic substances belonging to the group of plant products loosely termed as 'secondary metabolites', the products of a plant's secondary metabolism (Kuc and Rush, 1985). The secondary metabolites or secondary products do not appear to have a generalized role in the process of photosynthesis, respiration, solute transport, translocation, nutrient assimilation or differentiation unlike primary metabolites, such as chlorophyll, amino acids, nucleotides, simple carbohydrates or membrane lipids although many of them may have a well defined function in a certain group of plants e.g. *Thellungiella halophila* and *Arabidopsis thaliana* (Pedras and Adio, 2008).

Various type of phytoalexins like Pterostilbene, belonging to a group of phenolic compounds known as stilbenes, has been identified in several plant species such as the heartwood of sandalwood (Seshadri, 1972), leaves of *Vitis vinifera* (Langcake et al., 1979), peanuts (Medina-Bolivar et al., 2007), infected grape berries of varieties Chardonnay and Gamay (Adrian et al., 2000), healthy and immature berries of varieties Pinot Noir and Gamay (Pezet and Pont, 1988) and berries of some *Vacciunium* species (Pezet and Pont, 1988). In addition to its antifungal role (Pezet and Pont, 1990; Mazullo et al., 2000), pterostilbene presents other biological activities also including antihyperglycemic (Manickam et al., 1997), antioxidative (Roupe et al., 2006; Remsberg et al., 2008), anticancer (Remsberg et al., 2008; Pan et al., 2007; Nanjoo et al., 2007), anti-inflammatory (Remsberg et al., 2008), anticholesterol (Mizuno et al., 2008), hypolipidemic (Mazullo et al., 2000) and analgesic (Mazullo et al., 2000) activities.

The chemical structure of phytoalexins is diverse but these small organic compounds are synthesized from any one of three secondary metabolic pathways-the acetate-mevalonate, actetate-malonate or shikimic acid pathways. Most of the legume phytoalexins have an isoflavonoid skeleton derived from mixed acetate–malonate and shikimate pathways. Among these isoflavonoids are isoflavones, isoflavanones, pterocarpans, stilbenes and chalcones (Harborne, 1999; Farooq and Tahara, 1999). These pathways are common to all the plants (Kuc and Rush, 1985).

(a) The acetate-mevalonate pathway

This pathway leads to the formation of some aromatic compounds terpenoids also named as isoprenoids, mostly monoterpenes for example, rishitin, ipomeamarone (Stoessl, 1982). They represents the chemically and functionally most diversified class of low molecular mass lipids in plants, both primary and secondary metabolites (Iriti and Faoro, 2006). They include electron carriers (quinones), membrane constituents (sterols), vitamins (A, D, E and K), plant hormones (side chain of cytokinins, abscisic acid, gibberellins and brassinosteroids), photosynthetic pigments (chlorophyll, phytol and carotenoids) and essential oils (Sacchettini and Poulter, 1997).

(b) The acetate/malonate pathway (polyketide pathways)

This pathway leads to the formation of some plant quinones along with various large groups of flavonoids, for example, 6-methoxymellein, wyerone etc. (Strack, 1997). In polyketide pathway acetyl Co-A is the starting molecule. Ferrer et al. (1999) revealed the structure of chalcone synthase (CHS) and the molecular basis of plant polyketide biosynthesis. CHS is pivotal for its biosynthesis and its structure elucidation. The chemical basis provides a framework for engineering CHS- like enzymes to produce new products.

(c) The shikimate/arogenate pathway

The shikimate pathway is found only in microorganisms and plants, never in animals (Herrmann et al., 1999). This pathway leads to the formation of phenyl propane derivatives (phenylpropanoids) for example, chlorogenic acid etc. (Strack, 1997). Phenylpropanoids are a class of phenylalanine derivatives with a basic C6-C3 (phenyl-propane) skeleton. Therefore, the essential amino acid phenylalanine as well as the other aromatic amino acids tyrosine and tryptophan arise from the shikimate pathway (Iriti and Faoro, 2009). Precursors of this pathway are phosphoenolpyruvate, from glycolysis, and erythrose 4-phosphate from pentose phosphate pathway, leading to two important intermediates, shikimic and chorismic acid. In further steps, after a branch point, phenylalanine and tyrosine are synthesized from prephenic and arogenic acid, whereas, tryptophan from anthranilic acid (Weaver and Hermann, 1997).

The removal of an amino group from L-phenylalanine (deamination) via the step catalyzed by the enzyme phenylalanine ammonia-lyase (PAL) leads to cinnamic acid, which is the keystone step in phenylpropanoid biosynthesis (Jones, 1984; Dixon et al., 1994). This cinnamic acid serves as a precursor of hydroxycinnamates namely coumaric, ferulic and sinapic acids after a series of hydroxylation of the benzene ring. The downstream products of the flavonoid pathway include the flavones, flavanols, flavanones, anthocyanins, and deoxyanthocyanidins.

The shikimate pathway and the polyketide pathways are the most important ones in biosynthesis of the plant phenolics (Strack, 1997). But, much attention to shikimic acid pathway activated during pathogen attack has been given due to secondary metabolites production such as phytoalexins, which are responsible for adding mechanical rigidity and strength to cell walls and for providing barriers to infection by pathogen (Tan et al., 2004; Coneeica et al., 2006). The synthesis of a phytoalexins by more than one of the major biosynthetic pathways requires regulation and coordination of all contributing pathways (Sharma et al., 2011). Thus the deficiency or absence of a precursor from any one pathway could become rate limiting or block synthesis of the phytoalexin.

MAJOR FACTORS AFFECTING PLANT DEFENSE SYSTEM

Phenylalanine Ammonia Lyase (PAL)

Phenylalanine ammonia-lyase (PAL, EC 4.3.1.5) is one of the main regulatory enzyme of plants defense system which by participating in phenylpropanoid pathway, serves as a precursor for synthesis of various secondary metabolites including phenols, phenylpropanoids (Tomás-Barberán and Espín, 2001), which has been shown to accumulate in cells undergoing the hypersensitive response (Dorey et al., 1997) and to be essential for local and systemic resistance (Delaney et al., 1995).

The enzyme is widely distributed in higher plants (Sarma et al., 1998; Sarma and Sharma, 1999; Chen and McClure, 2000), some fungi and yeast (D'Cunha et al., 1996). However, the enzyme is absent in true bacteria and animal tissues. PAL has been purified and characterized from a number of plant and fungal sources (Camm and Towers, 1973). Using SDS mercaptoethanol gel electrophoresis, Havir and Hanson (1973, 1975) showed that PAL is a tetrameric enzyme with either four identical sub-unit or sub-unit that differ in molecular weight less than 5%.

PAL catalyzes the first step of phenylpropanoid pathway in plants i.e. nonoxidative deamination of L-phenylalanine (L-Phe) to form trans-cinnamic acid and free ammonium. This reaction leads to the biosynthesis of a large range of phenylpropanoid- derived secondary products in plants that have diverse functions in plants, notably in defense, such as cell wall strengthening and repair (e.g. lignin), antimicrobial activity (e.g. flavonoids, isoflavonoids, phytoalexins etc.), as signalling compounds such as salicylic acid (Howles et al., 1996) and wound-protective hydroxycinnamic acid esters including salicylic acid (Wen et al., 2005). Lim et al. (1997) also characterized PAL using SDS-PAGE. They showed that this enzyme consist of 4 subunits each having an estimated molecular weight of about 40,000 dalton on SDS-PAGE. In bean (*Phaseolus vulgaris* L.), PAL is encoded by a family of three genes (PAL 1, PAL 2 and PAL 3). Corresponding differential pattern of synthesis of specific PAL polypeptide isoforms were observed by gel electrophoretic analysis (Liang et al., 1989). SDS-PAGE analysis of three different purified recombinant proteins showed that the limits of detection were protein specific (Nishihara and Champion, 2002).

Because of the diverse roles played by phenylpropanoid-derived compounds, phenylpropanoid metabolism is under both environmental and developmental controls (Dixon and Paiva, 1995). Phenylpropanoid synthesis is activated as a response to stress, which includes elicitor treatment (Cui et al., 1996; Heinz et al., 1998; Joos and Hahlbrock, 1992; Sharma et al., 2011), pathogen infection (Habereder et al., 1989; Hahlbrock and Scheel, 1989), wounding (Lamb et al., 1989; Logemann et al., 1995), and UV irradiation (Lawton and Lamb, 1987). Using transgenic plants, it has been shown that PAL activity is a major control point for regulating the phenylpropanoid pathway (Maher et al., 1994; Strack, 1997) and the regulation of the enzyme activity is important in modulating phenylpropanoid biosynthesis in plants (Nagaranthna et al., 1993). Therefore, this proves that light, UV, wounding, nutrient and salt stress, nitrogen starvation, fungal elicitor, and fungal infection alters PAL activity which ultimately affects the phenylpropanoid pathway (Hahlbrock and Scheel, 1989; Dixon et al., 1994; Orczyk et al., 1996). PAL isozymes in *Arabidopsis thaliana* are synthesized de novo in response to UV irradiation, microbial attack and wounding (Li et al., 1993).

The reactions catalyzed by PAL are fundamental to processes in normal growth and development as well as in defense responses. Some authors reported that PAL may serve as a marker for induced resistance of plants to diseases (Tyuterev, 2002) and demonstrated its presence in pathogen-infected plants (Chen et al., 2000). Nita-Lazar et al. (2004) also demonstrated a rapid and transient increase in PAL activity in *Rubus fructicos* after treatment with an oligosaccharide isolated from *Fusarium oxysporum* L.

OXIDATIVE BURST

The oxidative burst is generally defined as a rapid production of high levels of ROS in response to external stimuli (Jones and Dangl, 1996; Bolwel et al., 1995). Reactive oxygen species (ROS) play a central role in plant defense against various pathogens (Mittler et al., 2004). Superoxide anion (O_2^-) and hydrogen peroxide (H_2O_2) and hydroxyl radical are the three major forms of ROS (Apel and Hirt, 2004). These molecules are highly reactive and toxic and can lead to the oxidative destruction of cells (Asada and Takahashi, 1987). The rapid accumulation of plant ROS at the pathogen attack site is toxic to pathogens directly (Lamb and Dixon, 1997) and can lead HR that results in a zone of host cell death, which prevents further spread of biotrophic pathogens (Heath, 2000; Gechev et al., 2006).

In addition to the described direct effects, ROS can also serve as signals that lead to the activation of other defense mechanisms (Dat et al., 2000; Grant and Loake, 2000). Various ROS-scavenging systems, including ascorbate peroxidases, glutathione, superoxide dismutases, and catalases maintain ROS homeostasis in different compartments of the plant cell (Mittler et al., 2004; Apel and Hirt, 2004; Passardi et al., 2004; Mika et al., 2004). These enzymes could restrict the ROS-dependent damage or maintain the ROS-dependent signal transduction. Differential regulation of these enzymes, in part mediated by SA, may contribute to increases in ROS and activation of defenses following infection (Dorey et al., 1998; Mittler et al., 1999; Klessig et al., 2000).

The first report on the rapid ROS production appeared in 1983, demonstrating the generation of superoxide radical (O_2^-) by potato (*Solanum tuberosum*) tuber discs that is rapidly transformed into H_2O_2 only in response to inoculation with an incompatible race of *Phytophthora infestans* or with hyphal wall components, but not with a compatible race (Doke, 1983). Similarly, H_2O_2 production was also observed during avirulent interaction between the bacteria *Pseudomonas syringae* strain DC3000 and Arabidopsis (Alvarez et al., 1998). Since then, further research has shown that pathogens induce a ROS production in plants, which thought to play an important signaling role in the activation and establishment of plant defense (Levine et al., 1994). The oxidative burst is considered as one of the earliest events following elicitation. This reaction was observed in plants challenged with pathogenic micro-organisms, including fungi, bacteria and viruses, as well as in cultured cells treated with elicitor preparations, pathogens or plant cell-wall fragments or in response to mechanical stress (Low and Merida, 1996). Huckelhoven and Kogel (2003) demonstrated that barley (*Hordeum vulgare*) leads to the formation of defensive barriers against powdery mildew by the production of reactive oxygen species.

PEROXIDASE

Peroxidase (PO) is a heme protein, which is a member of oxidoreductases [E.C.1.11.1.7] and catalyses the oxidation of a wide variety of organic and inorganic substrates in the presence of hydrogen peroxide (Banci, 1997; Köksal and Gulcin, 2008). The plant peroxidases (POs) are considered to catalyze the generation of aromatic oxyl radicals from several aromatic compounds (Takahama and Yoshitama, 1998), and the PO-dependent production of such organic radicals often results in the generation of reactive oxygen species (ROS) (Kagan et al., 1990). Plant POs catalyzes the single one-electron oxidation of several substrates at the expense of H_2O_2 (Almagro et al., 2009):

$$2RH + H_2O_2 \rightarrow 2R^* + 2H_2O$$

Peroxidases are widely distributed in living organisms including microorganisms, plants and animals. POs are involved in a broad range of physiological processes throughout the plant life cycle, probably due to the high number of enzymatic isoforms (isoenzymes) and to the versatility of their enzyme-catalysed reactions (Passardi et al., 2005). They play an important role in various physiological processes, such as construction, rigidification and eventual lignifications of cell walls (Quiroga et al., 2000), suberization (Bernards et al., 1999), phenol oxidation (Lagrimini, 1991), cross-linking of cell wall proteins (Schnabelrauch et al., 1996), protection of tissue from damage and infection by pathogenic microorganisms (Sakharov et al., 2000; Gulcin and Yildirim, 2005; Sat, 2008). Peroxidase plays an important role in the resistance mechanism of plant (Siddiqui & Mahmood, 1992; Mantoo & Siddiqui, 1996; Lin and Kao, 2001). Peroxidases catalyze the final polymerization step of lignin synthesis and, therefore, may be directly associated with the increased ability of systemically protected tissue to lignify (Chittoor et al., 1999) after pathogen attack or physical injury. This enzyme also participates in the formation of phytoalexins when plants are infected or wounded (Dixon and Paiva, 1995; Köksal and Gulcin, 2008). Therefore, higher peroxidase activity resulted in an increase in the phenolic contents of plant, which plays an important role in the resistance of cultivar (Mahmood & Saxena, 1986). Accumulation of lignin and phenolic compounds has been correlated with disease resistance in a number of plant-pathogen interactions. These include wheat-*Fusarium graminearum* (Mohammadi and Kazemi, 2002) and cucumber-*Pythium aphanidermatum* (Chen et al., 2000). They are also involved in the oxidation of isophenols to various other forms that are more toxic towards the pathogens (Takahama and Hirota, 2000). This may further limit the penetration of pathogen toxins into the cells and thus the spread of the infection (Lurie et al., 1997). Peroxidase due to their multifunctional nature considered as the sensitive markers of stress conditions. More recently, Ye and Ng (2002) demonstrated for the first time that a plant peroxidase (from *P. vulgaris* cv. Kentucky wonder) exhibits antifungal activity against various fungi including *Coprinus comatus*, *Mycospharella arachidicola*, *Fusarium oxysporum* and *Botrytis cinerea*. Moreover, under the influence of pathogenic microorganisms or other stress factors, peroxidases are the first enzymes to alter their activity and/or the composition of their isoenzymes (Lamb and Dixon, 1997; Ye et al., 1990). Xue et al. (1998) found a positive correlation between enhanced peroxidase activity and systemic protection against *Rhizoctonia solani* and *Colletotrichum lindemuthianum* in bean (*Phaseolus vulgaris*) plants.

POLYPHENOL OXIDASE

Polyphenol oxidase – PPO (EC 1.10.3.2) is an enzyme of broad distribution among plants, which catalyzes the hydroxylation of monophenols to o-diphenols and their oxidation to o-diquinones (Mayer and Harel, 1979). These quinones are highly reactive electrophiles that can undergo complex secondary reaction pathways, in particular the 1, 4 additions of *o*-quinones to cellular nucleophiles and the reversed disproportionation of quinones to semiquinone radicals that may lead to generation of reactive oxygen species (ROS). PPO-generated quinones and ROS can play an array of defense-related functions simultaneously.

The PPO activity can be induced by abiotic and biotic factors, such as damage caused by herbivores, fungal and bacterial infections, mechanical damage, insect regurgitation and by treatments with compounds which signal the octadecanoid pathway. Recently, Li and Steffens (2002) have obtained direct evidence of such a role for PPO in plants. These authors observed that transgenic plants of tomato overexpressing PPO had a higher oxidizing capacity and displayed increased resistance to *Pseudomonas syringae* pv. tomato. A positive correlation between polyphenol oxidase activity and disease resistance has been suggested in many reports (Constabel et al., 2000; Haruta et al., 2001; Li and Steffens, 2002; Shimizu, 2004). The mode of action proposed for PPO in defense is based on its capacity to oxidize phenolic compounds when the tissue is damaged. The breakdown of plastids membrane after pathogen attack releases PPO enzyme which ultimately comes in direct contact with the phenolic compounds released by rupture of the vacuole, the main storage organelle of these compounds (Mayer and Harel, 1979). PPO activity also leads to direct toxicity to plant and pathogen cellular macromolecules by quinone-mediated covalent modification or direct anti-microbial toxicity of H_2O_2 in the vicinity of pathogen attack, which ultimately may restrict disease progression (Thipyapong et al., 2007). Moreover, protein bioavailability to pathogens may be reduced due to the alkylation of plant proteins (Felton et al., 1989).

In addition to role in direct defense response, PPO generates H_2O_2 which could also be an important component of signalling processes. H_2O_2 plays a role in signalling by acting as a diffusible inducer of cellular protectant genes, phytoalexin biosynthesis, and salicylic acid and ethylene production, as well as a trigger of cell death resulting in restricted lesions delimited from surrounding healthy tissue. In addition, other plant defense genes and ultimately plant immunity may be elicited by ROS-mediated systemic signalling network (Grant and Loake, 2000; Garcia-Olmedo et al., 2001; Thipyapong et al., 2004).

SALICYLIC ACID

Salicylic or 2-dihydroxybenzoic acid (SA) is an endogenous growth regulator which occurs naturally in plants in very low amounts. It plays an important role in fulfilling numerous functions in plants under normal conditions and also participates in the regulation of physiological processes in plant such as stomatal closure, nutrient uptake, chlorophyll synthesis, protein synthesis, inhibition of ethylene biosynthesis, transpiration, photosynthesis heat production, flowering, germination and pathogen resistance (Raskin, 1992; Khan et al., 2003; Shakirova et al., 2003).

SA is the systemic signal molecule in plants that is induced by a number of biotic and abiotic stresses. A lot of data exist on the protective effect of SA against ultraviolet light (Yalpani et al., 1994), salinity (Shakirova et al., 2003), drought (Singh and Usha, 2003), heavy metal toxicity (Metawally et al., 2003), high temperatures (Dat et al., 1998), paraquat (Ananieva et al., 2002) and pathogen stress (Wang et al., 2005). It has been shown to play an important signalling role in the activation of various plant defense responses following pathogen attack (Raskin, 1992). These responses include the induction of local and systemic disease resistance, the potentiation of host cell death, and the limitation of pathogen spread (Shah, 2003; Panina et al., 2005). In the last two decades, the role of SA in pathogen resistance has been studied extensively (Durrant and Dong, 2003; Raskin, 1992).

SA can activate other resistance mechanisms such as pathogenesis-related (PR) proteins, phytoalexin production, proteinase inhibitors, or cell wall strengthening and lignification. The induction of synthesis of PR proteins and/or other components of SAR in tobacco and cucumber by SA were well documented (Malamy et al., 1990; Yalpani et al., 1991). When tobacco cultivars (NN genotype) resistant to tobacco mosaic virus (TMV) are inoculated with TMV, the HR is elicited along with increase in level of SA and the spread of the virus is restricted (Malamy et al., 1990). SA can also be detected in the phloem exudate of excised tobacco leaves following TMV inoculation (Yalpani et al., 1991). The appearance of SA in the phloem is also accompanied by the increase in the level of SA in uninoculated leaves above the TMV inoculated leaf (Malamy et al., 1990; Yalpani et al., 1991). This confirms the role of SA in disease resistance by directly relating increases in leaf SA to greater TMV resistance and by showing that SA levels naturally present during SAR are sufficient for the induction of resistance to TMV. Following the primary infection, the inoculated plant becomes resistant to subsequent pathogen attack, both locally and systemically, in pathogen-free leaves. Generally, mutants with constitutively high SA levels are resistant to biotrophic pathogens, whereas, those unable to accumulate SA are susceptible (Zhang et al., 2007; Shah et al., 2001; Zhang et al., 2003; Shirano et al., 2002; Heidel et al., 2004).

SA is a downstream metabolite of the phenypropanoid pathway. The biosynthetic pathway of SA appears to begin with the conversion of phenylalanine to transcinnamic acid (t-CA) catalyzed by PAL (Figure 3.1). The conversion of t-CA into SA has been proposed to proceed via chain shortening to produce benzoic acid (BA). Two routes have been proposed for the conversion of t-CA to BA for the formation of SA. The side chain of t-CA could be oxidatively shortened, which would produce *trans*-cinnamoyl-CoA as an intermediate. Support for the existence of this pathway comes from early studies showing that acetyl-CoA stimulated the conversion of CA to BA (Alibert and Ranjeva, 1971). The side chain of t-CA could also be shortened by a "nonoxidative" mechanism, which is characterized by the presence of *p*-hydroxybenzaldehyde as an important metabolic intermediate. Such a nonoxidative mechanism for the formation of *p*-hydroxybenzoic acid has been demonstrated in cell cultures of carrot (Schnitzler et al., 1992) and in cell-free extracts of *Lithospermum erythrorhizon* (Yazaki et al., 1991) and potato (French et al., 1976).

Like other phenolics in plants, SA is rapidly conjugated to an O-glucoside to form 2-*O*-β-D-glucosylsalicylic acid (SAG), which serves as a biologically inert reservoir of SA that can be hydrolyzed as needed (Enyedi and Raskin, 1993). SA is also present in plants as methyl-salicylate, which can also be conjugated to glucose (Lee et al., 1995). It has been shown that methyl-salicylate may function as an airborne signal, which activates disease resistance and expression of defense-related genes in neighbouring plants and healthy tissues of the infected plant (Shulaev et al., 1997). It acts by being converted back to SA. In tobacco, volatile methyl salicylate (MeSA) is produced from SA after infection and can induce defence responses by conversion to SA (Leon et al., 1993). Exogenous application of SA to plants can also confer resistance to pathogen by inducing the appearance of PR proteins, some of which have defense-related functions (Ward et al., 1991). Kim et al. (2003) also showed that SA induces PR protein synthesis in Chinese cabbage.

PATHOGENESIS RELATED PROTEINS

Pathogenesis related (PR) proteins were first described in the 1970s by Van Loon, who observed accumulation of various novel proteins in leaves of tobacco (*Nicotiana tabacum* cv Samsun NN and Xanthi-nc, respectively) after tobacco mosaic virus infection and were assumed to limit multiplication and/or spread of the invading virus (Van Loon and Van Kammen, 1970; Van Loon and Van Strien, 1999). PRs are distinguished by specific biochemical properties. They are low-molecular proteins (6-43 kDa), extractable and stable at low pH (< 3), thermostable, and highly resistant to proteases (Van Loon, 1999). These physicochemical properties enable them to resist to acidic pH and proteolytic cleavage and thus able to survive in the harsh environments where they occur, the vacuolar compartment or cell wall or intercellular spaces (Van Loon, 1999).

PR proteins are plant species-specific proteins induced specifically in pathological or related situations (Antoniw and Pierpoint, 1978; Van Loon et al., 1994). Besides being induced by pathogens, PRs synthesis can be affected by abiotic stresses such as chemicals (salicylic, polyacrylic), fatty acids, inorganic salts, as well as physical stimuli (wounding, UV-B radiation, osmotic shock, low temperature, water deficit and excess).

They display a great variety in their primary structure, in species specificity, and in the mechanism of action (Leiter et al., 2005). Induction and accumulation of various PR proteins is important feature of the plant defense response to pathogens (Van Loon et al., 2006). Induction of PR proteins is accompanied by a massive alteration in the pattern of gene expression and activation of other defense responses such as phytoalexin accumulation, lignin deposition and synthesis of cell wall hydroxyproline-rich glycoproteins (Cramer et al., 1985; Lawton and Lamb, 1987). Several studies have investigated PR proteins in soybean (Li et al., 2000), tomato (Ramamoorthy et al., 2002), wheat (Freitas et al., 2003) and capsicum (Guevara-Morato et al., 2010). Even in the homologous symbiotic interaction, accumulation of PRs has been described as part of the mechanism by which the legume controls infection and regulates nodulation (Vasse et al., 1993). They are not only accumulated locally in the infected leaf, but are also induced systemically, and are associated with the development of SAR against further infection by fungi, bacteria and viruses. It is generally thought that SAR results from the concerted effects of many PR proteins rather than a specific PR protein. Van Loon and Antoniw (1982) had shown that PR genes serve as useful molecular markers for the onset of SAR.

Being first detected in tobacco, PRs have subsequently been identified in numerous monocotyledonous and dicotyledonous plants across different genera, and hence can be considered as ubiquitously distributed in plant kingdom.

Originally, five main classes of PRs (PR-1±5) were characterized by both biochemical and molecular-biological techniques in tobacco (Bol et al., 1990, Van Loon et al., 1987). Later, other families of PR-proteins were reviewed and recognized (Yun et al., 1997; Datta and Muthukrishnan, 1999; Broekaert et al., 2000). Now, 17 families of PR proteins have been classified (Table 2.2) (Van Loon et al., 2006). Brunner et al. (1998) showed that PR proteins comprise four families of chitinases (PR-3, -4, -8 and -11), one of â-1,3-glucanases (PR-2), one of proteinase inhibitors (PR-6),one endoproteinase (PR-7) and one specific peroxidase (PR-9), as well as the PR-1 family with unknown biochemical properties, the thaumatin-like PR-5 family, and one of the ribonuclease belongs to PR-10 family. The PR-12 type defensins, PR-13 type thionins and PR-14 type lipid transfer proteins (LTPs) all exhibit antifungal and antibacterial activity (Bohlmann, 1994; Broekaert et al., 1997; Garcßa-Olmedo et al., 1995). Germins and germin-like proteins (GLPs) have been classified as PR-15 and PR-16 (Van Loon and Van Strien, 1999; Selitrennikoff, 2001; Bernier and Berna, 2001; Park et al., 2004 a, b).

The first PR-1 protein was discovered in 1970. Since then, a number of PR-1 proteins have been identified in *Arabidopsis, Hordeum vulgare* (barley), *Nicotiana tabacum* (tobacco), *Oryza sativa* (rice), *Piper longum* (pepper), *Solanum lycopersicum* (tomato), *Triticum* sp. (wheat) and *Zea mays* (maize) (Liu and Xue, 2006). PR-1 proteins have antifungal activity at the micromolar level against a number of plant pathogenic fungi, including *Uromyces fabae, Phytophthora infestans,* and *Erysiphe graminis* (Niderman et al., 1995).

Chitinases and β-1, 3-glucanases are present in many higher plants. Both possess the potential antifungal activity, which collectively plays a role in inhibiting pathogen growth, multiplication and/or spread, and can also be responsible for the state of SAR (Kombrink and Somssich, 1997; Ryals et al., 1997). They lead to weakening of fungal cell walls (containing glucans, chitin and proteins) and lysis of the fungal cell wall that would ultimately elicit various defense mechanisms in the plants (Frindlender et al., 1993). In *Arabidopsis thaliana,* the expression of PR-1, PR-2 and PR-5 is required for increased protection against *Pernospore parasitica* and *Pseudomonas syringae.* It has also been reported that induction of PR-3 and PR-4 is associated with induced resistance to *Alternaria brassicicola, Botrytis cinerea* and *Erwinia carotovora* (Van Loon and Van Strien, 1999). Further, the activities of these enzymes were also measured in chickpea (Saikia et al., 2005). Xu et al., (2008) observed significant stimulation in the activities of chitinase and β-1,3-glucanases in peach seeds upon infection with *Puchia membranaefaciens, Cryptococcus laurentii, Candida guilliermondii* and *Rhodotorula glutinis* and suggested that antioxidant defense response may be involved in the mechanisms of microbial biocontrol agents against fungal pathogen. In another experiment the transgenic wheat lines carrying a combination of a wheat chitinase and b-1,3-glucanases exhibited delayed symptoms of *Fusarium* head blight (Anand et al., 2003).

GENETIC BASIS OF DISEASE RESISTANCE

Particular cultivars of plant species possess the ability to recognize certain strains or races of the pathogen species and, consequently, activate an efficient resistance response (race:cultivar-specific resistance) (Heath, 1997; Flor, 1971; De Wit, 1997). Race-specific pathogen recognition is determined by the action of complementary pairs of (semi) dominant resistance (*R*) genes in the host plant and (semi) dominant avirulence (*avr*) genes in the pathogen (Flor, 1971; De Wit, 1997). Expression of the *avr* gene triggers plant defense responses governed by the product of the R gene. Lack or nonfunctional products of either gene would result in colonization of the plant.

The genetic evidence for the gene-for-gene relationship was first provided by Flor's (1955) work. He explained gene-for-gene relationship by studying the interaction between flax and the causal agent of flax rust, the phytopathogenic fungus *Melampsora lini*. He proposed that the resistance results from the combination of a dominant avirulence (*Avr*) gene in the pathogen and a cognate resistance (*R*) gene in the host. A biochemical interpretation of this gene-for-gene concept implies a receptor:ligand-like interaction between plant *R* gene products and the corresponding *avr* gene products from the pathogen (De Wit, 1997; Keen, 1990). The interaction of both gene products leads to the activation of host defence responses, such as the hypersensitive response, transcriptional activation of defense-related genes, such as production of lytic enzymes, phytoalexin biosynthesis, development of the HR, expression of PR proteins and systemic acquired resistance that arrests the growth of fungi (Hammond-Kosack and Jones, 1996; Ebel and Scheel, 1997; Dempsey et al., 1999; Kombrink and Schmelzer, 2001).

This gene-for-gene concept has been experimentally demonstrated for a number of pathosystems, mainly involving biotrophic fungi, with a number of avirulent genes identified (De wit et al., 2009). The *avrNIP1* gene from the barley leaf scald causing fungus, *Rhynchosporium secalis*, was shown to contribute to virulence of the pathogen on susceptible barley cultivars (Rohe et al., 1995). Similarly, a number of bacterial avr genes were also shown to be indispensible for full virulence in compatible host plants (Alfano et al., 1997; Ritter and Dangl, 1995; Yang et al., 1996). The *avrBs2* gene from *Xanthomonas campestris* pv. *vesicatoria* appears to be important for the pathogen to cause disease on its host, pepper, as deletion of the gene resulted in reduced pathogenicity (Kearney and Staskawicz, 1990). Sequence similarity of the *avrBs2* gene product to *Agrobacterium tumefaciens* agrocinopine synthase suggests a role of this protein in pathogen nutrition during infection (Swords et al., 1996). Obviously, the role of *avr* genes and their gene products as avirulence determinants is coincidental and disadvantageous for the pathogen. This situation may reflect rather interestingly the plant's ability to recognize a pathogen and activate its pathogen defense machinery through components that are important for the life cycle of the pathogen (De wilt, 1997; Knogge, 1996).

The identification and characterization of many R genes and in many cases their corresponding effect or proteins have increased research into the molecular basis of gene-for-gene resistance (Cohn et al., 2001; Martin et al., 2003). Most of R genes encode proteins with a predicted trimodular structure (Inohara and Nunez, 2003; Martin et al., 2003). These molecules act as receptors which mediate Avr protein recognition. At their carboxy terminus, they carry a Leucine-rich repeat (LRR) domain believed to be the initial recognition domain and mediate protein-protein interactions (Kobe and Kajava, 2001). Various studies indicate that the pathogen specificity resides in this domain (Thomas et al., 1997; Jia et al., 2000; Seear and Dixon, 2003).

Different plants have different spectrum of *R* genes which work against different *Avr* genes present differentially in pathogens. Hence the incorporation of *R* gene from resistant plant to susceptible plant leads to resistance to pathogen carrying corresponding *Avr* gene (Grover and Gowthaman, 2003). Therefore, many plant resistance genes (R-genes) have been cloned and characterized (Dangl and Jones, 2001). R genes from maize, tobacco, tomato and flax have been cloned using transposon-based gene tagging techniques. The first cloned plant R genes was the Hm1 gene of maize. This gene encodes a HC-toxin reductase which inactives HC-toxin produced by *Cochliobolus carbonum* race 1 isolated as a pathogenicity factor (Johal and Briggs, 1992). Therefore, the cloned R gene controls resistance in maize against *C. carbonum* race 1. Further, R genes from tomato and *Arabidopsis* have been cloned using the map-based positional cloning technique. The small size of the *Arabidopsis* (150 Mb) and tomato (950 Mb) genomes and the presence of small numbers of repeated sequences in these plants help to positionally clone two R genes in these plants (Staskawicz et al., 1995).

Plant resistance which is not conferred by a single gene but results from involvement of many genes is called polygenic. An example of polygenic resistance gene products is PR proteins which are strongly linked to plant resistance. These have enzyme activities e.g. β-1,3 glucanase, endochitinase, peroxidase etc (Fritig et al., 1998). A wide range of plant antimicrobial proteins have been described and enhanced resistance has been obtained by introducing the corresponding genes into crop species to produce transgenic lines (Fritig et al., 1998). Transgenic tomato plants expressing a *Lycopersicon chilense* chitinase gene was shown to have improved resistance to *Verticillium dahlia* race 2 compared to non transgenic plants (Tabeizadeh et al., 1999).

The defense response genes in plants have been studied and classified with the aim of manipulating the plant signals that regulate an array of defense responses (Cheng, 1998; Vidhyasekaran, 1998). Development of genetic engineering technology and molecular characterization of plant defense responses have provided strategies for controlling plant diseases in addition to those based on chemical control or classical breeding programmes. Genetic engineering techniques provide new tools and methods to produce new, disease-resistant crop varieties (Honee, 1999).

CONCLUSION

From the review of the available knowledge in the literature, it can be concluded that the infection in the plants with microbial system induced an up regulation of plant defense mechanisms. This resulted in increased accumulation of antifungal phenolic compounds, salicylic acid along with increase in the activities of PAL, polyphenol oxidase, peroxidase and total proteins which are known to inhibit fungal growth. This would be a fundamental step in controlling the spread of the infection within the host.

REFERENCES

Anubhuti Sharma, Neha Joshi, Annu Maheswari, Pratibha Sharma and Sandhya Sharma, Induction of Defense Related Metabolites in Four Different Cultivars of Chickpea (*Cicer arietinum*) by *Macrophomina phaseolina. Indian Journal of Mycology and Plant Pathology,* 41 (1): 91-96, 2011.

Anubhuti Sharma, Sandhya Sharma, Neha Joshi and Pratibha Sharma, Alteration in Biochemical Response in *Sesamum indicum* Upon Different Plant-pathogen Interactions. *International J. of agri. Sci. and tech.* 5(6), 2011.

Adrian M, Jeandet P, Douillet-Breuil A, Tesson L and Bessis R (2000) Stilbene Content of Mature *Vitis vinifera* Berries in Response to UV-C elicitation. *J. Agr. Food Chem.* 48: 6103-6105.

Agrios GN (1997) Plant Pathol, 4th ed. San Diego: Academic Press, pp: 93-114.

Aist JR (1976) Papillae and Related Wound Plugs of Plant Cells. *Annu Rev Phytopathol.* 14: 145-163.

Alfano JR, Kim HS, Delaney TP and Collmer A (1997) Evidence that the *Pseudomonas syringae* pv. *Syringae* hrp- linked hrmA gene Encodes an Avr-like Protein that Acts in an hrp-dependent Manner within Tobacco Cells. *Mol. Plant-Microbe Interact.* 10: 580-588.

Alibert G and Ranjeva R (1971) Recherches sur les enzymes catalysant la biosynthese des Acides phenoliques chez *Quercus pedunculata* (ehrh.): I-formation des premiers termes des series cinnamique et benzoique. *FEBS Lett.* 19: 11-14.

Almargo L, Gomez Ros LV, Belchi-Navarro S, Bru R, Barcelo AR and Pedreño MA (2009) Class III Peroxidases in Plant defebce Reactions. *Journal of Experimental Botany.* 60(2): 377-390.

Alvarez ME, Pennell RI, Meijer P-J, Ishikawa A, Dixon RA and Lamb C (1998) Reactive Oxygen Intermediates Mediate a Systemic Signal Network in the Establishment of Plant Immunity. *Cell.* 92: 773-784.

Anand A, Zhou T, Trick HN, Gill BS and Bockus WW *et al.* (2003) Greenhouse and Field Testing of Transgenic Field Plants Stably Expressing Genes for Thaumatin Like Protein, Chitinase and Glucanase Against *Fusarium graminearum. J. Exp. Bot.* 54: 1101-1111.

Ananieva EA, Alexieva VS and Popova LP (2002) Treatment with Salicylic Acid Decreases the Effects of Paraquat on Photosynthesis. *J. Plant Physiol.* 159: 685-693.

Angelova Z, Georgiev S and Roos W (2006) Elicitation of Plants. *Biotechnol. & Biotechnol. Eq.* 20: 72-83.

Antoniw JF and Pierpoint WS (1978) Purification of a Tobacco Leaf Protein Associated with Resistance to Virus Infection. *Biochemical Society Transactions.* 6: 248-250.

Apel K and Hirt H (2004) Reactive Oxygen Species: Metabolism, Oxidative Stress, and Signal Transduction. *Annu Rev Plant Biol.* 55: 373-399.

Asada K and Takahashi M (1987) Production and Scavenging of Active Oxygen in Photosynthesis. *In* DJ Kyle, CB Osmond, CJ Amtzen, eds, Photoinhibition (Topics in Photosynthesis), Vol. 9. Elsevier, Amsterdam, pp. 227-287.

Baker JC, Mock N, Glazener J and Orlandi E (1993) Physiological Evidences Associated with Hypersensitive Response. *Physiol. Mol. Plant Pathol.* 43: 81-94.

Banci L (1997) Structural Properties of Peroxidases. *Journal of Biotechnology.* 53: 253-263.

Bernards MA, Fleming WD, Llewellyn DB, Priefer R, Yang X, Sabatino A and Plourde GL (1999) Biochemical Characterization of the Suberization-associated Anionic Peroxidase of Potato. *Plant Physiol.* 121: 135-145.

Bernier F and Berna A (2001) Germins and Germin-like Proteins, Plant do-all Proteins. But what do they Exactly? *Plant Physiology and Biochemistry.* 39: 545-554.

Bohlmann H (1994) The Role of Thionins in Plant Protection. *Crit Rev Plant Sci.* 13: 1-16.

Bol JF, Linthorst HJM and Cornelissen BJC (1990) Plant Pathogenesis-related Proteins Induced by Virus Infection. *Annu. Rev. Phytopathol.* 28: 113-138.

Boller T (1995) Chemoperception of Microbial Signals in Plant Cells. *Annu. Rev. Plant Physiol. Plant Mol Biol.* 46: 189-214.

Bolwell GP, Butt VS, Davies DR and Zimmerlin A (1995) The Origin of the Oxidative Burst in Plants. *Free Radic Res.* 23: 517-532.

Bradley DJ, Kjellbom P and Lamb CJ (1992) Elicitor- and Wound-induced Oxidative Cross-linking of a Proline-rich Plant Cell Wall Protein: A Novel Rapid Defense Response. *Cell.* 70: 21-30.

Broekaert WF, Cammue BPA, De Bolle MFC, Thevissen K, de Samblanx GW and Osborn RW (1997) Antimicrobial Peptides from Plants. *Cri Rev Plant Sci.* 16: 297-323.

Broekaert WF, Terras FRG and Cammue BPA (2000) Induced and Preformed antimicrobial Proteins. In Mechanisms of Resistance to Plant Diseases. Edited by Slusarenko, A.J., Fraser, R.S. and van Loon, L.C. pp. 371-477. Kluwer Academic Publishers, Dordrecht.

Brunner F, Stintzi A, Fritig B and Legrand M (1998) Substrate Specificities of Tobacco Chitinases. *The Plant Journal.* 14: 225-234.

Camm EL and Towers GHN (1973) Review Article: Phenylalanine Ammonia Lyase. *Phytochemistry.* 12: 961-73.

Carbone D and Arnaudi C (1930) L'immunità nelle piante. Monografie dell'Istituto Sieroterapico Milanese, Milano.

Chen CQ, Belanger RR, Benhamou N and Paulitz TC (2000) Defense Enzymes Induced in Cucumber Roots by Treatment with Plant Growth-promoting Rhizobacteria (PGPR) and *Pythium aphanidermatum. Physiological and Molecular Plant Pathology.* 56: 13-23.

Chen M and McClure JW (2000) Altered Lignin Composition in Phenylalanine ammonia-lyase-inhibited Radish Seedlings: Implications for Seed-derived Sinapyl esters as lignin precursors. *Phytochemistry.* 53: 365-370.

Cheng, J, Smith Becker J and Keen NT (1998) Genetics of Plant Pathogen Interactions. *Curr. Opin. Biotechnol.* 9: 202-207.

Chittoor JM, Leach JE and White FF (1999) Induction of Peroxidase during Defense Against Pathogens. In: Pathogenesis Related Proteins in Plants. S.K. Datta and S. Muthukrishnan, eds. CRC Press. Boca Raton, FL, U.S.A, pp. 171-193.

Cohn J, Sessa G, Martin GB (2001) Innate Immunity in Plants. *Curr. Opin. Immunol.* 13: 55-62.

Conceicao LF, Ferreres F, Tavores RM and Dios AC (2006) Induction of Phenolic Compounds in *Hypericum pertoralum* L. cells by *Colletotricohum gloeosprioides* Elicitation. *Phytochemistry.* 67: 149-155.

Constabel CP, Yip L, Patton JJ and Christopher ME (2000) Polyphenol Oxidase from Hybrid Poplar: Cloning and Expression in Response to Wounding and Herbivory. *Plant Physiol.* 124: 285-295.

Cramer CL, Ryder TB, Bell JN and Lamb CJ (1985) Rapid Switching of Plant Gene Expression by Fungal Elicitor. *Science.* 227: 1240-1243.

Cui Y, Magill J, Frederiksen R and Magill C (1996) Chalcone Synthase and Phenylalanine Ammonia lyase mRNA following Exposure of Sorghum Seedlings to Three Fungal Pathogens. *Physiological and Molecular Plant Pathology.* 49: 187-199.

D'Cunha GB, Satyanarayan V and Nair PM (1996) Stabilization of Phenylalanine Ammonia lyase Containing *Rhodotorula glutinis* Cells for the Continuous Synthesis of L-phenylalanine methyl-ester. *Enzyme Microb. Technol.* 19: 421-427.

Da Cunha L, Aidan AM and Mackey D (2006) Innate Immunity in Plants: A Continuum of Layered Defenses. *Microbes and Infection.* 8: 1372-1381.

Dakora FD and Phillips DA (1996) Diverse Functions of Isoflavonoids in Legumes Transcend Anti-microbial Definitions of Phytoalexins. *Physiol Mol Plant Pathol.* 49: 1-20.

Dangl JL and Jones JD (2001) Plant Pathogens and Integrated Defence Responses to Infection. *Nature.* 411: 826-833.

Dat J, Vandenabeele S, Vranova E, Van Montagu M, Inze D and Van Breusegem F (2000) Dual Action of the Active Oxygen Species during Plant Stress Responses. *Cell Mol Life Sci.* 57: 779-795.

Dat JF, Lopez-Delago H, Foyer CH and Scott IM (1998) Parallel Changes in H_2O_2 and Catalase during Thermotolerance Induced by Salicylic Acid or Heat Acclimation in Mustard Seedlings. *Plant Physiol.* 116: 1351-1357.

Datta SK and Muthukrishnan S (1999) Pathogenesis-related Proteins in Plants. CRC Press LLC, 2000 Corporate Blvd, N.W, Boca Raton, Florida 33431.

De Wit PJ, Mehrabi R, Van den Burg HA and Stergiopoulos I (2009) Fungal Effector Proteins: Past, Present and Future. *Molecular Plant Pathology.* 10(6): 735-747.

De Wit PJGM (1997) Pathogen Avirulence and Plant Resistance: A Key Role for Recognition. *Trends Plant Sci.* 2: 452-458.

Delaney TP, Friedrich L and Ryals JA (1995) Arabidopsis Signal Transduction Mutant Defective in Chemically and Biologically Induced Disease Resistance. *Proceeding of National Academy of Sciences USA.* 92: 6602-6606.

Dempsey D, Shah J and Klessig DF (1999) Salicylic Acid and Disease Resistance in Plants. *Crit. Rev. Plant Sci.* 18: 547-575.

Dixon RA and Paiva NL (1995) Stress-induced phenylpropanoid Metabolism. *Plant Cell.* 7: 1085-1097.

Dixon RA, Harrison MJ and Lamb CJ (1994) Early Events in the Activation of Plant Defense Responses. *Annu Rev Phytopathol.* 32: 479-501.

Doke N (1983) Involvement of superoxide anion Generation in the Hypersensitive Response of Potato Tuber Tissues to Infection with an Incompatible Race of *Phytophthora infestans* and to the hyphal Wall Components. *Physiol Plant Pathol.* 23: 345-357.

Dorey S, Baillieul F, Pierrel MA, Saindrenan P, Fritig B and Kauffmann S (1997) Spatial and Temporal Induction of Cell Death, Defense Genes, and Accumulation of Salicylic Acid in Tobacco Leaves Reacting Hypersensitively to a Fungal Glycoprotein Elicitor. *Mol Plant-Microbe Interact.* 10: 646-655.

Dorey S, Baillieul F, Saindrenan P, Fritig B and Kauffmann S (1998) Tobacco Class I and II Catalases are Differentially Expressed during Elicitor Induced Hypersensitive Cell Death and Localized Acquired Resistance. *Mol Plant Microbe Interact.* 11: 1102-1109.

Durrant WE and Dong X (2004) Systemic Acquired Resistance. *Annu Rev Phytopathol.* 42: 185-209.

Ebel J and Cosio EG (1994) Elicitors of Plant Defense Responses. *Int. Rev. Cytol.* 148: 1-36.

Ebel J and Scheel D (1997) Signals in Host-parasite Interactions. In: Carrol GC, Tudzynski P (eds), The Mycota, Vol. V Part A, Springer-Verlag, Berlin, Heidelberg, New York, pp. 85-105.

Ehrenfeld N, Cañón P, Stance C, Medina C, Arce-Johnson P (2005) *Tobamovirus* Coat Protein CPCg Induces an HR-like Response in Sensitive Tobacco Plants. *Mol and Cells.* 19: 418-427.

Enyedi AJ and Raskin I (1993) Induction of UDP-g1ucose: Salicylic Acid Glucosyltransferase Activity in TMV-inoculated Leaves. *Plant Physiol.* 101: 1375-1380.

Farooq A and Tahara S (1999) Fungal Metabolism of Flavonoids and Related Phytoalexins. *Curr. Top. Phychem.* 2: 1-33.

Felton GW, Donato KK, Del Vecchio RJ and Duffey SS (1989) Activation of Plant Foliar Oxidases by Insect Feeding Reduces Nutritive Quality of Foliage for Noctuid Herbivores. *J.Chem. Ecol.* 15: 2667-2694.

Ferrer JL, Jez JM, Bowman ME, Dixon RA and Noel JP (1999) Structure of Chalcone Synthase and the Molecular Basis of Plant Polyketide Biosynthesis. *Nature Structural and Molecular Biology.* 6: 775-784.

Firdous SS, Rehana A, Hague MI and Afzal SN (2007) Development of Hypersensitive Response by *Xanthomonas campestris* pv. *sesami* on *Lycopersicon esculentum* L., and *Solanum tuberosum* L., leaves. *Pak. J. Bot.* 39(6): 2135-2139.

Flor HH (1955) Host-parasite Interactions in Flax Rust - Its Genetics and Other Implications. *Phytopathology.* 45: 680-685.

Flor HH (1971) Current Status of the Gene-for-gene Concept. *Annu. Rev. Phytopathol.* 9: 275-296.

Freitas LB, Koehler-Santos P and Salzano FM (2003) Pathogenesis-related Proteins in Brazilian Wheat Genotypes: Protein Induction and Partial Gene Sequencing. *Cienc. Rural.* 33: 497-500.

French CJ, Vance CP and Towers GHN (1976) Conversion of p-coumaric Acid to p-hydroxybenzoic Acid by Cell Free Extracts of Potato Tubers and *Polyporus hispidus. Phytochemistry.* 15: 564-566.

Friend J (1980) Plant Phenolics, Lignification and Plant Disease. *Pragr. Phytochem.* 14: 197-261.

Frindlender M, Inbar J and Chet I (1993) Biological Control of Soilborne Plant Pathogens by a β-1,3-glucanase Producing Pseudomonas cepacia. *Soil Biol. Biochem.* 25: 1211-1221.

Fritig B, Heitz T and Legrand M (1998) Antimicrobial Proteins in Induced Plant Defense. *Current Opinion in Immunology.* 10: 16-22.

Garcia-Olmedo F, Molina A, Segura A and Mooreno M (1995) The Defensive Role of Non specific Lipid-transfer Proteins in Plants. *Trend Microbiol.* 3: 72-75.

Garcia-Olmedo F, Rodriguez-Palenzuela P, Molina A, Alamillo JM, Lopez-Solanilla E, Berrocal-Lobo M and Poza-Carrion C (2001) Antibiotic Activities of Peptides, Hydrogen Peroxide and Peroxynitrite in Plant Defence. *FEBS Letters.* 498: 219-222.

Gechev TS, Van Breusegem F, Stone JM, Denev I and Laloi C (2006) Reactive Oxygen Species as Signals that Modulate Plant Stress Responses and Programmed Cell Death. *Bioessays.* 28: 1091-1101.

Gilchrist DG (1997) Mycotoxins Reveal Connections Between Plants and Animals in Apoptosis and Ceramide Signaling. *Cell Death Differ.* 4: 689-698.

Glazebrook J, Rogers EE and Ausubel FM (1997) Use of *Arabidopsis* for Genetic Dissection of Plant Defence Responses. *Annu Rev Genet.* 31: 547-569.

Grant JJ and Loake GJ (2000) Role of Reactive Oxygen Intermediates and Cognate Redox Signaling in Disease Resistance. *Plant Physiol.* 124: 21-29.

Grayer RJ and Kokubun T (2001) Plant-fungal Interactions: The Search for Phytoalexins and Other Antifungal Compounds from Higher Plants. *Phytochemistry.* 56: 253-263.

Grover A and Gowthaman R (2003) Strategies for Development of Fungus-resistant Transgenic Plants. *Current Science.* 84(3): 330-340.

Guevara-Morato MA, de Lacoba MG, García-Luque I and Serra MT (2010) Characterization of a Pathogenesis-related Protein 4 (PR-4) Induced in *Capsicum Chinense* L[3] Plants with dual RNase and DNase Activities. *Journal of Experimental Botany.* 61(12): 3259-3271.

Gülçin I and Yildirim A (2005) Purification and Characterization of Peroxidase from *Brassica oleracea* var. Acephala. *Asian J. Chem.* 17: 2175-2183.

Habereder H, Schroder G and Ebel J (1989) Rapid Induction of Phenylalanine Ammonia-lyase and Chalcone Synthase mRNAs during Fungus Infection of Soybean (*Glycine max* L.) Roots or Elicitor Treatment of Soybean Cell Cultures at the Onset of Phytoalexin Synthesis. *Planta.* 177: 58-65.

Hahlbrock K and Scheel D (1989) Physiology and Molecular Biology of Phenylpropanoid Metabolism. *Annu. Rev. Plant Physiol Mol. Biol.* 40: 347-369.

Hahn MG (1996) Microbial Elicitors and Their Receptors in Plants. *Annu. Rev. Phytopathol.* 34: 387-412.

Hammond-Kosack KE and Jones JDG (1996) Resistance Gene-dependent Plant Defense Responses. *Plant Cell.* 8: 1773-1791.

Hammond-Kosack KE and Jones JDG (2000) Response to Plant Pathogens. *In* BB Buchanan, W Gruissem, RL Jones, eds, Biochemistry and Molecular Biology of Plants. ASPP Press, Rockville, MD, pp. 1102-1156.

Harborne JB (1975) Biochemical Systematics of Flavanoids. In The Flavanoids (eds.) Harborne JB, Mabrg TJ and Mabry H. Chapman and Hall, London, pp. 1056-1095.

Haruta M, Pedersen JA and Constabel CP (2001) Polyphenol Oxidase and Herbivore Defense in Trembling Aspen (*Populus tremuloides*): cDNA Cloning Expression and Potential Substrates. *Physiol.Plant.* 112: 552-558.

Havir EA and Hanson KR (1973) L-Phenylalanine Ammonia- lyase (Maize and Potato). Evidence that the Enzyme is Composed of Four Subunits. *Biochemistry.* 12: 1583-1591.

Havir EA and Hanson KR (1975) L-Phenylalanine Ammonia-lyase (Maize, Potato, and *Rhodotorula glutinis*). Studies of the Prosthetic Group with Nitromethane. *Biochemistry.* 14: 1620-1626.

Heath MC (1997) Evolution of Plant Resistance and Susceptibility to Fungal Parasites. In G.C. Carroll and P. Tudzynski (Eds.) The Mycota Vol. V. Plant Relationships Part B. Springer-Verlag. Berlin/Heidelberg, pp. 257-276.

Heath MC (1998) Apoptosis, Programmed Cell Death and the Hypersensitive Response. *Eur J Plant Pathol.* 104: 117-124.

Heath MC (2000) Hypersensitive Response-related Death. *Plant Molecular Biology.* 44: 321-334.

Heidel AJ, Clarke JD, Antonovics J and Dong X (2004) Fitness Costs of Mutations Affecting the Systemic Acquired Resistance Pathway in *Arabidopsis thaliana*. *Genetics.* 168: 2197-2206.

Heinz R, Lee SW, Saparno A, Nazar RN and Robb J (1998) Cyclical Systemic Colonization in *Verticillium*-infected Tomato. *Physiological and Molecular Plant Pathology.* 52: 385-396.

Herrmann A, Löwer CF and Schachtel GA (1999) A New Tool for Entry and Analysis of Virulence Data in Plant Pathogens. *Plant Pathology.* 48: 154-158.

Honee G (1999) Engineered Resistance Against Fungal Plant Pathogens. *Euro. J. Plant pathol.* 105: 319-326.

Howles PA, Sewalt VJH, Paiva NL, Elkind Y, Bate NJ, Lamb C and Dixon RA (1996) Overexpression of L-phenylalanine Ammonia-lyase in Transgenic Tobacco Plants Reveals Control Points for Flux into Phenylpropanoid Biosynthesis. *Plant Physiology.* 112: 1617-1624.

Huckelhoven R and Kogel KH (2003) Reactive Oxygen Intermediates in Plantmicrobe Interactions: Who is who in Powdery Mildew Resistance? *Planta.* 216: 891-902.

Hutcheson S (1998) Current Concepts of Active Defense in Plants. *Ann. Rev. Phytopathology.* 36: 59-90.

Iakimova E, Atanassov A and Woltering E (2005) Chemical and Pathogen Induced Programmed Cell Death in Plants. *Biotechnol and Biotechnol. Eq.* 19: 124-138.

Ingham JL (1976) 3,5,4′-Trihydroxystilbene as a Phytoalexin from Groundnut (*Arachis hypogaea*). *Phytochemistry.* 15: 1791-1793.

Inohara N and Nunez G (2003) NODs: Intracellular Proteins Involved in Inflammation and Apoptosis. *Nature Rev Immunol.* 3: 371-382.

Iriti M and Faoro F (2006) Lipid Biosynthesis in Spermatophyta. In *Floriculture, Ornamental and Plant biotechnology;* Teixeira da Silva, J.A., Ed.; Global Science Books; London, UK, 2006; Vol. 1, Chapter 40, p. 359.

Jia Y, McAdams SA, Bryan GT, Hershey HP and Valent B (2000) Direct Interaction of Resistance Gene and Avirulence Gene Products Confers Rice Blast Resistance. *EMBO J.* 19: 4004-4014.

Johal GS and Briggs SP (1992) Reductase Activity Encoded by the HM7 Disease Resistance Gene in Maize. *Science.* 258: 985-987.

Jones AM and Dangl JL (1996). Logjam at the Styx: Programmed Cell Death in Plants. *Trends Plant Sci.* 1: 114-119.

Jones DH (1984) Phenylalanine Ammania-lyase: Regulaton of its Induction, and Role in Plant Development. *Phytochemistry.* 23: 1349-1359.

Joos HJ and Hahlbrock K (1992) Phenylalanine Ammonia-lyase in Potato (*Solanum tuberosum* L.): Genomic Complexity, Structural Comparison of Two Selected Genes and Modes of Expression. *Eur. J. Biochem.* 204: 621-629.

Kagan VE, Serbinova EA and Packer L (1990) Generation and Recycling of Radicals from Phenolic Antioxidants. *Arch. Biochem. Biophys.* 280: 33-39.

Kearney B and Staskawicz BJ (1990) Widespread Distribution and Fitness Contribution of *Xanthomonas campestris* Avirulence gene *avrBs2*. *Nature.* 346: 385-386.

Keen NT (1975) Specific Elicitors of Plant Phytoalexin Production: Determinants of Race Specificity in Pathogens? *Science.* 187: 74-75.

Keen NT (1990) Gene-for-gene Complementarity in Plant Pathogen Interactions. *Annu Rev Genet.* 24: 447-463.

Khan W, Prithiviraj B and Smith DL (2003) Photosynthetic Response of Corn and Soybean to Foliar Application of Salicylates. *J. Plant Physiol.* 160: 485-492.

Kim HN, Cha JS, Cho T and Kim HY (2003) Salycylic Acid and Wounding Induce Defense-related Proteins in Chinese Cabbage. *Korean J. Biol. Sci.* 7: 213-219.

Klessig DF, Durner J, Noad R, Navarre DA, Wendehenne D, Kumar D, Zhou JM, Shah J, Zhang S and Kachroo P, et al (2000) Nitric Oxide and Salicylic Acid Signaling in Plant Defense. *Proc Natl Acad Sci USA.* 97: 8849-8855.

Knogge W (1996) Fungal Infection of Plants. *The Plant Cell.* 8: 1711-1722.

Kobe B and Kajava AV (2001) The Leucine-rich Repeat as a Protein Recognition Motif. Curr. *Opin. Struct. Biol.* 11: 725-732.

Köksal E and Gülçin (2008) Purification and Characterization of Peroxidase from Cauliflower (*Brassica oleracea* L.) buds. *Protein Peptide Lett.* 15(4): 320-326.

Kombrink E and Schmelzer E (2001) The Hypersensitive Response and its Role in Local and Systemic Disease Resistance. *European Journal of Plant Pathology*. 107: 69-78.

Kombrink E and Somssich IE (1997) Pathogenesis-related Proteins and Plant Defense. In: G.C. Carrol & P. Tudzynski (eds), The Mycota V part A, Plant Relationships. Springer-Verlag, Berlin, pp. 107-128.

Kortekamp A and Zyprian E (2003) Characterization of *Plasmopara-resistance* in Grapevine Using *in vitro* Plants. *J Plant Physiol*. 160: 1393-1400.

Kuc J and Rush JS (1985) Phytoalexins. *Arch. Biochem. Biophys.* 236: 455-472.

Kuc´ J (1972) Phytoalexins. *Annu. Rev. Phytopathol.* 10: 207-232.

Lagrimini LM (1991) Wound-induced Deposition of Polyphenols in Transgenic Plants Overexpressing Peroxidase. *Plant. Physiol.* 96: 577-583.

Lamb C and Dixon RA (1997) The Oxidative Burst in Plant Disease Resistance. *Annu Rev Plant Physiol Plant Mol Biol.* 48: 251-275.

Lamb CJ, Lawton MA, Dron M and Dixon RA (1989) Signals and Transduction Mechanisms for Activation of Plant Defenses Against Microbial Attack. *Cell*. 56: 215-224.

Langcake P, Cornford CA and Pryce RJ (1979) Identification of Pterostilbene as a Phytoalexin from *Vitis vinifera* Leaves. *Phytochemistry*. 18: 1025-1027.

Lawton MA and Lamb CJ (1987) Transcriptional Activation of Plant Defense Genes by Fungal Elicitor, Wounding and Infection. *Mol Cell Biol*. 7: 335-341.

Lee HI, León J and Raskin I (1995) Biosynthesis and Metabolism of Salicylic Acid. *Proc Natl Acad Sci USA*. 92: 4076-4079.

Legendre L, Rueter S, Heinstein PF and Low PS (1993) Characterization of the Oligogalacturonide-induced Oxidative Burst in Cultured Soybean (*Glycine max*). *Cells Plant Physiology*. 102: 133-140.

Leiter E, Szappanos H, Oberparleiter C, Kaiserer L, Sernoch L, Pusztahelyi T, Emri T, Po´csi I, Salvenmoser W and Marx F (2005) Antifungal Protein PAF Severely Affects the Integrity of the Plasma Membrane of *Aspergillus nidulans* and Induces an Apoptosis-Like Phenotype. *Antimicrob. Agents Chemother.* 49 (6): 2445-2453.

León J, Yalpani N, Raskin I and Lawton MA (1993) Induction of Benzoic Acid 2-hydroxylase in Healthy and Virus-inoculated Tobacco. *Plant Physiol*. 103: 323-328.

Levine A, Pennell RI, Alvarez ME, Palmer R and Lamb C (1996) Calcium-mediated Apoptosis in a Plant Hypersensitive Disease Resistance Response. *Curr Biol*. 6: 427-437.

Levine A, Tenhaken R, Dixon R and Lamb C (1994) H_2O_2 from the Oxidative Burst Orchestrates the Plant Hypersensitive Disease Resistance Response. *Cell*. 79: 583-593.

Li J, Ou-Lee TM, Raba R, Amoundson RG and Last RL (1993) Arabidopsis Flavonoid Mutants are Hypersensitive to UV-B irradiation. *Plant Cell*. 5: 17-79.

Li L and Steffens JC (2002) Overexpression of Polyphenol Oxidase in Transgenic Tomato Plants Results in Enhanced Bacterial Disease Resistance. *Planta*. 215: 239-247.

Li S, Hartman GL, Lee B and Wildholm JW (2000) Identification of a Stress-induced Protein in Stem Exudates of Soybean Seedlings Root-infected with *Fusarium solani* f. sp. *glycines*. *Plant Physiol Biochem.* 38: 803-809.

Liang X, Dron M, Cramer CL, Dixon RA and Lamb CJ (1989) Differential Regulation of Phenylalanine Ammonia-lyase Genes during Plant Development and by Environmental Cues. *Journal of Biological Chemistry.* 264: 14486-14492.

Lim MJ, Patton WF, Lopez MF, Spofford KH, Shojaee N and Shepro D (1997) A Luminescent Europium Complex for the Sensitive Detection of Proteins and Nucleic Acids Immobilized on Membrane Supports. *Anal Biochem.* 245: 184-195.

Lin CC and Kao CH (2001) Abscisic Acid Induced Changes in Cell Wall Peroxidase Activity and Hydrogen Peroxide Level in Roots of Rice Seedlings. *Plant Sci.* 160: 323-329.

Liu Q and Xue Q (2006) Computational Identification of Novel PR-1-type Genes in *Oryza sativa*. *Journal of Genetics.* 85: 193-198.

Logemann E, Parniske M and Hahlbrock K (1995) Modes of Expression and Common Structural Features of the Complete Phenylalanine Ammonia-lyase Gene Family in Parsley. *Proc Natl Acad Sci USA.* 92: 5905-5909.

Low PS and Merida JR (1996) The Oxidative Burst in Plant Defense: Function and Signal Transduction. *Physiol Plant.* 96: 533-542.

Lurie S, Fallik E, Handros A and Shapira R (1997) The Possible Involvement of Peroxidase in Resistance to *Botrytis cinerea* in Heat Treated Tomato Fruit. *Physiol Mol Plant Pathol.* 50: 141-9.

Maher EA, Bate NJ, Ni W, Elkind Y, Dixon RA and Lamb CJ (1994) Increased Disease Susceptibility of Transgenic Tobacco Plants with Suppressed Levels of Preformed Phenylpropanoid Products. *Proc. Natl. Acad. Sci. U.S.A.* 91: 7802-7806.

Mahmood I and Saxena SK (1986) Relative Susceptibility of Different Cultivars of Tomato to *Rotytenchulus reniformis* in Reaction to Changes in Phenolics. *Revue Nematol.* 9: 89-91.

Malamy J, Carr JP, Klessig DF and Raskin I (1990) Salicylic Acid: A Likely Endogenous Signal in the Resistance Response of Tobacco to Viral Infection. *Science.* 250: 1002-1004.

Malolepsza U and RÓzalaska S (2005) Nitric Oxide and Hydrogen Peroxide in Tomato Resistance. Nitric Oxide Modulates Hydrogen Peroxide Level in O.hyd roxyethylorutin-induced Resistance to *Botrytis cinerea* in Tomato. *Plant Physiol Biochem.* 43: 623-635.

Manickam M, Ramanathan M, Jahromi MAF, Chansouria JPN and Ray AB (1997) Antihyperglycemic Activity of Phenolics from *Pterocarpus marsupium*. *Journal of Natural Products.* 60: 609-610.

Mantoo MA and Siddiqui MN (1996) Reaction of Chickpea Varieties to Root-knot Nematode and Their Effect on Peroxidase Activity and Protein Content. *Indian J Plant Pathol.* 14(1-2): 41-45.

Maarten H. Stuiver & Jerome H.H.V. Custers (2001) Progress Engineering Disease Resistance in Plants. *Nature* 411, 865-868.

Martin GB, Bogdanove AJ and Sessa G (2003) Understanding the Functions of Plant Disease Resistance Proteins. *Annu. Rev. Plant Biol.* 54: 23-61.

Mayer AM and Harel E (1979) Polyphenol Oxidases in Plants. *Phytochemistry*. 31: 193-215.

Mazullo A, Stefano DiM, Osti F and Cesari A (2000) Bioassays on the Activity of Resveratrol, Pterostilbene and Phosphorous Acid Towards Fungal Associated with Esca of Grapevine. *Phytopathol. Mediterr.* 39: 357-365.

Medina-Bolivar F, Condori J, Rimando AM, Hubstenberger J, Shelton K, O'Keefe S, Bennett S and Dolan MC (2007) Production and Secretion of Resveratrol in Hairy Root Cultures of Peanut. *Phytochemistry*. 68: 1992-2003.

Mehdy MC (1994) Active Oxygen Species in Plant Defense Against Pathogens. *Plant Physiol*. 105: 467-472.

Metwally A, Finkemeier I, Georgi M and Dietz K (2003) Salicylic Acid Alleviates the Cadmium Toxicity in Barley Seedlings. *Plant Physiology*. 132: 272-281.

Mika A, Minibayeva F, Beckett R and Luthje S (2004) Possible Functions of Extracellular Peroxidases in Stress-induced Generation and Detoxification of Active Oxygen Species. *Phytochem Rev*. 3: 173-193.

Mittler R, Herr EH, Orvar BL, van Camp W, Wilikens H, Inze´ D and Ellis BE (1999) Transgenic Tobacco Plants with Reduced Capability to Detoxify Reactive Oxygen Intermediates are Hyperresponsive to Pathogen Infection. *Proc Natl Acad Sci USA*. 96: 14165-14170.

Mittler R, Vanderauwera S, Gollery M and Breusegem FV (2004) Reactive Oxygen Gene Network of Plants. *Trends Plant Sci*. 9: 490-498.

Mizuno CS, Ma G, Khan S, Patny A, Averyc MA and Rimando AM (2008) Design, Synthesis, Biological Evaluation and Docking Studies of Pterostilbene Analogs Inside PPARa. *Bioorg. Med. Chem.* 16: 3800-3808.

Mohammadi M and Kazemi H (2002) Changes in Peroxidase and Polyphenol Activity in Susceptible and Resistant Wheat Heads Inoculated with *Fusarium graminearum* and Induced Resistance. *Plant Science*. 162: 491-498.

Montesano M, Brader G and Palva ET (2003) Pathogen Derived Elicitors: Searching for Receptors in Plants. *Mol. Plant Pathol.* 4: 73-79.

Muller KO and Börger H (1940) Experimentelle Untersuchungen Fiber die *Phytoph*thora-Resistenz der Kartoffel. *Arb. biol. Reichsanst. Land-u. Forstwirlsch., Berl.* 23: 189-231.

Nagarathna KC, Shetty SA and Shetty HS (1993) Phenylalanine Ammonia-lyase Activity in Pearl Millet Seedlings and its Relation to Downy Mildew Disease Resistance. *J. Exp. Bot.* 44: 1291-1296.

Nanjoo S, Shiby P, Xingpei H, Simi B, Xiao H, Rimando AM and Reddy BS (2007) Pterostilbene, an Active Constituent of Blueberries, Suppresses Aberrant Crypt foci Formation in the Azoxymethane-induced Colon Carcinogenesis Model in Rats. *Clin. Cancer Res.* 13: 350-355.

Niderman T, Genetet I, Bruyere T, Gees R, Stintzi A, Legrand M, Fritig B and Mosinger E (1995) Pathogenesis-related PR-1 Proteins are Antifungal. Isolation and Characterization of Three 14-kilodalton Proteins of Tomato and of a Basic PR-1 of Tobacco with Inhibitory Activity Against *Phytophthora infestans*. *Plant Physiol.* 108: 17-27.

Nishihara JC and Champion KM (2002) Quntitative Evaluation of Proteins in One and Two Dimensional Polyacrylamide gels Using a Fluorescent Stain. *Electrophoresis.* 23: 2203-2215.

Nita-Lazar M, Heyraud A, Gey C, Braccini I and Lienart Y (2004) Novel Oligosaccharides Isolated from *fusarium oxysporum* L. Rapidly Induce pal Activity in Rubus Cells. *Acta Biochim. Pol.* 51: 625-634.

Nürnberger T (1999) Signal Perception in Plant Pathogen Defense. *Cell. Mol. Life Sci.* 55: 167-182.

Nürnberger T and Scheel D (2001) Signal Transmission in the Plant Immune Response. *Trends Plant Sci.* 6: 372-379.

Orczyk W, Hipskind J, deNeergaard E, Goldsbrough P and Nicholson RL (1996) Stimulation of Phenylalanine Ammonia-lyase in Sorghum in Response to Inoculation with *Bipolaris maydis. Physiol Mol Plant Pathol.* 48: 55-64.

Ortega X, Velasquez JC and Pérez LM (2005) IP3 Production in the Hypersensitive Response of Lemon Seedlings Against *Alternaría alternata* Involves Active Protein Tyrosine kinases but not a G-protein. *Biol Res.* 38: 89-99.

Pan MH, Chang YH, Badmaev V, Nagabhushanam K and Ho CT (2007) Pterostilbene Induces Apoptosis and Cell Cycle Arrest in Human Gastric Carcinoma Cells. *J. Agric. Food Chem.* 55: 7777-7785.

Panina YS, Gerasimova NG, Chalenko GI, Vasyukova NI and Ozeretskovskaya OL (2005) Salicylic Acid and Phenylalanine Ammonia-Lyase in Potato Plants Infected with the Causal Agent of Late Blight. *Russian Journal of Plant Physiology.* 52(4): 511-515.

Park CJ, An JM, Shin YC, Kim KJ, Lee BJ and Paek KH (2004a) Molecular Characterization of Pepper Germin-like Protein as the Novel PR-16 Family of Pathogenesis-related Proteins Isolated during the Resistance Response to Viral and Bacterial Infection. *Planta.* 219: 797-806.

Park CJ, Kim KJ, Shin R, Park JM, Shin YC and Paek KH (2004b) Pathogenesis-related Protein 10 Isolated from Hot Pepper Functions as a Ribonuclease in an Antiviral Pathway. *The Plant Journal.* 37: 186-98.

Passardi F, Cosio C, Penel C and Dunand C (2005) Peroxidases have more Functions than a Swiss Army Knife. *Plant Cell Rep.* 24: 255-265.

Passardi F, Longet D, Penel C and Dunand C (2004) The Class III Peroxidase Multigenic Family in Rice and its Evolution in Land Plants. *Phytochemistry.* 65: 1879-1893.

Pedras MSC and Adio AM (2008) Phytoalexins and Phytoanticipins from the Wild Crucifers *Thellungiella halophila* and *Arabidopsis thaliana*: Rapalexin A, wasalexins and camalexins. *Phytochem.* 69: 889-893.

Perrin D and Bottomley W (1962) Studies on Phytoalexins. V. The Structure of Pisatin from *Pisum sativum. Journal of the American Chemical Society.* 84: 1919-1922.

Pezet R and Pont V (1988) Identification of Pterostilbene in Grape Berries of *Vitis vinifera. Plant Physiol. Biochem.* 26: 603-607.

Pezet R and Pont V (1990) Ultrastructural Observations of Pterostilbene Funcgitoxicity in Dormant Conidia of *Botrytis cinera* Pers. *J. Phytopathol.* 129: 19-30.

Pozo MJ, Cordier C, Dumas-Gaudot E, Gianinazzi S, Barea JM and Azcón-Aguilar C (2002) Localized versus Systemic Effect of Arbuscular Mycorrhizal Fungi on Defence Responses to *Phytophthora* Infection in Tomato Plants. *J Exp Bot.* 53: 525-534.

Quiroga M, Guerrero C, Botella MA, Barcelo A, Amaya I, Medina MI, Alonso FJ, Milrad DE, Forchetti S, Tigier H and Valpuesta V (2000) A Tomato Peroxidase Involved in the Synthesis of Lignin and Suberin. *Plant Physiol.* 122: 1119-1127.

Rajab R, Rajan SS, Satheesh LS, Harish SR, Sunukumar SS, Sandeep BS, Kishor Mohan TC and Murugan K (2009) Hypersensitive Response of *Sesamum prostratum* Retz. Elicitated by *Fusarium oxysporum f. sesame* (Schelt) Jacz Butler. *Indian journal of Experimental Biology.* 47: 834-838.

Ramamoorthy V, Raguchander T, Samiyappan R (2002) Induction of Defense-related Proteins in Tomato Roots Treated with *Pseudomonas fluorencens* Pf1 and *Fusarium oxysporum* f.sp. *lycopersici. Plant and Soil.* 239: 55-68.

Raskin I (1992) Role of Salicylic Acid in Plants. *Ann. Rev. Plant Physiol. Plant Mol. Biol.* 43: 439-463.

Remsberg CM, Yáñez JA, Ohgami Y, Vega-Villa KR, Rimando AM and Davies NM (2008) Pharmacometrics of pterostilbene: preclinical pharmacokinetics and Metabolism, Anticancer, Antiinflammatory, Antioxidant and Analgesic Activity. *Phytother. Res.* 22: 169-179.

Ritter C and Dangl JL (1995) The avrRpm1 gene of Pseudomonas Syringae pv. Maculicola is Required for virulence on Arabidopsis. *Mol. Plant-Microbe Interact.* 8: 444-453.

Rohe M, Gierlich A, Hermann H, Hahn M, Schmidt B, Rosahl S and Knogge W (1995) The Race Specific Elicitor, NIP1, from the Barley Pathogen, *Rhynchosporium secalis,* Determines Avirulence on Host Plants of the *Rrs1* Resistance Genotype. *EMBO J.* 14: 4168-4177.

Ross AF (1966) Systemic Effects of local Lesion Formation. In: A.B.R. Beemster & J. Dijkstra (Eds.), Viruses of Plants, pp. 127-150. North-Holland Publishing, Amsterdam.

Roupe KA, Remsberg CM, Yáñez JA and Davies NM (2006) Pharmacometrics of Stilbenes: Seguing Towards the Clinic. *Curr. Clin. Pharm.* 1(1): 81-101.

Ryals J, Neuenschawander UH, Willits MG, Molina A, Steiner HY and Hunt M (1996) Systemic Acquired Resistance. *Plant Cell.* 8: 1809-1819.

Ryals J, Uknes S and Ward E *(*1994*)* Systemic Acquired Resistance. Plant Physiol. 104: 1109-1112.

Ryals J, Weymann K, Lawton K, Friedrich L, Ellis D, Steiner HY, Johnson J, Delaney TP, Jesse T, Vos P and Uknes S (1997). The Arabidopsis NIM1 Protein Shows Homology to the Mammalian Transcription Factor Inhibitor IkB. *Plant Cell.* 9: 425-439.

Sacchettini JC and Poulter CD (1997) Creating Isoprenoid Diversity. *Science.* 277: 1788-1789.

Saikia R, Yadav M, Singh BP, Gogoi DK, Singh T and Arora DK (2006) Induction of Resistance in Chickpea by Cell Wall Protein of *Fusarium oxysporum* f. sp. *ciceri* and *Macrophomina phaseolina. Current Science.* 91(11, 10): 1543-1546.

Sakharov IY, Castillo JL, Areza JC and Galaev IY (2000) Purification and Stability of Peroxidase of African Oil Palm *Elaies guineensis*. *Bioseperation*. 9: 125-132.

Sarma AD, Sreelakshimi Y and Sharma R (1998) Differential Expression and Properties of Phenylalanine Ammonia-lyase Isoforms in Tomato Leaves. *Phytochemistry*. 49: 2233-2243.

Sarma AD and Sharma R (1999) Purification and Characterization of UV-B Induced Phenylalanine Ammonia-lyase from Rice Seedlings. *Phytochemistry*. 50: 729-737.

Sat IG (2008). The Effect of Heavy Metals on Peroxidase from Jerusalem Artichoke (*Helianthus tuberosus* L.) tubers. *Afr. J. Biotechnol*. 7: 2248-2253.

Schnabelrauch LS, Kieliszewski M, Upham BL, Alizedeh H and Lamport DTA (1996) Isolation of pI 4.6 Extension Peroxidase from Tomato Cell Suspension Cultures and Identification of Val-Tyr-Lys as Putative Intermolecular Cross-link Site. *Plant J*. 9: 477-489.

Schnitzller JP, Madlung J, Rose A and Seitz HU (1992) Biosynthesis of p-hydroxybenzoic Acid in Elicitor-treated Carrot cell Cultures. *Planta*. 188: 594-600.

Seear PJ and Dixon MS (2003) Variable leucine-rich Repeats of Tomato Disease Resistance Genes Cf-2 and Cf-5 Determine Specificity. *Mol Plant Pathol*. 4: 199-202.

Selitrennikoff CP (2001) Antifungal Proteins. *Applied Environ. Microbiol*. 67: 2883-2894.

Seshadri TR (1972) Polyphenols of *Pterocarpus* and *Dalbergia woods*. *Phytochemistry*. 11: 881-898.

Shah J (2003) The Salicylic Acid Loop in Plant Defense. *Curr. Opin. Plant Biol*. 6: 365-371.

Shah J, Kachroo P, Nandi A and Klessig DF (2001) A Recessive Mutation in the *Arabidopsis SSI2* gene Confers SA- and *NPR1*-independent Expression of *PR* Genes and Resistance Against Bacterial and Oomycete Pathogens. *Plant J*. 25: 563-574.

Shakirova FM, Sakhabutdinova AR, Bezrukova MV, Fathudinova RA and Fathutdinova DR (2003) Changes in Hormonal Status of Wheat Seedlings Induced by Salicylic Acid and Salinity. *Plant Sci*. 164: 317-322.

Shimizu MM (2004) Polifenoloxidase como fator de resistência dassoja a 'nematóide e na oxidação do palmito. Doctorate Thesis, Universidade Estadual de Campinas, Capinas/SP, Brazil, pp. 107.

Shirano Y, Kachroo P, Shah J and Klessig DF (2002) A gain-of-function Mutation in an Arabidopsis Toll interleukin1 Receptor-nucleotide Binding Site-leucine-rich Repeat type R gene Triggers Defence Responses and Results in Enhanced Disease Resistance. *Plant Cell*. 14: 3149-3162.

Shirasu K, Nakajima H, Rajasekhar VK, Dixon RA and Lamb CJ (1997) Salicylic Acid Potentiates an Agonist-dependent Gain Control that Amplifies Pathogen Signals in the Activation of Defence Mechanisms. *The Plant Cell*. 9: 261-270.

Shulaev V, Silverman P and Raskin I (1997) Airborne Signaling by Methyl Salicylate in Plant Pathogen Resistance. *Nature*. 385: 718-721.

Siddiqui ZA and Mahmood I (1992) Response of Chickpea Cultivars to *Meloidogyne incognita* Race 3 and Their Effect on Peroxidase Activity. *Pak. J. Nematol.* 10(2): 113-117.

Singh B and Usha K (2003) Salicylic Acid Induced Physiological and Biochemical Changes in Wheat Seedlings Under Water Stress. *Plant Growth Regul.* 39: 137-141.

Staskawicz BJ, Ausubel FM, Baker BJ, Ellis JG and Jones JDG (1995) Molecular Genetics of Plant Disease Resistance. *Science.* 268: 661-667.

Sticher L, Mauch-Mani B and Metraux JP (1997) Systemic Acquired Resistance. *Annual Review of Plant Pathology.* 35: 235-270.

Stoessl A (1982) Biosynthesis of Phytoalexins. In: Bailey JA, Mansfield JW, eds, Phytoalexins. Glasgow and London, UK:Blackie & Son Ltd., pp. 141-150.

Strack D (1997) Plant Biochemistry. In: Phenolic Metabolism. Dey PM, Harborne JB (eds). London, Academic Press, pp. 387-416.

Swords KM, Dahlbeck D, Kearney B, Roy M and Staskawicz BJ (1996) Spontaneous and Induced Mutations in a Single Open Reading Frame Alter both Virulence and Avirulence in *Xanthomonas campestris* pv. *vesicatoria avrBs2*. *J. Bacteriol.* 178: 4661-4669.

Tabaeizadeh Z, Agharbaoui Z and Harrak H (1999) Transgenic Tomato Plants Expressing a *Lycopersicon chilense* Chitinase Gene Demonstrate Improved Resistance to *Verticillium dahaliae* race2. *Plant cell reports.* 19: 197-202.

Takahama U and Hirota S (2000) Deglucosidation of Quercetin Glucosides to the Aglycone and Formation of Antifungal Agents by Peroxidase-dependent Oxidation of Quercetin on Browning of Onion Scales. *Plant Cell Physiol.* 41: 1021-9.

Tan JB, Schneider A, Svatos P, Bendnarek JL and Hahlbrock K (2004) Universally Occurring Phenylpropanoid and Specific Indolic Metabolites in Infected and Uninfected *Arabidopsis thaliana* Roots and Leaves. *Phytochemistry.* 65: 691-699.

Thakker JN, Patel N and Kothari IL (2007) *Fusarium oxysporum* Derived Elicitor-induced Changes in Enzymes of Banana Leaves Against Wilt Disease. *J. of Mycology Pl. Pathol.* 37(3): 510-513.

Thipyapong P, Hunt MD and Steffens JC (2004) Antisense Down Regulation of Polyphenol Oxidase Results in Enhanced Disease Susceptibility. *Planta.* 220: 105-117.

Thipyapong P, Melkonian J, Wolfe DW and Steffens JC (2004) Suppression of Polyphenol Oxidases Increases Stress Tolerance in Tomato. *Plant Sci.* 167: 693-703.

Thipyapong P, Stout MJ and Attajarusit J (2007) Functional Analysis of Polyphenol Oxidases by Antisense/Sense Technology. *Molecules.* 12: 1569-1595.

Thomas CM, Jones DA, Parniske M., Harrison K, Balint-Kurti PJ, Hatzixanthis K and Jones JD (1997). Characterization of the Tomato Cf-4 gene for Resistance to *Cladosporium fulvum* Identifies Sequences that Determine Recognitional Specificity in Cf-4 and Cf-9. *Plant Cell.* 9: 2209-2224.

Thomma BP, Penninckx, IA, Broekaert WF and Cammue BP (2001) The Complexity of Disease Signaling in *Arabidopsis*. *Curr. Opin. Immunol.* 13: 63-68.

Tomas-Barberan F and Espin JC (2001) Phenolic Compounds and Related Enzymes as Determinants of Quality of Fruits and Vegetables. *J. Sci. Food and Agric.* 81: 853-876.

Tyuterev SL (2002) in *Nauchnye osnovy indutsirovannoi bolezneustoichivosti rasteniya* (Scientific Bases of Induced Resistance of Plants to Diseases), St. Petersburg: VIZR, pp. 167-175.

Van Loon LC (1997) Induced Resistance in Plants and the Role of Pathogenesis-related Proteins. *European Journal of Plant Pathology.* 103: 753-765.

Van Loon LC (1999) Occurrence and Properties of Plant Pathogenesis-related Proteins. In: Pathogenesis-related Proteins in Plants. Eds. S.K. Datta, S. Muthukrishnan, CRC Press LLC, Boca Raton, pp. 1-19.

Van Loon LC and Antoniw JF (1982). Comparison of the Effects of Salicylic Acid and Ethephon with Virus-induced Hypersensitivity and Acquired Resistance in Tobacco. *Neth. J. Plant Pathol.* 88: 237-256.

Van Loon LC and Van Kammen A (1970) Polyacrylamide disc Electrophoresis of the Soluble Leaf Proteins from *Nicotiana tabacum* var. "Samsun" and "Samsun NN" II. Changes in Protein Constitution After Infection with Tobacco Mosaic Virus. *Virology.* 40: 199-211.

Van Loon LC and Van Strien EA (1999) The Families of Pathogenesis-related Proteins, Their Activities, and Comparative Analysis of PR-1 Type Proteins. *Physiol. Mol. Plant Pathol.* 55: 85-97.

Van Loon LC, Pierpoint WS, Boller T and Conejero V (1994) Recommendations for Naming Plant Pathogenesis-related Proteins. *Plant Mol. Biol. Reporter.* 12: 245-264.

Van Loon LC, Rep M and Pieterse CMJ (2006) Significance of Inducible Defense Related Proteins in Infected Plants. *Annu. Rev. Phytopathol.* 44: 135-162.

Vasse J, de Billy F and Truchet G (1993) Abortion of Infection during the *Rhizobium meliloti*-alfalfa Symbiotic Interaction is Accompanied by a Hypersensitive reaction. *Plant J.* 4: 555-566.

Vidhyasekaran P (1998) Molecular Biology of Pathogenesis and Induced Systemic Resistance. *Indian phytopath.* 51(2): 111-120.

Wang D, Weaver ND, Kesarwani M and Dong X (2005) Induction of Protein Secretory Pathway is Required for Systemic Acquired Resistance. *Science.* 308: 1036-1040.

Ward ER, Uknes SJ, Williams SC, Dincher SS, Wiederhold DL, Alexander DC, Ahl-Goy P, Métraux JP and Ryals JA (1991) Coordinate gene Activity in Response to Agents that Induce Systemic Acquired Resistance. *Plant Cell.* 3: 1085-1094.

Ward HM (1902) On the Relations Between Host and Parasite in the Bromes and Their Brown Rust, *Puccinia dispersa* (Erikss.). *Ann. Bot.* 16: 233-315.

Weaver LM and Hermann KM (1997) Dynamics of the Shikimate Pathway in Plants. *Trends in Plant Science.* 2: 346-50.

Wen PF, Chen JY, Kong WF, Pan QH, Wan SB and Huang WD (2005) Salicylic Acid Induced the Expression of Phenylalanine Ammonia- lyase Gene in Grape Berry. *Plant Science.* 169: 928-934.

Wharton PS and Nicholson RL (2000) Temporal Synthesis and Radiolabelling of the Sorghum 3-deoxyanthocyanidin Phytoalexins and the Anthocyanin, Cyaniding 3-dimalonyl glucoside. *New Phytol.* 145: 457-469.

Wilkens A, Paulsen J, Wray V and Winterhalter P (2010) Structures of Two Novel Trimeric Stilbenes Obtained by Horseradish Peroxidase Catalyzed Biotransformation of Trans-resveratrol and (-)-e-viniferin. *J. Agric. Food Chem.* 58: 6754-6761.

Wingard SA (1928) Hosts and Symptoms of Ringspot, a Virus Disease of Plants. *Journal of Agricultural Research.* 37: 127-153.

Xu X, Qin G and Tian S (2008) Effect of Microbial Biocontrol Agents on Alleviating Oxidative Damage of Peach Fruit Subjected to Fungal Pathogen. *Int. J. Food Microbiol.* 126: 153-158.

Xue L, Charest PM and Jabaji-Hare SH (1998) Systemic induction of peroxidases, 1,3-β-glucanases, Chitinases and Resistance in Bean Plants by Binucleate *Rhizoctonia* species. *Phytopathology.* 88: 359-365.

Yalpani N, Silverman P, Wilson TMA, Kleier DA and Raskin I (1991) Salicylic Acid as a Systemic Signal and an Inducer of Pathogenesis-related Proteins in Virus-infected Tobacco. *Plant Cell.* 3: 808-818.

Yang Y, Yuan Q and Gabriel DW (1996) Watersoaking Function(s) of XcmH1005 are Redundantly Encoded by Members of the *Xanthomonas avr/pth* Gene Family. *Mol. Plant-Microbe Interact.* 9: 105-113.

Yazaki K, Heide L and Tabata M (1991) Formation of p-hydroxybenzoic Acid from p-coumaric Acid by Cell Free Extract of *Lithospemum erythrorhizon* Cell Cultures. *Phytochemistry.* 30: 2233-2236.

Ye XS, Pan SQ and Kuc' J (1990) Activity, Isozyme Pattern, and Cellular Localization of Peroxidase as Related to Systemic Resistance of Tobacco to Blue Mold (*Peronospora tabacina*) and to Tobacco Mosaic Virus. *Phytopathology.* 80: 1295-9.

Ye XY and Ng TB (2002) Isolation of a Novel Peroxidase from French Bean Legumes and First Demonstration of Antifungal Activity of a Non-milk Peroxidase. *Life Sci.* 71: 1667-1680.

Yun DJ, Bressan RA and Hasegawa PM (1997) Plant Antifungal Proteins. *Plant Breed Rev.* 14: 39-88.

Zhang X, Dai Y, Xiong Y, Defraia C, Li J, Dong X and Mou Z (2007) Overexpression of *Arabidopsis* MAP Kinase Kinase 7 Leads to Activation of Plant Basal and Systemic Acquired Resistance. *Plant J.* 52: 1066-1079.

Zhang Y, Goritschnig S, Dong X and Li X (2003) A Gain-of-function Mutation in a Plant Disease Resistance Gene Leads to Constitutive Activation of Downstream Signal Transduction Pathways in *Suppressor of npr1-1, Constitutive 1. Plant Cell.* 15: 2636-2646.

Pages: 58-85

SEED TECHNOLOGY, PLANT GROWTH AND CROPPING SYSTEM

Edited by: **Dr. Pawan Kumar Tyagi; Dr. Pawan Kumar 'Bharti'**

ISBN: 978-93-5056-738-8

Edition: **2015**

Published by: **Discovery Publishing House Pvt. Ltd., New Delhi (India)**

Role of Botanicals in Plant Disease Management

Sanjeev Kumar and **Archana Rani***

ABSTRACT

The blanket use of most of the synthetic fungicides has created different types of environmental and toxicological problems. Of late, in India and other parts of the world, attention has been paid towards exploitation of higher plant products as novel chemotherapeutants in plant protection. The popularity of botanical pesticides is once again increasing and some plant products are being used globally as green pesticides. A considerable number of trees, shrubs and herbs are known as botanicals that can be used in control of varieties of pathogens like fungi, bacteria and nematodes. Among numerous botanical pesticides, neem, onion, garlic ocimum, eucalyptus etc. are some of the most widely used for the management of plant diseases.

Department of Plant Pathology, Jawaharlal Nehru Krishi Vishwa Vidyalaya, Jabalpur - 482 004, Madhya Pradesh (India).

* Department of Agricultural Biotechnology and Molecular Biology, (FBS & H), Rajendra Agricultural University, Pusa - 848 125, Bihar (India).

Although botanicals have often been suggested as an alternative for chemical control, it is unlikely that botanicals alone would be able to produce required level of control. Botanicals may be effectively used in integrated disease management programmes where a combination of traditional practices, cultural practices, use of chemicals and biocontrol brought about by other agents. Botanical pesticides are best suited for use in organic food production in industrialized countries but can play a much greater role in the production and post harvest protection of food products in developing countries.

INTRODUCTION

Future agricultural and rural development is, to a large extent, influenced by the fast increasing food demand of 2.5 billion people expected to swell the world population by 2020. In developing countries, agriculture is the driving force for broad-based economic growth. Achieving food sufficiency in a sustainable manner is a most important challenge for farmers, agro-industries, researchers and governments (Schillhorn van Veen, 1999). One of the major tribulations with agriculture now-a-days is demand for production of more and more in order to provide food for the population which is in permanent augmentation. In realizing this, one of the stumbling blocks seems to be the yield losses due to diseases. In spite of the use of all available means of plant protection, about one-third of the yearly harvest of the world is destroyed by the pests. Losses at times are so severe so as to lead to famine in large areas in many countries of the world.

SYNTHETIC FUNGICIDES AND THEIR SIDE EFFECTS

Fungicides are the primary means of controlling diseases. With regard to acute toxicity, fungicides are reported to be less hazardous compared to insecticides and herbicides, though the mercurial compounds could be exceptional in this instance, and they are gradually being replaced. Repeated use of certain chemical fungicides on crop has led to the appearance of fungicide resistant populations of pathogens. Of late, there has been considerable pressure by consumers to reduce or eliminate chemical fungicides in foods. Further, the use of synthetic chemicals to control post harvest biodeterioration has been restricted due to their carcinogenicity, high and acute residual toxicity, teratogenecity, long degradation period, hormonal imbalance, environmental pollution and their adverse effects on food and side effects on humans (Brent and Hollomon, 1998; Dubey *et al.*, 2007; Kumar *et al.*, 2007). The use of synthetic chemicals as antimicrobials for the management of plant pathogens has undoubtedly increased crop protection but with some deterioration of environmental quality and human health (Cutler and Cutler, 1999). Their uninterrupted and indiscriminate use has not only led to the development of resistant strains but accumulation of toxic residues on food grains used for human consumption has led to the health problems (Sharma and Meshram, 2006).

Another method is the use of synthetic fumigants, which has also led to increased cost of application, pest resistance, lethal effects on non target organisms and toxicity to users (Okonkwo and Okoye, 1996). For most fungicides it has proved impossible to demonstrate symptoms of acute poisoning in toxicological tests. Chronic effects on humans of long term exposure to chemicals for disease control have not been determined directly. High doses on animals have been shown to be mutagenic, antimitotic, teratogenic or carcinogenic, however, these doses are highly unlikely to be used under practical conditions. Some fungicides are known to have phytotoxic side effects. Specifically acting fungicides have been observed to cause pathogen resistance. One example of this is the complete failure of the benzimidazole fungicides (benomyl, thiabendazole, carbendazin, thiophanate methyl) due to the development of resistance in a number of pathogenic fungi.

BOTANICAL PESTICIDES AS ALTERNATIVES TO SYNTHETIC PESTICIDES

Of late, in different parts of the world, attention has been paid towards exploitation of plant products as novel chemotherapeutants in plant protection. Because of non phytotoxicity, systemicity, easy biodegradability and stimulatory nature of host metabolism, plant products possess the potential to be of value in pest management (Mishra and Dubey, 1994). During the past few decades, the interest in the use of plant products has increased; chiefly natural origin with low mammalian toxicity (Subramanyam and Roesli, 2000). Many tropical medicinal plants and spices have been used as disease control agents (Lale, 1992). Numerous studies have documented about antifungal (Suhr and Nielson, 2003; Mishra and Dubey, 1994; Elgayyar *et al.*, 2001) and antibacterial (Canillac and Mourey, 2001) effect of plant essential oils. Examination of indigenous local herbs and plant materials have also been reported from around the world example, India (Ahmad and Beg, 2001), Australia (Cox *et al.*, 1998), Argentina (Penna *et al.*, 2001) and Finland (Rauha *et al.*, 2000).

Higher plants contain a wide spectrum of secondary metabolites such as phenols, flavonoids, quinones, tannins, essential oils, alkaloids, saponins and sterols. Such plant-derived chemicals may be exploited for their different biological properties. Biologicals, because of their natural origin are biodegradable and do not leave toxic residues or by products. Botanicals have long been touted as attractive alternatives to synthetic chemical pesticides for disease management because botanicals pose little threat to the environment or to human health. The body of scientific literature documenting bioactivity of plant derivatives to fungal and bacterial diseases continues to expand, yet only a handful of botanicals are currently used in agriculture in the industrialized world, and there are prospects for commercial development of new botanical products. Pyrethrum and neem are well established commercially, pesticides based on plant essential oils have recently entered in the market, and the use of rotenone appears to be waning. Several factors appear to limit the success of botanicals, most notably regulatory barriers and the availability of competing products that are cost-effective and relatively safe compared with their predecessors. In the context of agricultural diseases & pest management, botanical pesticides are best suited for use in organic food production in industrialized countries but can play a much greater role in the production and postharvest protection of food in developing countries (Isman, 2006).

Accordingly, use of green pesticides particularly for post harvest diseases are being recommended globally and use of essential oils seem to be the best choice. Studies have shown that essential oils are readily biodegradable and less detrimental to non-target organisms as compared to synthetic pesticides (Baysal, 1997). Application of plant products especially essential oils is a very attractive method for controlling post harvest diseases. Essential oils and their components are gaining increasing interest because of their relatively safe status, their wide acceptance by the consumers and their exploitation for potential multi-purpose functional use. (Oxenham, 2003).

The problem of the development of resistant strains of fungi may be solved by the use of essential oils of higher plants as fumigants in the management of diseases and pests because of synergism between different components of the oils (Varma and Dubey, 1999; Dubey *et al.*, 2007). Although various essential oils have been screened for their pesticidal activity against various pests but detailed studies *viz.* antifungal, insecticidal, repellency, oviposition, ovicidal, antiaflatoxigenic activity, phytochemistry and safety limit profile have not been done properly with most of the oils.

Therefore, there is urgent need to bioprospect the pesticidal property of different essential oils and detailed *in vitro* and *in vivo* investigations are required for their recommendation of their practical application as pesticides for the control of pre and post harvest biodeterioration of food commodities and thereby enhancing shelf life of the commodities. Most of the active compounds of essential oils are specific to particular pathogens groups and not to mammals (Isman, 2000), many of them are not dangerous to humans. They should be considered in diseases and pest management strategies.

BOTANICAL PESTICIDES

Disease and pest killers derived from plant extracts is called botanical pesticides or botanicals. Botanical pesticides are derived from plants which have been shown to have pesticidal properties. They are also very close chemically to those plants from which they are derived., so they are easily decomposed by a varietiy of microbes common in most soils. Botanical pesticides are good alternatives to chemical pesticides. Botanical pesticides are ecofriendly, economic, target specific and biodegradable. They are safer to the user and the environment because they break down into harmless compounds within hours or days in the presence of sunlight.

SOURCES OF BOTANICALS

The pesticidal effects of many natural products from plants have long been known and are being used in today"a agriculture also. There are number of useful agrochemicals that are derived from plants. These compounds may provide useful templates to produce more active agrochemicals with less environmental risk. The presence of antifungal compounds in higher plants has long been recognized as an important factor to disease resistance (Mahadevan,1982; Singh & Dwivedi, 1987; Kurucheve *et al*., 1997). Such compounds being biodegradable and selective in their toxicity are considered valuable for controlling different plant diseases (Sing & Dwivedi, 1987). There are many herbs, shrubs ad trees are useful as sources of botanical pesticides (Table 4.1). Botanicals pesticides or botanicals which are used in plant disease control are listed below (Table 4.2) Among numerous botanical pesticides, neem, onion, garlic Ocimum, Eucalyptus etc. are some of the most widely used for the management of plant diseases. Such botanicals effectively fit into concept of IDM, in tune of recent needs.

PREPARATION OF AQUEOUS EXTRACTS

For water extraction, respective plant parts (fresh or air dried or sun dried) are washed thoroughly in distilled water , air dried and macerated in equal volume (w/v) of water in a grinder to get crude extract. The plant material can be surface sterilized with 0.1 percent aqueous solution of mercuric chloride (Hgcl2) followed by three washings in distilled water. The crude extract is partially purified by passing through double layer of cheese cloth followed by centrifugation at 5000 g for 10 min, the supernatant is collected and filter sterilized through Whatman filter paper No.1 into a sterilized vial to get 100 percent concentrations of the extract. Requsite quantity of sterile distilled water is generally added to this 100 percent extract , to get desired concentration of the extract.

Inhibitory effect of aqueous extracts of neem oil cake and garlic leaf extract has been reported against wilt of lentil, caused by *Fusarium oxysporum f.sp. lentis*.(Khan *et al*., 1973, 1974). Meena *et al*, (2004) also reported significant reduction in mycelia growth of *Alternaria brassicae* using aqueous extract of *Allium sativum* (bulb) and *Acacia nilotica* (leaf) *in vitro*.

Table 4.1: List of Botanicals Known to Control Plant Diseases

Plant	Plant Parts Used	Form of Use	Disease Controlled	References
Garlic (*Allium sativum*)	Clove	Extract	Wilt of pigeonpea	Singh & Singh (1983)
			Alternaria blight of sonflower	Chattopadhyay (1999)
			Late blight of potato	Coa & Ariena (2001)
			Grey mildew of cotton	Ponnanna & Adiver (2001)
			Basal stem rot of coconuts	Srinivasulu *et al.* (2002)
			Banded leaf & Sheath blight of maize	Meena *et al* (2003)
			Wilt of pea	Verma & Dohroo (2003)
			Wilt of lentil	Sinha & Sinha (2004)
			Wilt of chickpea	Chand & Singh (2005)
			Wilt of cowpea	Sahayaraj *et al* (2006)
			Late & Early blight of potato	Abd-El-Khair and Waha (2007)
Neem (*Azadirachta indica*)	Leaf	Extract	Leaf spot of chilli	Maharishi (1993)
			Rust of groundnut	Suresh *et al.* (1997)
			Sheath rot of rice	Pramanick & Phookan (1998)
			Grey mildew of cotton	Ponnanna & Adiver (2001)
			Early blight of potato	Patil *et al.* (2003)
			Collar rot cauliflower	Prasad *et al.* (2003)
			Maydis leaf blight of maize	Jha *et al.* (2004)
			Wilt of lentil	Sindha & Sinha (2004)
			Collar rot of pigeonpea	Suryawanshi *et al.* (2007)

(Table Contd…)

Plant	Plant Parts Used	Form of Use	Disease Controlled	References
		Cake	Sheath blight of rice	Prasad *et al.* (1998)
			Anthracnose of sorghum	Akhtar & Dwuvedi (2000 & 2002)
	Seed	Kernel Extract	Leaf spot of groundnut	Lokhande *et al.* (1998)
			Leaf curl of tomato	Somasekhara *et al.* (1998)
			Early blight of potato	Patil *et al.* (2003)
Onion (*Allium cepa*)	Seed	Extract	Maydis leaf blight	Jha *et al.* (2004)
			Early & Late blight of potato	Abd- El-Khair & Wafaa (2007)
Chilli (*Capsicum annum*)	Seed	Extract	Fusarium wilt of muskmelon	Bower & Locke (2000)
			Early & Late blight of potato	Abd- El-Khair & Wafaa (2007)
Tulsi (*Ocimum sanctum*)	Leaf	Extract	Wilt of cowpea	Ushamalini *et al.* (1997)
			Sheath blight of rice	Pramanick & Phookan (1998)
Eucalyptus (*Eucalyptus citriodora*)	Leaf	Extract	Sheath rot of rice	Pramanick & Phookan (1998)
			Collar rot of cauliflower	Prasad *et al* (2003)
Calotropsis sp.	Leaf	Extract	Root knot of chickpea	Jain & Triveidi (1997)
		Manure	Sheath blight of rice	Prasad *et al* (1998)
Lemon grass (*Cymbopogon citrates*)	Leaf	Exract	Bacterial soft rot of cabbage	Acedo *et al.* (1999)
			Early & Late blight of potato	Abd- El-Khair & Wafaa (2007)
			Alternaria blight of mustard	Patni *et al.* (2005)

(Table Contd…)

Plant	Plant Parts Used	Form of Use	Disease Controlled	References
Peppermint (*Mentha arvensis*)	Oil	Extract	Post harvest rot of citrus	Tripathi *et al.* (2004)
	Leaf		Early & Late blight of potato	Abd- El-Khair & Wafaa (2007)
Datura (*Datura fastuosa*)	Leaf	Extract	Root diseases of cauliflower	Ehteshamal Haque *et al.* (1998)
Cotton (*Hibiscus sp.*)	Seed	Cake	Root diseases of cauliflower	Ehteshamal Haque *et al.* (1998)
Ground nut (*Arachis hypogeal*)	Seed	Cake	Stalk rot of sorghum	Hundekar *et al.* (1998)
Safflower	Seed	Cake	Stalk rot of sorghum	Hundekar *et al* (1998)
Mustard (*Brassica sp.*)	Leaf	Extract	Wilt of muskmelon	Boers & Locke (2000)
Ginger (*Zingiber officinale*)	Oil		Post harvest rot of citrus	Tripathi *et al.* (2004)
Brahami (*Centella asiatica*)	Leaf	Extract	TUMV of radish	Sharma *et al.* (2007)
			TUMV of radish	Sharma *et al.* (2007)
Castar (*Ricinis communis*	Leaf	Extract	Collar rot of pigeonpea	Suryawanshi *et al.* (2007)

Table 4.2: Common Herbs Employed in Disease Control

Botanical Name	Common Name	Method of Preparation	Diseases Controlled
Allium sativum	Garlic	Chop the cloves finely, soak in 2 teaspoons of oil for oneday, then mix with half a lit of soapy water and filter. Mix 1 part solution with 20 partswater, then spray.	Damping off , Stem and root rot , Wilt, Curly top. Fruit rot, Early blight, Purple blotch, Leaf spot, Frog eye leaf spot, Anthracnose, Smudge, Leaf blight.
Cassiaalata	Acapulco	Extract the juice of *Cassia alata* leaves and spray at the rate of 1 cup juice/lit of water.	Damping off , Stem and root rot , Wilt, Curly top. Fruit rot, Early blight, Purple blotch, Leaf spot, Frog eye leaf spot, Anthracnose, Smudge, Leaf blight.
Allium cepa	Red onion	Chop Allium cepa bulb finely, soak in two teaspoons of oil for a day. Then mix with half a lit of soapy waterand filter. Mix one part solution with 20 parts water, and spray.	Early blight, Leaf mold, Leaf spot, Frog-eye leaf spot, Anthracnose, Fruit rot, Smudge, Fruit and stem rot, Damping off, Root rot, wilt, curly top.
Amaranthus gracilis	Amaranth	Extract the juice from 1 kg of Amaranth leaves, then mix juice with 3 litres of water and spray.	Fruit rot, Early blight, Purple blotch, Leaf spot, Leaf mould, Frog eye leaf spot, Anthracnose, Smudge, Leaf blight.
Moringaoleifera	Drumstick	Extract the juice of 1 kg leaves of drum stick, then mix juice with 3 litres of water, and use as spray.	Fruit rot, Early blight, Purpleblotch, Leaf spot, Anthracnose, Fruit rot, Smudge, Fruit and stem rot.
Impatiensbalsamina	Kamantigi	Extract the juice (1 Kg of *Impatiens balsamina*) leaves, then mix the juice with 3 litres of water, and use as spray.	Fruit rot, Early blight, Purple blotch, Leaf spot leaf mould and frog- eye leaf blight.
Centella asiatica L.)	Apiaceae	Extract the juice from 1 Kg of *Centella asiatica* with 3 litres of water, and use as spray.	Damping off, Stem and root rot, Early blight, Wilt, Curly top, Leaf blight.
Jatropha multifida	Wild castor	Extract the juice of 1 Kg of *Jatropha* leaves, mix the juice with 3 lit of water, and use as spray.	Fruit and stem rot, Damping off, Stem and root rot, Early blight. Wilt and curly top.

(Table Contd...)

Botanical Name	Common Name	Method of Preparation	Diseases Controlled
Carica papaya	Papaya.	Pound and soak leaves of papaya in water and use infusion as spray.	Leaf mold, Leaf spot, Early blight, Frogeye leaf spot, Fruit and stem rot.
Mimosa pudica	Touch me	Pound, soak the whole plant in water overnight and use infusion as spray.	Fruit and stem rot, Leaf spot.
Artemisiavulgaris	Damong maria	Extract the juice of *Artemisia vulgaris* leaves and use as spray at the rate of 2 to 5 table spoons juice per lit of water.	Fruit rot, Early blight, Purple blotch, and Leaf spot
Zingiber officinale	Ginger.	Extract the 500 gm Ginger rhizome juice, add one lit of cow urine and 10 litres of water mix well and use as spray.	Leaf mold, Leaf spot, Early blight, Frog-eye leaf spot.
Gliricidia sepium.		Extract the juice of *Gliricidia sepium* from 1 kg leaves, and then mix juice with 3 litres of water, and use as spray. Fresh stems with leaves can be placed between plants to deter insects.	Leaf mold, Leaf spot, Early blight, Frog-eye leaf spot.
Vitex negundo		Extract juice of 1 kg of *Vitexnegundo* leaves, then mix juice with 3 litres of water, and useas spray.	Leaf mold, leaf spot, Early blight, frog-eye leaf spot.

EXTRACTION, ISOLATION, CHARACTERIZATION OF BIOACTIVE COMPOUNDS FROM PLANTS'

Extraction

Extraction is the crucial first step in the analysis of medicinal plants, because it is necessary to extract the desired chemical components from the plant materials for further separation and characterization. The basic operation included steps, such as pre-washing, drying of plant materials or freeze drying, grinding to obtain a homogenous sample and often improving the kinetics of analytic extraction and also increasing the contact of sample surface with the solvent system. Proper actions must be taken to assure that potential active constituents are not lost, distorted or destroyed during the preparation of the extract from plant samples. If the plant was selected on the basis of traditional uses (Fabricant and Farnsworth, 2001), then it is needed to prepare the extract as described by the traditional healer in order to mimic as closely as possible the traditional 'herbal' drug. The selection of solvent system largely depends on the specific nature of the bioactive compound being targeted. Different solvent systems are available to extract the bioactive compound from natural products. The extraction of hydrophilic compounds uses polar solvents such as methanol, ethanol or ethyl-acetate. For extraction of more lipophilic compounds, dichloromethane or a mixture of dichloromethane/methanol in ratio of 1:1 are used. In some instances, extraction with hexane is used to remove chlorophyll (Cos *et al.,* 2006).

As the target compounds may be non-polar to polar and thermally labile, the suitability of the methods of extraction must be considered. Various methods, such as sonification, heating under reflux, soxhlet extraction and others are commonly used (United States Pharmacopeia and National Formulary, 2002; Pharmacopoeia of the People's Republic of China, 2000). The Japanese Pharmacopeia, 2001) for the plant samples extraction. In addition, plant extracts are also prepared by maceration or percolation of fresh green plants or dried powdered plant material in water and/or organic solvent systems. The other modern extraction techniques include solid-phase micro-extraction, supercritical-fluid extraction, pressurized-liquid extraction, microwave-assisted extraction, solid-phase extraction, and surfactant-mediated techniques, which possess certain advantages. These are the reduction in organic solvent consumption and in sample degradation, elimination of additional sample clean-up and concentration steps before chromatographic analysis, improvement in extraction efficiency, selectivity, and/ kinetics of extraction. The ease of automation for these techniques also favors their usage for the extraction of plants materials (Huie, 2002).

IDENTIFICATION AND CHARACTERIZATION

Due to the fact that plant extracts usually occur as a combination of various type of bioactive compounds or phytochemicals with different polarities, their separation still remains a big challenge for the process of identification and characterization of bioactive compounds. It is a common practice in isolation of these bioactive compounds that a number of different separation techniques such as TLC, column chromatography, flash chromatography, Sephadex chromatography and HPLC, should be used to obtain pure compounds. The pure compounds are then used for the determination of structure and biological activity. Beside that, non-chromatographic techniques such as immunoassay, which use monoclonal antibodies (MAbs), phytochemical screening assay, Fourier-transform infrared spectroscopy (FTIR), can also be used to obtain and facilitate the identification of the bioactive compounds.

CHROMATOGRAPHIC TECHNIQUES

Thin-layer Chromatography (TLC) and Bio-autographic Methods

TLC is a simple, quick, and inexpensive procedure that gives the researcher a quick answer as to how many components are in a mixture. TLC is also used to support the identity of a compound in a mixture when the R_f of a compound is compared with the R_f of a known compound. Additional tests involve the spraying of phytochemical screening reagents, which cause color changes according to the phytochemicals existing in a plants extract; or by viewing the plate under the UV light. This has also been used for confirmation of purity and identity of isolated compounds.

Bio-autography is a useful technique to determine bioactive compound with antimicrobial activity from plant extract. TLC bioautographic methods combine chromatographic separation and *in situ* activity determination facilitating the localization and target-directed isolation of active constituents in a mixture. Traditionally, bioautographic technique has used the growth inhibition of microorganisms to detect anti-microbial components of extracts chromatographed on a TLC layer. This methodology has been considered as the most efficacious assay for the detection of anti-microbial compounds (Shahverdi, 2007). Bio-autography localizes antimicrobial activity on a chromatogram using three approaches: (*i*) direct bio-autography, where the micro-organism grows directly on the thin-layer chromatographic (TLC) plate, (*ii*) contact bio-autography, where the antimicrobial compounds are transferred from the TLC plate to an inoculated agar plate through direct contact and (*iii*) agar overlay bio-autography, where a seeded agar medium is applied directly onto the TLC plate (Hamburger and Cordell, 1987; Rahalison *et al.*, 1991). The inhibition zones produced on TLC plates by one of the above bioautographic technique will be use to visualize the position of the bioactive compound with antimicrobial activity in the TLC fingerprint with reference to *Rf* values (Homans and Fuchs, 1970). Preparative TLC plates with a thickness of 1mm were prepared using the same stationary and mobile phases as above, with the objective of isolating the bioactive components that exhibited the antimicrobial activity against the test strain. These areas were scraped from the plates, and the substance eluted from the silica with ethanol or methanol. Eluted samples were further purified using the above preparative chromatography method. Finally, the components were identified by HPLC, LCMS and GCMS. Although it has high sensitivity, its applicability is limited to micro-organisms that easily grow on TLC plates. Other problems are the need for complete removal of residual low volatile solvents, such as *n*-BuOH, trifluoroacetic acid and ammonia and the transfer of the active compounds from the stationary phase into the agar layer by diffusion (Cos *et al.*, 2006). Because bio-autography allows localizing antimicrobial activities of an extract on the chromatogram, it supports a quick search for new antimicrobial agents through bioassay-guided isolation (Cos *et al.,* 2006). The bioautography agar overlay method is advantageous in that, firstly it uses very little amount of sample when compared to the normal disc diffusion method and hence, it can be used for bioassay-guided isolation of compounds. Secondly, since the crude extract is resolved into its different components, this technique simplifies the process of identification and isolation of the bioactive compounds (Rahalison *et al.*, 1991).

HIGH PERFORMANCE LIQUID CHROMATOGRAPHY

High performance liquid chromatography (HPLC) is a versatile, robust, and widely used technique for the isolation of natural products (Cannell, 1998). Currently, this technique is gaining popularity among various analytical techniques as the main choice for fingerprinting study for the quality control of herbal plants (Fan *et al.,* 2006). Natural products are frequently isolated following the evaluation of a relatively crude extract in a biological assay in order to fully characterize the active entity. The biologically active entity is often present only as minor component in the extract and the resolving power of HPLC is ideally suited to the rapid processing of such multicomponent samples on both an analytical and preparative scale. Many bench top HPLC instruments now are modular in design and comprise a solvent delivery pump, a sample introduction device such as an auto-sampler or manual injection valve, an analytical column, a guard column, detector and a recorder or a printer.

Chemical separations can be accomplished using HPLC by utilizing the fact that certain compounds have different migration rates given a particular column and mobile phase. The extent or degree of separation is mostly determined by the choice of stationary phase and mobile phase. Generally the identification and separation of phytochemicals can be accomplished using isocratic system (using single unchanging mobile phase system). Gradient elution in which the proportion of organic solvent to water is altered with time may be desirable if more than one sample component is being studied and differ from each other significantly in retention under the conditions employed.

Purification of the compound of interest using HPLC is the process of separating or extracting the target compound from other (possibly structurally related) compounds or contaminants. Each compound should have a characteristic peak under certain chromatographic conditions. Depending on what needs to be separated and how closely related the samples are, the chromatographer may choose the conditions, such as the proper mobile phase, flow rate, suitable detectors and columns to get an optimum separation.

Identification of compounds by HPLC is a crucial part of any HPLC assay. In order to identify any compound by HPLC, a detector must first be selected. Once the detector is selected and is set to optimal detection settings, a separation assay must be developed. The parameters of this assay should be such that a clean peak of the known sample is observed from the chromatograph. The identifying peak should have a reasonable retention time and should be well separated from extraneous peaks at the detection levels which the assay will be performed. UV detectors are popular among all the detectors because they offer high sensitivity (Lia *et al.*, 2004) and also because majority of naturally occurring compounds encountered have some UV absorbance at low wavelengths (190-210 nm) (Cannell, 1998). The high sensitivity of UV detection is bonus if a compound of interest is only present in small amounts within the sample. Besides UV, other detection methods are also being employed to detect phytochemicals among which is the diode array detector (DAD) coupled with mass spectrometer (MS) (Tsao and Deng, 2004). Liquid chromatography coupled with mass spectrometry (LC/MS) is also a powerful technique for the analysis of complex botanical extracts (Cai *et al.*, 2002; He, 2000). It provides abundant information for structural elucidation of the compounds when tandem mass spectrometry (MS^n) is applied. Therefore, the combination of HPLC and MS facilitates rapid and accurate identification of chemical compounds in medicinal herbs, especially when a pure standard is unavailable (Ye *et al.*, 2007).

The processing of a crude source material to provide a sample suitable for HPLC analysis as well as the choice of solvent for sample reconstitution can have a significant bearing on the overall success of natural product isolation. The source material, e.g., dried powdered plant, will initially need to be treated in such a way as to ensure that the compound of interest is efficiently liberated into solution. In the case of dried plant material, an organic solvent (e.g., methanol, chloroform) may be used as the initial extractant and following a period of maceration, solid material is then removed by decanting off the extract by filteration. The filtrate is then concentrated and injected into HPLC for separation. The usage of guard columns is necessary in the analysis of crude extract. Many natural product materials contain significant level of strongly binding components, such as chlorophyll and other endogenous materials that may in the long term compromise the performance of analytical columns. Therefore, the guard columns will significantly protect the lifespan of the analytical columns.

NON-CHROMATOGRAPHIC TECHNIQUES

Immunoassay

Immunoassays, which use monoclonal antibodies against drugs and low molecular weight natural bioactive compounds, are becoming important tools in bioactive compound analyses. They show high specificity and sensitivity for receptor binding analyses, enzyme assays and qualitative as well as quantitative analytical techniques. Enzyme-linked immunosorbent essay (ELISA) based on MAbs are in many cases more sensitive than conventional HPLC methods. Monoclonal antibodies can be produced in specialized cells through a technique known as hybridoma technology (Shoyama *et al.,* 2006). The following steps are involved in the production of monoclonal antibodies via hybridoma technology against plant drugs:

1. A rabbit is immunized through repeated injection of specific plant drugs for the production of specific antibody, facilitated due to proliferation of the desired B cells.
2. Tumors are produced in a mouse or a rabbit.
3. From the above two types of animals, spleen cell (these cells are rich in B cells and T cells) are cultured separately. The separately cultured spleen cells produce specific antibodies against the plants drug, and against myeloma cells that produce tumors.
4. The production of hybridoma by fusion of spleen cells to myeloma cells is induced using polyethylene glycol (PEG). The hybrid cells are grown in selective hypoxanthine aminopterin thymidine (HAT) medium.
5. The desired hybridoma is selected for cloning and antibody production against a plant drug. This process is facilitated by preparing single cell colonies that will grow and can be used for screening of antibody producing hybridomas.
6. The selected hybridoma cells are cultured for the production of monoclonal antibodies in large quantity against the specific plants drugs.
7. The monoclonal antibodies are used to determine similar drugs in the plants extract mixture through enzyme-linked immunosorbent essay (ELISA).

FOURIER-TRANSFORM INFRARED SPECTROSCOPY (FTIR)

FTIR has proven to be a valuable tool for the characterization and identification of compounds or functional groups (chemical bonds) present in an unknown mixture of plants extract (Eberhardt *et al.,* 2007; Hazra *et al.,* 2007). In addition, FTIR spectra of pure compounds are usually so unique that they are like a molecular "fingerprint". For most common plant compounds, the spectrum of an unknown compound can be identified by comparison to a library of known compounds. Samples for FTIR can be prepared in a number of ways. For liquid samples, the easiest is to place one drop of sample between two plates of sodium chloride. The drop forms a thin film between the plates. Solid samples can be milled with potassium bromide (KBr) to and then compressed into a thin pellet which can be analyzed. Otherwise, solid samples can be dissolved in a solvent such as methylene chloride, and the solution then placed onto a single salt plate. The solvent is then evaporated off, leaving a thin film of the original material on the plate.

BIOASSAY AND EVALUATION OF BOTANICALS

Various techniques for evaluationg the antimicrobial properties of chemical/botanical pesticides have been described from time to time by different workers. However, it is possible to consider a few which would serve the need of laboratory screening of most of the chemicals. Modifications in these techniques have also been made by researchers as per the need .Some such techniques have been described in this chapter.

POISONED FOOD TECHNIQUE

The principle involved in this technique is to poison the medium with fungicides and then allow a teat fungus to grow on such medium. (Nene & Thapliyal, 1997). The test may be conducted both on solid and liquid medium. In this method, Prepare Potato Dextrose Agar medium in flasks and sterilize. Add required amount of chemicals as to get a final desired concentration and thoroughly mixed. The medium is poured into sterilized Petri-plates and stored in refrigerator till required. A culture of test fungus is grown on PDA for a certain period at the optimum temperature for growth. Small disc of test fungus culture is cut with sterile cork borer and transferred ascetically in the centre of the Petri-dish containing the medium with desired fungicidal concentration. Suitable control are kept where the culture discs are grown under the similar conditions on PDA without fungicide. The fungal radial growth/colony diameter is measured at every 24 h. The radial growth / colony diameter compared with control is taken as measure of fungi toxicity.Evidences for the fungal activity in plant extracts using poison food technique have been provded by several workers. (Maji *et al.*, 2005; Sesha Kiran *et al.*, 2005; Yadav & Thrimurty, 2006; Sharma and Tripathi, 2006; Suryavanshi *et al.,* 2007; and Razeena and Ahmad, 2007)

INHIBITION ZONE TECHNIQUE

It is a simple satisfactory method employed to test the effectiveness of antimicrobial agents against selected test organisms. In this method, a sterile filter paper disc impregnated with an antimicrobial agent is place on a pathogen inoculated agar plate. Thes plates are kept for incubation and are looked for zone of inhibition. The presence of a clear zone of inhibition surrounding the disk indicates the inhibitory activity of the material under study. Bauer *et al,* (1996) and Salie *et al* , (1996) have reported the antimicrobial activity of aqueous and methanol extracts of different plant species using agar disc diffusion method.

Slide germination technique: In this technique, spore suspension of the test pathogen from fresh culture, is prepared in sterile water. Concentration of the spores is adjusted to 20-25 spores per microscopic field at low magnification. A drop of suspension is place on a clean grease free cavity slide and then one drop of double concentration of the test chemical is added to. Both the drops are mixed thoroughly in cavity using inoculation/ dissecting needle. The cavity slides are placed in moist chambers and incubated at desired temperature. After terminating the incubation period, germinataed and ungerminated spores in 10-20 microscopic fields are counted and percent inhibition of spore germination is calculated. Raghuvansi *et al* (2006) used the slide germination technique to test the efficacy of leaf extracts of some plants against spore germination of *Colletotrichum falcatum*, the red rot pathogen of sugarcane. They reported significant inhibition of conidial germination of *C. falcatum* by leaf extract of neem, bhang and shisham. Similarly , Maji *et al* (2005) also used the slide germination method for *in vitro* screening of twenty plants species against four fungal pathogens *viz., Peridiospora mori* (Brown rust), *Phyllactinia corylea* (Powdery mildew), and *Pseudocercospora mori* (Black leaf spot).

WELL DIFFUSION METHOD

In this method, wells are made in the pathogen seededplates with the help of a sterile cork borer. The test compounds are introduced into the wells under strict aseptic conditions and then these plates are incubated at the temperature required for the growth of test pathogen and are looked for zone of inhibition. Microbial growth is determined by measuring the diameter of the zone of inhibition. Perez *et al.* (1990); Noir and Chanda (2005) and Satish *et al* (1999) had determined the antibacterial activity of aqueous and methanol extracts of different plants species by agar well diffusion methods.

DELIVERY SYSTEM

Seed and Seedling Treatment

The seed and seedling treatment is essential because a large number of disease causing pathogens are associated with seed and whenever such seeds are used for sowing, these pathogens also become active and cause either seed rot and seedling mortality. The purpose of seed and seedling treatments is to destroy these pathogens , which cause seed decays and seedling blights and also to protect te germinating seed from the attack of certain soil inhabiting microbes. The advantages of seed and seedling treatment have been well established through the years. In fact , treatment of seeds af all crops should be done as a routine practice since it is type of cheap insurance against possible diseases at a later stage (Nene and Thapliyal, 1997).

Ash from leaves of Azadirachta, Melia indica and *Vernonia amygdalina* protects seeds and seedlng from pre and post emergence rot of wheat caused by Sclerotium rolfsii (Enikuomehin *et al.*, 1998). Similarly, seed treatment with 5 percent leaves extract of marigold, neem and garlic bulb extract significantly reduces the wilt disease complex in lentil (Sinha and Sinha, 2004). Seed soaking in aqueous extracts of neem seeds reduces penetration by *Meloidogyne incognita.* The reduction is directly proportional to the concentration and soaking time. (Mojumder and Mishra, 1992). Treatment of rice seedlings with oil extracted from the seeds of *Azadirachta indica* (neem oil) and *Annona* app. (custard apple oil) significantly shortened the life span of *Nephotettix virescens* carrying rice *tungro* and ther by significantly reduced the incidence of transmission of the virus (Mariappan , 1998 and Saxena *et al.,* 1987)

B. SOIL APPLICATION

Soil harbours a very large number of plant pathogens. So the purpose of soil treatment is to eradicate or reduce the inoculum density of soil-borne plant pathogens. Soil amendment with botanicals is one of the most effective and adopted method to control various soil borne plant diseases. Plants ,leaves and oil cakes applied as manure were very effective against not only insects but diseases as well. Farmers in Bengal apply leaves of *Cleistanthus collinus* for management of brown leaf spot disease of paddy (Mandal, 2001). Leaves of Acacia catechu (Khair) placed at the water inlet of paddy fields control brown spot disease of paddy (Pereira, 1993). Use of organic amendments viz., cotton, neem, groundnut and safflower cakes reduced the inoculums levels of *Macrophomina phaseolina and Fusarium moniliforme* in the soil and subsequently reduced the incidence of stalk rot of sorghum (Hundekar *et al.,* 1998). Similarly, soil amendment with seed cakes of neem, cotton, *Datura fastuosa* and *Steochospeimum marginatum* significantly reduced *Fusarium solani* infection of sunflowers in Pakistan. However, seed cakes of neem and cotton were also effective against *Macrophomina phaseolina* and *Rhizoctonia solani*, while *S. marginatum* and *D. fastuosa* were effective against *R. solani* infection of sunflower roots (Ehteshamal Haque *et al.*, 1998). Application of neem coated urea @ 60 kg N/ha significantly reduced the incidence of blast disease of rice. (Hooda and Srivastava, 1998). Surviaval of sclerotia of Rhizoctonia solani adversely effected in soil with the application of neem cake and Calotropsis (Prasad *et al.*, 1998). Population of plant parasitic nematodes , including *Meloidogyne incognita, Rotylenchulus reniformis, Tylenchorhynchus brassicae* and *Helicotylenchus indicus*, pathogenic on mungbean and chickpea, is reduced significantly with soil application of oil cakes of castor, neem and mustard. (Tyagi and Alam, 1995). Similarly, soil amended with *Azadirachta indica, Calotropsis procera, Lawsonia inermis, Ocimum sanctum* and *Parthenium hysterophorus* showed increase in growth parameters of chickpea plants and nematicidal activity against root knot nematode infecting chickpea. These amendments showed a marked decline in number of root galls, eggs per egg mass and final nematode population indicating a reduction in severity of disease (Jain and Trivedi, 1997). Planting of dhaincha as green manure before landing the rice residues incidence of sheath blight (Ahuja ad Ahuja , 2008).

C. FOLIAR APPLICATION

Application of chemicals on the stem leaves flowers and fruits are called vegetative or foliar application. It is carried out in the form of spraying, dusting and pastes. It is more prevalent for fungal disease than for bacterial and viral diseases of the foliage. A larfe number of botanicals possess antiviral substances which when aprayed on tobacco early in the season give good protection against tobacco mosaic virus infection (Nagarajan, 1990). Spraying crude extract of *Azadirachta indica* was most potent in reducing bean common mosaic virus infectivity under field conditions (Tripathi and Tripathi, 1982). Similarly, nee seed extract and neem oil can be used for the management of leaf spot of ground nut, caused by *Mycosphaeralla arachidis* (Lokhande *et al.*, 1998). Pre inoculation spray of neem product inhibits leaf spots, mildews, rusts, rot diseases and mould (Mariappan, 1998). Neem product is also found effective in reducing the white fly population, a vector of tomato leaf curl (Somasekhara *et al* 1998). Pre inoculation spray of *Ocimum sanctum, Azadirachta indica* and *Eucalyptus citirodora* restrict the development of sheath rot of rice (Pramanick and Phookan, 1998). *Eucalyptus globus* spray was also found effective for the management of *Alternaria* blight of mustard (Patni *et al.*, 2005). Similarly, spray of bael and tulsi leaf extract was recommended. Similarly, spray of bael and tulsi leaf extract was recommended for the control of blast of rice by CRRI, Cuttack, Orissa (Ahuja and Ahuja, 2008).

INDUCTION OF SYSTEMIC RESISTANCE

Systemic acquired response is the increased resistance of a plant to a wide range of pathogens following infection by one pathogen. This has been termed as induced resistance, acquired resistance , acquired immunity, and immunization by various authors.Biologically active compound present in plant products act as elicitors and induce systemic resistaance in host plants resulting in reduction in disease development (Vidhyasekaran, 1992). There are several reports of plant extracts having resistance inducing activity in plants.(Doubrara *etal* , 1988 and Yamada *et al.*, 1990). Aqueous extract of healthy barley leaves induced papillae formation which in tune provides resistance against powdery mildew in barley seedlings (Yokoyamma *et al.*, 1991). Similarly, Doubrava *et al.,* (1988) found that seed treatment of first leaves with spinach extracts provide resistance against *Colletotrichum orbiculare* in cucumber. Chakraboty *et al.,* (2007) reported that the foliar application of aqueous extract of *Cathranthus roseus* induced a high level of three defense enzymes, viz., β-1,3 glucanase, chitinase and phenlyalalanine ammonia lyase in tea plants along with rapid and distinct accumulation of phenolics which in turn leads to reduction in disease incidence in foliar blight of tea. Similarly, barley treated with leaf extract of *Azadirachta indica* resulted in induction of protection against leaf strip disease pathogen involve accumulation of proteins in the intercellular spaces, and the treated leaf exhibited significantly high acativity of enzyme phenlyalalanine ammonia lyase, tyrosine ammonia lyase along with rapid accumulation of fungitoxic phenols (Paul and Sharma, 2002). Induction of peroxidase, PAL, chitinase and ., β-1,3 glucanase has been observed in rice plants followed by application of leaf extracts of Datura metel and challenge incolation with *Rhizoctonai solani* (Kagale *et al.*, 2004). According to Sing and Pritihiviraj (1997), neemazal, a product of neem (5 percent azadirachtin solution) induced resistance in pea against *Erysiphe pisi* and the disease development correlated with increased PAL activity in pea leaf following treatment with neemazal. These enzymes exert ltic action of pathogens, and may conduce to the formation of toxic barrier against subsequent fungal attack (Mauch *et al* ., 1988).

CONCLUSION

Plants have coevolved with their pests and pathogens. As a consequence they display resisatnce against harmful organisms manifested through various mechanisms including production fo toxic chemicals . Some of these chemicals are produced constitutively whereas others are elicited as a result of injury or infection. As they are derived from plants and kill, inhibit, reduce fertility or repel other organisms, such chemicals are botanical useful as disease control agents. A considerable number of trees, shrubs and herbs are known as botanicals that can be used in control of varieties of pathogens like fungi, bacteria and nematodes. Plants and their extracts have long been used in disease control in traditional agricultural practices. With the realization of the harmful impacts of chemicals used in agriculture, chemicals extracted from plants have been viewed as the best alternatives. Although botanicals have often been suggested as an alternative for chemical control, it is unlikely that botanicals alone would be able to produce required level of control. Botanicals may be effectively used in integrated disease management programmes where a combination of traditional practices , cultural practices, use of chemicals and biocontrol brought about by other agents. Identification of active compounds may lead to their chemical synthesis and also to use biotechnological approaches to enhance productivity and to minimize cost of production. As diverse plants produe diverse chemicals , conservation of biodiversity becomes extremely important. Once the plants producing usedful chemicals are identified, it may be necessary to cultivate the plant in commercial scale in order to reduce the pressure on natural populations. Further modern technology has been employed in certain cases where the product may be extracted from cell, callus and hairy root cultures.Certain useful botanicals are tissue specific and produced through complex biochemical pathways. Genetic manipulation can also be useful in generating new variants of plants producing chemicals that are originally produced by other organisms and also to generate overproducers of exising botanicals.

REFERENCES

Abd-El-Khair, H. and Waff, M.H., 2007. Application of Some Egyptian Medicinal Plants Extracts Against Potato Late and Early Blights. Research Journal of Agriculture and Biological Sciences, 3 (3): 166-175.

Acedo, A.L. Jr., Acedo, J.Z. and Evangelio, M.F.N., 1999. Post Harvest biocontrol of bacterial soft rot of cabbage using botanicals. Philippine Journal of Crop Science, 24 (1): 12.

Ahmad, I. and Beg, A.Z. 2001. Antimicrobial and Phytochemical Studies on 45 Indian Medicinal Plants Against Multi-drug Resistant Human Pathogens. *Journal of Ethnopharmacology*, 74: 113-123.

Ahuja, S.C. and Ahuja, Uma., 2008. Learning from Farmers: Traditional Rice Production.

Akhtar, J. and Divedi, R.R., 2002. Effect of Different Oil Cakes on Radial Growth and Mycelia Dry Weight of Colletotrichum Graminicola in vitro Conditions. Indian Phytopath., 55(3): 383.

Bauer, A.W., Kirby, W.M.M. and Sherris, J.C., 1996. Antibiotic Susceptibility Testing by a Standardized Single Disk Method. Am. J. Clin. Pathol., 493-496.

Baysal, O. 1997. Determination of Microorganisms Decomposing Essential Oils of *Thymbra spicata* L. var. spicata and Effect of These Micro-organisms on Some Soil Borne Pathogens. M.Sc. Thesis, Akdenniz University, Antalya.

Bowers, J.H., and Locke, J.C., 2000. Effect of Botanical Extracts on the Population Density of Fusarium Oxysporum in Soil and Control of Fusarium Wilt in the Green House. Plant Dis. 84: 300-305.

Brent, K.J. and Hollomon, D.W. 1998. Fungicide Resistance: The Assessment of Risk. FRAC, *Global Crop Protection Federation, Brussels, Monograph*, 2: 1-48.

Canillac, N. and Mourey, A. 2001. Antibacterial Activity of the Essential Oil of *Picea excelsa* on *Listeria, Staphylococcus aureus* and Coliform Bacteria. *Food Microbiology*, 18: 261-268.

Cannell R J P. Natural Products Isolation. New Jersey: Human Press Inc; 1998. pp. 165-208.

Chakraboty, B.N., Biswas. R.D. and Sharma, M., 2007. Induction of Resistance in Tea Plants Against Alternaria Alternate by Foliar Application of Leaf extracts. J.Mycol. Pl. Pahtol. 37 (1): 60-64.

Chand, H. and Singh , S., 2005. Control of chickpea wilt using bioagents and plant extracts. Indian J. of Agric. Sci. 75 (2): 115-116.

Chattopadhyay, C., (1999) Yield Loss Attribute to Alternaria Blight of Sunflower in India and Some Potentially Effective Control Measures . Int. J. Pest Manag. 45(1): 15-21.

Coa, K.Q. and Ariena, H.C. Van B.(2001) Inhibitory Efficacy of Several Plant Extracts and Plant Products on Phytophthora Infestans. J.of Ahric. Univ. of Hebei. 24(2): 1-9.

Cosa P, Vlietinck A J, Berghe D V, Maes L. Anti-infective Potential of Natural Products: How to Develop a Stronger *in vitro* 'proof-of-concept' J Ethnopharmacol. 2006;106: 290-302.

Cox, S.D., Gustafson, J.E., Mann, C.M., Markham, L., Liew, Y. C., Hartland, R.P., Bell, H.

C., Warmington, J.R., and Wyllie, S.G. 1998. Tea Tree Oil Causes K+ Leakage and Inhibits Respiration in *Escherichia coli. Letters in Applied Microbiology*, 26: 355-358.

Doubrara, N.S., Dean, R.A. and Kuc, J., 1998. Induction of Systemic Induced Resistance to Anthracnose Caused by Colletotrichum Lagenarium in Cucumber by Oxalate and Extracts from Spinach and Rhubarb Leaves. Physiol. And Mol. Pl. Pathol. 33: 69-79.

Dubey, R.K., Rajesh, K.Jaya, and Dubey, N.K. 2007. Evaluation of *Eupatorium cannabinum* Linn. Oil in Enhancement of Shelf Life of Mango Fruits from Fungal Rotting. *World Journal of Microbiology and Biotechnology*.

Dubey, S.C., Suresh, M. and Singh, B. 2007. Evaluation of *Trichoderma* Species Against *Fusarium oxysporum* f. sp. *ciceris* for Integrated Management of Chickpea. *Biological Control*, 40: 118-127.

Eberhardt T L, Li X, Shupe T F, Hse C Y. Chinese Tallow Tree (Sapium Sebiferum) Utilization: Characterization of Extractives and Cell-wall Chemistry. Wood Fiber Sci. 2007; 39: 319-324.

Ehteshamul Hague, Zaki, M.J., Vahidy, A.A and Abaul Graffas., 1998. Effect of Organic Amendments on the Efficacy of Pseudomonas Aeruginosa in the Control of Root Rot Diseases of Sunflower. Pakistan J.Botany, 30 (1): 45-50.

Elgayyar, M., Draughon , F.A., Golden, D.A. and Mount, J.R. 2001. Antimicrobial Activity of Essential Oils from Plants Against Selected Pathogenic and Saprophytic Microorganisms. *Journal of Food Protection*, 64: 1019-1024.

Enikuomehin, O.A., Ikotun, T. and Ekpo, E. J.A., 1998. Evaluation of Ash from Some Tropical Plants of Nigeria for the Control of Sclerotium Rolfsii sacc. On Wheat. Mycopathologia. 142(1): 81-87.

Esteshamul Hague, Zaki, M.J., Vahidy, A.A. and Abaul Graffas., 1998. Effect of Organic Amendments on the Efficacy of Pseudomonas Aeruginosa in the Control of Root Rot Diseases of Sunflower. Pakistan J.Botany, 30 (1): 45-50.

Fabricant D S, Farnsworth N R. The Value of Plants Used in Traditional Medicine for Drug Discovery. Environ Health Perspect. 2001; 109: 69-75.

Fan X H, Cheng Y Y, Ye Z L, Lin R C, Qian Z Z. Multiple Chromatographic Fingerprinting and its Application to the Quality Control of Herbal Medicines. Anal Chim Acta. 2006; 555: 217-224.

Hamburger M O, Cordell G A. A Direct Bioautographic TLC Assay for Compounds Possessing Antibacterial Activity. J Nat Prod. 1987; 50: 19-22.

Homans A L, Fuchs A. Direct Bioautography on Thin-layer Chromatograms as a Method for Detecting Fungitoxic Substances. J Chromatogr. 1970; 51: 327-329.

Hooda, K.S. and Srivastava, M.S., 1998. Impact of Neem Coatd Urea and Potash on the Incidence of Rice Blast. Plant Dis. Research. 13(1).

Huie C W. A Review of Modern Sample-preparation Techniques for the Extraction and Analysis of Medicinal Plants. Anal Bioanal Chem. 2002; 373: 23-30.

Hundekar, A.R., Anahosur, K.H., Patil, M.S., Kalapannavar. I.K. and Chattannavar, S.N., 198. *In vitro* Evaluation of Organic Amendments Against Stalk Rot of Sorghum. J.Mycol. and Pl. Path. 28 (1): 26-30.

Hundekar, A.R., Anahosur, K.H., Patil, M.S., Kalapannavar. I.K. and Chattannavar, S.N., 1998. *In vitro* Evaluation of Orgnic Amendments Against Stalk Rot of Sorghum. J.Mycol. and Plant Pathol. 28 (1): 26-30.

Isman, M.B. 2006. Botanical Insecticides, Deterrents, and Repellents in Modern Agriculture and an Increasingly Regulated World. *Annual Review of Entomology*, 51: 45-66.

Jain, C. and Trivedi, P.C., 1997. Nematicidal Activity of Certain Plants Against Root Knot Nematode, Meloidogyne Incognita Infecting Chickpea, Cicer Arietinum. Annals of Plant Protection Sciences, 5(2): 171-174.

Jain, C. and Trivedi, P.C., 1997. Nematicidal Activity of Certain Plants Extracts Against Root Knot Nematode, Meloidogyne Incognita Infection Chickpea. Annals of Plant Protection Sciences, 5 (2): 171-174.

Jha, M.M., Kumar , S. and Hasan, S., 2004. Effect of Botanicals on maydis Leaf Blight of Maize *in vitro*. Annals of Biology. 20 (2): 173-176.

Kagale, S., Marimuthu, T., Thayumanavan, B., Nandakumar, R. and Samiyappan, R., 2004. Antimicrobial Activity and Induction of Systemic Acquired Resistance in Rice by Leaf extract of Datura Metel Against Rhi.

Kumar, R., Mishra, A. K., Dubey, N. K. and Tripathi, Y. B. 2007. Evaluation of *Chenopodium ambrosoides* Oil as a Potential Source of Antifungal, Antiaflatoxigenic and Antioxidant Activity. *International Journal of Food Microbiology*, 115: 159-164.

Kurucheve, V., Ezhilan, J.G. and Newaskar. V.B., 1988. Effect of Different Fungicides and Neem Products for Control of Leaf Spot of Groundnut. J.Soils and Crops. 8 (1): 44-49.

Lale, N.E.S. 1992. A Laboratory Study of the Comparative Toxicity of Products from Three Spices to the Maize Weevil. *Postharvest Biology and Technology*, 2: 612-664.

Li H B, Jiang Y, Chen F. Separation Methods Used for *Scutellaria baicalensis* Active Components. J Chromatogr B. 2004; 812: 277-290.

Lokhande, N.M., Lanjewar . R.D. and Newaskar. V.B. 1998. Effect of Different Fungicides and Neem Products for the Control of Leaf Spot of Groundnuts. J.Soils and Crops. 8(1): 44-49.

Lokhande,. N.M., Lanjewar, R.D. and Newaskar.V.B., 1889; Effect Odifferent Fungicides and Neem Products for Control of Leaf Spot of Groundnut. J. Soils and Crops. 8 (1): 44-49.

Mahadevan, A 1982 Biochemical Aspects of Disease Resistance part I. Performed Inhibitory Substances Prohibitions. Today and Tomorrow's Printers and Publishers, New Delhi, India, 425 p.

Maji , M.D., Chattopadhyay, S., Kumar. P. and Saratchandra, B., 2005. *In vitro* Screening of Some Plant Extracts Against Fungal Pathogens of Mublberry. Archies of Phytopathology and Plant Protection. 38 (3): 157-164.

Mararishi, R.P., 1993. Management of Chilli Diseases by Neem Based Preparations. World Neem Conference. Bangalore, India: 34.

Mariappan, V., 1998. Neem for the Management of Crop Diseases. Associated Publishing Company, New Delhi. pp. 220.

Mauch, F., Mauch-mani, B. and Boller, T., 1998. Antifungal Hydrolases in Pea Tissue. II. Inhibition of Funga Growth by Combinations of Chitinase and β-1,3-glucanase. Plant Physiol. 88: 936-942.

Meena, R.L., Rathore, R.S. and Kusum, M., (2003). Evaluation of Fungicides and Plant Extracts Against Banded Leaf and Sheath Blight of Maize. Ind. J. Plant. Prot. 31(1): 94-97.

Mishra, A.K. and Dubey, N.K. 1994. Evaluation of Some Essential Oils for Their Toxicity Against Fungi Causing Deterioration of Stored Food Commodities. *Applied and Environmental Microbiology*, 60: 1101-1105.

Mji, M.D., Chattopadhyay, S., Kumar, P. and Saratchandra, B., 2005. *In vitro* Screening of Some Plant Extracts Against Fungal Pathogens of Mulberry. Archies of Phytopathology and Plant Protection. 38 (3): 157-164.

Mojumdar, V. and Mishra, S.D., 1992. Effect of Seed Soaking in Aqueous Extracts of Neem Seed on Germination on Ungbean and Penetration of Second Stage Juveniles of Meloidogyne Incognita. Annals of Agricultural Research, 13: 297-299.

Nagarajan (1990). Effect of Plant Extracts and Oils on Rice Yellow Dwarf Infection. Madras Agric. J. 77: 197-201.

Nair, R and Chanda, S., 2005. Anticonidial Activity of Punica Granatum Exhibited in Different Solvents. Pharm. Biol. 43: 21-25.

Nene, Y.L. and Thapliyal, P.N., 1987. Fungicides in Plant Disease Control. Oxford and IBH Publishing Co. Pvt. Ltd. New Delhi, pp. 691.

Okonkwo, E.U. and Okoye, W.I. 1996. The Efficacy of Four Seed Powders and the Essential Oils as Protectants of Cowpea and Maize Grains Against Infestation by *Callosobruchus maculatus* (Fabricius) (Coleoptera: Bruchidae) and *Sitophilus zeamais* (Motschulsky) (Coleoptera: Curculionidae) in Nigeria. *International Journal of Pest Management*, 42: 143-146.

Oxenham, S. K. 2003. Classification of an *Ocimum basilicum* Germplasm Collection and Examination of the Antifungal Effects of the Essential Oil of Basil. Ph.D. Thesis, University of Glasgow, Glasgow, UK.

Patil, M.J., Ukey, S.P. and Raut, B.T., 2003. Evaluation of Fungicides and Botanicals for the Management of Early Blight of Tomato. PKV Research Journal. 25 (1): 49-51.

Patni C.S., Kolte, S.J and Awasthi , R.P., 2005 b. Inhibitory Effect of Some Plant Extracts Against Alternaria Brassicae, Causing Alternaria Blight of Mustard. Journal of Research SKUAT-J, 4 (1), 71-79.

Patni, C.S., Kolte, S.J and Awasthi, R.P., 2005a.Efficacy of Botanicals Against Alternaria Blight of Mustard. Indian Phtopath. 58 (4): 426-430.

Paul, P.K and Sharma, P.D., 2002. Azadirachta Indica Leaf Extract Induces Resistance in Barley Against Leaf Stripe Disease. Physiol. Mol. Pl. Pathol. 61: 3-13.

Penna, C., Marino, S., Vivot, E., Cruanes, M. C., Munoz, J. de D., Cruanes, J., Ferraro, G., Gutkind, G. and Martino, V. 2001. Antimicrobial Activity of Argentine Plants Used in the Treatment of Infectious Diseases. Isolation of Active Compounds from *Sebastiania brasiliensis*. *Journal of Ethnopharmacology*, 77: 37-40.

Perez, C., Paul, M. and Bazerque, P., 1990. An Antibiotic Assay for the Agar Well Diffusion Method. Acta Biol. Med. Exp. 15: 113-115.

Pharmacopoeia of the People's Republic of China, Author. The Pharmacopeia Commission of PRC. English ed. Beijing: 2000.

Ponnana, K.M. and Adiver, S.S., (2001). Fungicidal Management of Grew Mildew of Cotton. Pl. Pathol. News letter., 19: 6-8.

Ponnanna, K.M. and Adiver, S.S., 2001. Fungicidal Management of Grey Mildew of Cotton. Plant Pathology Newsletter., 19: 6-8.

Pramanick, T.C. and Phookan, A.K., 1998. Effect of Plant Extracts in the Management of Sheath Rot of Rice. J.Agric. Sci. North East India. 11(1): 85-87.

Prasad , C.S., Gupta, V., Tyagi, A. and Pathak, S., 2003. Biological Control of Sclerotium rolfsii Sacc., the Incitant of Cauliflower Collar Rot. Annals. of Plant Protection Sciences. 11(1): 61-63.

Prasad , M.S., Lakshmi, B.S. and Shaik Mohiddin 1998. Survival of Sclerotia of Rhizoctonia Solani in Rice Soils Amended with Oil Cakes and Green Leaf Manures. Ann. Agric. Res., 19(1): 44-48.

Prasad, M.S., Lakshmi, B.S. and Shaik Mohiddin 1998. Survival of Sclerotia of Rhizoctonia Solani in Rice Soils Amended with Oil Cakes and Green Leaf Manures. Ann. Agric. Res., 19(1): 44-88.

Raghuvanshi, N.S., Dubey, K.S. and Kumar, B., 2006. Effect of Soil Extracts Amended with Some Organic Materials on Conidial Germination of Colletotrichum Falcatum. Indian J. Plant Pathology. 24 (1 & 2): 117-118.

Rahalison L, Hamburger M, Hostettmann K, Monod M, Frenk E. A Bioautographic Agar Overlay Method for the Detection of Antifungal Compounds from Higher Plants. Phytochem Anal. 1991; 2: 199-203.

Rauha, J.P., Remes, S., Heinonen, M., Hopia, A., Kahkonen, M., Kujala, T., Pihlaja, K., Vuorela, H. and Vuorela, P. 2000. Antimicrobial Effects of Finnish Plant Extracts Containing Flavonoids and Other Phenolic Compounds. *International Journal of Food Microbiology*, 56: 3-12.

Razeena, B.P.M and Ahmad, R., 2007 Control of Seed Borne Fungi of Okra with Pseudomonas Fluorescens and Aqueous Extract of Heena . J.Mycol. Pl. Pathol. 37 (3): 485-487

Sahayaraj, K., Mamasivayam, S.K.R, and Borgio, J.A.F., 2006 Influence of Three Plant Extracts on Fusarium Oxysporum f. sp. ciceris mycelia growth. J.Plant Ptotec. Res. 46(4): 235-238.

Salie, F., Eagles, P.F.K. and leng, H.M.F., 1996. Preliminary Antimicrobial Screening of Four South African Asteraceae species. J. Ethonopharmacol, 52: 27-33.

Satish, S., Raveesha, K.A. and Janardhana, G.R., 1999/Antibacterial Activity of Plant Extracts on Phytopathogenic Xanthomonas Campestris Pathovars. Letters in Applied Microbiology. 28: 145-147.

Saxena, R.C., Khan, Z.R. and Bajet, N.B., 1987. Reduction of Tungro Virus Transmission by Nephotettix Virescens in Neem Cake Treated Rice Seedlings. J.Econ. Entomol. 80 (5): 1079-1082.

Schillhorn van Veen, T.W. (1999). Agricultural Policy and Sustainable Livestock Development. *Int. J. Parasitol.*, 29: 7-15, ISSN: 0020-7519.

Sesha Kiran, K., Ligaraju, S. and Adiver, S.S, 2006. Effect of Plant Extracts on Slerotium Rolfsii, the Incitant of Stem Rot of Groundnut. J. Mycol. Pl. Pathol. 36 (1): 77-78.

Shahverdi A R, Abdolpour F, Monsef-Esfahani H R, Farsam H A. TLC Bioautographic Assay for the Detection of Nitrofurantoin Resistance Reversal Compound. J Chromatogr B. 2007; 850: 528-530.

Sharma, N. and Tripathi, A., 2006; Fungitoxicity of the Essential Oils of Citrus Sinensis on Post Harvest Pathogens. Worls J. Microbiol. Biotech. 22(6): 587-593.

Sharma, U., Thakur, P.D., Handa, A., Bhalik, A. and Gupta, D., 2007. Effect of Centella Asiatica and Vitex Negundo Against TUMV Infectiong Radish. J.Pl.Dis. Sci. 2(1): 22-25.

Shoyama Y, Tanaka H, Fukuda N. Monoclonal Antibodies Against Naturally Occurring Bioactive Compounds. Cytotechnology. 2003; 31: 9-27.

Singh, U.P. and Prithiviraj, B., 1997. Neem Azal. A product of Neem, Induces Resistance in Pea Against Erysiphe Pisi. Physiological and Molecular Plant Pathology, 51(3): 181-194.

Singh, N and Singh, R.S., (1983) Inhibition of Fusarium Udum (Pigeon Pea Wilt) by ether distillate of margosa cake amended soil. Indian Journal of Mycol. & Pl.Pathol., 13(3): 329-330.

Singh P.K and Dwivedi, R.S., 1987. Effect of Oils on Sclerotium Rolfsii Causing Root Rot of Barle. Indian Phytopath. 40: 531-533.

Sinha, R.K.P. and Sinha, B.B.P., 2004, Effect of Potash, Botanicals and Fungicides Against Wilt Disease Complex of Lentil. Annls. Pl. Protec. Sci. 12(20: 454-455.

Somasekhara, Y.M., Natishan, B.M and Muniyappa, V., 1998. Evaluation of Neem Products and Insecticides Against White Fly a Vector of Tomato Leaf Curl Geminivirus Diseases. Neem Mews Letter. 15 (2): 16.

Somasekhara, Y.M., Natishan, B.M and Muniyappa, V., 1998. Evaluation of Neem Products and Insecticides Against West Fly (Bemesia tabaci) a Vector of Tomato Leaf Curl Geminivirus Diseases. Neem Newsletter. 15 (2): 16.

Srinivasulu, B., Doraiswamy, S., Aruna, K., Rao, D.V.R., Rabindran, R., (2002). Efficacy of Biocontrol Agen, Chemicals and Botanicals on Ganoderma sp., the Coconut Basal Stem Rot Pathogen. J. Planta. Crops. 30(3): 57-59.

Suhr, K.I. and Nielsen, P.V. 2003. Antifungal Activity of Essential Oils Evaluated by Two Different Application Techniques Against Rye Bread Spoilage Fungi. *Journal of Applied Microbiology*, 94: 665-674.

Suresh, G., Narasimhan, N.S. and Masilamani, S., 1997. Antifungal Fractions and Compounds from Uncrushed Green Leaf *Azdirachta indica*. Phytoparasitica 25(1): 33-39.

Suryavanshi, A.P., Ladkat, G.M., Dhoke, P.K., Surayawanshi, S.D. and Pensalwar, S.N., 2007. Antifungal Fractions and Compounds from Uncrushed Green Leaves of Azadirachta Indica. Phytoparasitica. 25 (1): 33-39.

Suryawanshi, A.P., Ladkat, G.M., Dhoke, P.K., Surayawanshi , S.D. and Pensalwar, S.N., 2007. Evaluation of Some Plant Extracts Against Sclerotium Rolfss on Pigeonpea. J.Pl. Sis. Sci. 2(1): 32-33.

Tripathi, P., Dubey, N.K., Banerji, R, and Chansouria, J.P.N., 2004. Evaluation of Some Essential Oils as Botanical Fungitoxicvants in Management of Post Harvest Rotting of Citrus Fruits. World J. Microbiol. Biotech.20 (3): 317-21.

Tripathi, R.K.R. and Tripathi, R.N., 1982. Reduction in Bean Common Mosaic Virus (BCMV) Infectivity *vis-a vis* Crude Leaf Extracts of Some Higher Plants. Experimentia. 38 (3): 349.

Tsao R, Deng Z. Separation Procedures for Naturally Occurring Antioxidant Phytochemicals. J Chromatogr B. 2004; 812: 85-99.

Tyagi, S.A. and Alam M.M., 1995. Efficacy of Oil Seed Cakes Against Plant Parasitic Nematodes and Soil Inhabiting Fungi on Mungbean and Chickpea. Bioresource Technology, 51: 233-239.

Ushamalini, C., Rajappan,K. and Gangadhran, K., 1997. Suppression of Charcoal Rot and Wilt Pathogens of Cowpea by Botanicals. Plant Disease Research. 12(2): 113-117.

Varma, J. and Dubey, N.K. 1999. Perspective of Botanical and Microbial Products as Pesticides of Tomorrow. *Current Science*, 76: 172-179.

Verma S. and Dohroo, N.P., 2003. Evaluation of Botanicals *in vitro* Against *Fusarium oxysporum f. sp. pisi* Causing Wilt of Pea. Plant Dis. Res. 18(2): 131-134.

Vidhyasekaran, P., 1992. Principles of Plant Pathology. CBS Printers and Publishers, New Delhi.

Yadav, V.K. and Thirmurty, V.S., 2006. Fungitoxicity of Some Medicinal Plant Extracts Against Sarocladium Sryze Causing Sheath Rot of Rice. Indin J.Plant Pathology. 24 (1 & 2): 93-96.

Yamada, T., Hiramotoa, T., Tobimatsu, T., Shiraishi, T. and Oku. H., 1990. Elicitor Like Substances Present in Barley and Wheat Seeds. J. Phytopathology. 128: 89-98.

Yokoyama, K., Aist, J.R. and Bayles, C.J., 1991: Plant Growth Regulating Extract that Induced Resistance to Barley Powdery Mildew. Physiol. And Mol. Pl. Pathol. 35: 166-175.

Pages: **86-104**

SEED TECHNOLOGY, PLANT GROWTH AND CROPPING SYSTEM

Edited by: **Dr. Pawan Kumar Tyagi; Dr. Pawan Kumar 'Bharti'**

ISBN: 978-93-5056-738-8

Edition: **2015**

Published by: **Discovery Publishing House Pvt. Ltd., New Delhi (India)**

5

Environmental Impact of Agriculture

Ndofor-Foleng H.M.*, and Osita C.O

INTRODUCTION

Agriculture generally plays a key role in land management and has a huge responsibility in the preservation of natural resources. It is one of the key aspects to the functionality of our society. Over the last few centuries the society has developed means to improve the efficiency of our agricultural practices which has increased the carry capacity of the earth and allowed for more people to survive on our planet. The practice of agriculture has been around for hundreds of years and has become a basic way of life for a majority of the world. Gradually over the years, agricultural processes have flourished and become more efficient. A new report from FAO says livestock production is one of the major causes of the world's most pressing environmental problems, including global warming, land degradation, air and water pollution, and loss of biodiversity. Using a methodology that considers the entire commodity chain, it estimates that livestock are

Department of Animal Science, University of Nigeria, Nsukka, Nigeria.

responsible for 18 percent of greenhouse gas emissions, a bigger share than that of transport. However, the report says, the livestock sector's potential contribution to solving environmental problems is equally large, and major improvements could be achieved at reasonable cost.

Environmental issues, linked to the production of animals farming systems, are usually discussed, using pigs, poultry and dairy cattle as examples. The principal livestock production factors influencing their environmental impact are identified as the balance between different farm animal types and the husbandry practices used for these species. Livestock provides countless people with sustenance and livelihood all over the world. However, with agriculture, animal farming in particular, comes great risk. Agriculture increases carbon dioxide levels making it one of the main sources of carbon dioxide emissions for decades. Animal waste from farms contains harmful pathogens such as *Cryptosporidium parvum* and *Giardia duodenalis* both of which are known to cause disease and infection. By getting into soil and water systems they create irreversible damage to land and pose health risks towards humans.

The production of large quantities of nitrogenous waste, resulting from the importation of large quantities of nitrogen to intensive animal production units, is identified as the major environmental problem for animal production. These problems lead both directly and indirectly to health risks, and may so many health disorders. Fertilizers also put forth several complications. They contain harmful elements such as nitrogen and phosphates, both of which negatively affect air and water quality. Its use causes the release of ammonia, nitrogen runoff and eutrophication, all of which have negative effects on the environment.

However, with new research and technological developments, scientists have found the negative effects that farms have had on the environment. All around the world, researchers have been discovering the problems by which farms have been plaguing our environment. The development of systems which allow these waste products to be re-used at sites of primary crop production is seen as a sustainable solution to this problem.The general trend towards more intensive and industrialised agriculture has a profound impact on the environment, including emissions to air and water, quality and quantity of surface water and groundwater, soil erosion, pollution due to large-scale use of pesticides, and loss of biodiversity and habitats. Environmental and agro ecological research is currently focusing on understanding the cause-consequence relationships between e.g. specificagricultural practices and land use and the responses at different levels of ecosystems. The chapter discusses briefly the key impacts of agriculture on the environment (biodiversity, leaching of nutrients to water, emissions to air, water availability and soil degradation and pollution) and the mitigations.

THE ENVIRONMENTAL IMPACT OF AGRICULTURE

The environmental impact of agriculture varies based on the wide variety of agricultural practices employed around the world.

(a) Environmental Impacts of Farming

Unsustainable agricultural and aquaculture practices present the greatest immediate threat to species and ecosystems around the world. Farmed areas – both on land and in the water – provide important habitats for manywild plants and animals. When farming operations are properly managed, they can help preserve and restore habitatsand improve soil health and water quality. But when practiced without care, farming presents the greatest threat to species and ecosystems.

Land Conversion, Habitat Loss and Desertification: The main impact from farming comes from clearing natural habitats for agriculture and aquaculture – especially for intensive monocultures. Agriculture is a major land use. Around 50% of the world's habitable land has already been converted to farming land. Overall, farmland covers 38% of the world's land area. This area is still expanding. It is predicted that in developing countries, a further 120 million hectares of natural habitats will be converted to farmland to meet demand for food by 2050. This will include land with high biodiversity value. Agricultural ecosystems provide important habitats for many wild plant and animal species. This is especially the case for traditional farming areas that cultivate diverse species.

However, rising demand for food and other agricultural products has seen large-scale clearing of natural habitats to make room for intensive monocultures. Recent examples include the conversion of lowland rainforests in Indonesia and Cameroon tooil palm plantations, and of large areas of the Amazon rainforest to soybean farms.

This ongoing habitat loss threatens entire ecosystems as well as many species. Expanding oil palm plantations in Indonesia , Malaysia and Cameroon for example, pose the most significant threats to endangered megafauna including elephant and tigers. On top of habitat loss due to clearing, unsustainable agricultural practices are seeing 12 million hectares of land lost each year to desertification.

WASTEFUL WATER CONSUMPTION

Globally, the agricultural sector consumes about 70% of the planet's accessible freshwater – more than twice that of industry (23%), and dwarfing municipal use (8%). Between 15-35% of water use by agriculture is estimated to be unsustainable. Moreover, agriculture wastes 60% or 1,500 trillion litres, of the 2,500 trillion litres of water it uses each year. Many big food producing countries like the US, China, India, Pakistan, Australia and Spain have reached, or are close to reaching, their renewable water resource limits.

The main causes of wasteful and unsustainable water use are leaky irrigation systems, wasteful field application methods and cultivation of thirsty crops not suited to the environment.

Aquaculture is also in direct competition with natural marine and freshwater habitats for space. For example, marine fish farms often need the shelter of bays and estuaries to avoid damage from storms and currents. In addition, farmed fish need good water quality, frequent water exchange, and other optimal environmental conditions. But these locations are also very often ideal for wild fish and other marine life.

Some African fish farms have been placed in the migratory routes of some fish species, while in Asia and Latin America, mangrove forests have been cleared to make space for shrimp farms.

Unsustainable water use harms the environment by changing the water table and/or depleting ground water supplies. Excessive irrigation can also increase soil salinity and wash pollutants and sediment into rivers – causing damage to freshwater ecosystems and species as well as those further downstream, including coral reefs and coastal fish breeding grounds.

Irrigation: Irrigation accounts for about 37 percent of US withdrawn freshwater use, and groundwater provides about 42 percent of US irrigation water. Irrigation water applied in production of livestock feed and forage has been estimated to account for about 9 percent of withdrawn freshwater use in the United States. Groundwater depletion is a concern in some areas because of sustainability issues (and in some cases, land subsidence and/or saltwater intrusion). However, where production relies on irrigation from groundwater reserves, water table monitoring is appropriate to provide timely warning if groundwater depletion occurs.

Arable Land Destroyed: It is estimated that since 1960, one-third of the world's arable land has been lost through erosion and other degradation. An example is seen in Enugu State, Nigeria where a large expanse of land is lost every year through erosion. The problem persists, with a reported loss rate of about 10 million hectares per year. In reality, the situation may be much more worrying. Over the last 5 decades, increases in agricultural productivity have made it possible to produce more crops on the same amount of land. But the problem is that because agricultural land is often degraded and almost useless, producers keep on moving to more productive land. Globally, the land used and abandoned in the last 50 years may be equal to the amount of land used today. There is also increase in flooding: Erosion caused by deforestation can also lead to increased flooding. In banana plantations, for example, flooding occurs partly because of deforestation (soil is no longer there to absorb the water) and partly because of poorly constructed plantation drainage systems.

Soil erosion and degradation: A major problem in Africa and in Europe is the degradation of soils and irreversible losses of soils due to soil sealing and erosion. The productive capacity of soils depends on the content of mineral nutrients, organic carbon, soil structure and texture. Erosion affects all these soil properties. Loss of organic matter, soil biodiversity and consequent deterioration of soil fertility are often driven by unsustainable agricultural practices, such as deep ploughing. Soil has many functions, including the capacity to remove contaminants from the environment by filtration and adsorption. Soil degradation, through its impact on soil organic matter, has also an influence on the release of CO_2 into the atmosphere and thus on global carbon cycling (EEA, 2003). Erosion commonly occurs following conversion of natural vegetation to agricultural land – carrying away fertile soil as well as fertilizers, pesticides and other agrochemicals. When natural vegetation is cleared and when farmland is ploughed, the exposed topsoil is often blown away by wind or washed away by rain. This leads to reduced soil fertility and degraded land.

(b) Environmental Impact of Animal Production

(*i*) *Deforestation:* One of the causes of deforestation is to clear land for pasture or crops. According to British environmentalist Norman Myers, 5% of deforestation is due to cattle ranching, 19% due to over-heavy logging, 22% due to the growing sector of palm oil plantations, and 54% due to slash-and-burn farming. In 2000 the Food and Agriculture Organization (FAO) found that deforestation can result from "a combination of population pressure and stagnating economic, social and technological conditions.The livestock sector is by far the single largest anthropogenic user of land. Grazing occupies 26 percent of the Earth's terrestrial surface, while feed crop production requires about a third of all arable land. About 70 percent of all grazing land in dry areas is considered degraded, mostly because of overgrazing, compaction and erosion attributable to livestock activity.Growing food and raising animals also uses resources from the earth. Humans impact the environment through deforestation, agricultural and livestock activities, urbanization and burning fossil fuels (Shepherd, 2011).This is because each livestock production system is different in the way it uses resources.

(*ii*) *Systems of Animal Farming:* The systems are often categorized into two types: extensive farming and intensive farming.

Extensive farming is a type of agriculture that is mainly a pasture-based and land-based system. In beef cattle production, for example, cattle in an extensive system would graze in a pasture. Intensive systems have more concentrated operations and are often more mechanized. Each of these systems occurs all around the world and each has an environmental impact.

The challenge for global livestock production is to improve environmental sustainability within each region. Extensive livestock production plays a critical role in land degradation, climate change, water and biodiversity loss. For example, grazing occupies 26 percent of the Earth's terrestrial surface, and feed-crop production requires about a third of all arable land, he said. Expansion of livestock grazing land is also a leading cause of deforestation, especially in Latin America, he added. In the Amazon basin alone, about 70 percent of previously forested land is used as pasture, while feed crops cover a large part of the remainder.

Intensive systems: Animals are contained and feed is brought to them. "Extensive systems" generally refer to grazing animals that live off the land. There has also been a large shift towards "confinement" operations. This again, is somewhat of an unfortunate term, since confinement simply means that the animals are being raised indoors. When animals are moved completely inside, they obviously loose some things like exposure to sunlight and grass. They are also usually housed in pens with less square feet per animal than in outdoor production systems. However, their environment can be better controlled indoors. It can be heated, ventilated and cooled. Feed consumption and animal health can be easily monitored. Exposure to direct sunlight seems like a great thing until you realize that pigs sunburn very easily.

Free-range animal production: It requires land for grazing, which in some places has led to land use change. According to the Food and Agriculture Organization (FAO), "Ranching-induced deforestation is one of the main causes of loss of some unique plant and animal species in the tropical rainforests of Central and South America as well as carbon release in the atmosphere." This for example has implications for meat consumption in Europe, which imports significant amounts of feed from Brazil. Raising animals for human consumption accounts for approximately 40% of the total amount of agricultural output in industrialized countries. Grazing occupies 26% of the earth's ice-free terrestrial surface, and feed crop production uses about one third of all arable land. Environmental effects of grazing can be positive or negative, depending on the quality of management, and grazing can have different effects on different soils and different plant communities. Grazing sometimes reduces, but sometimes increases biodiversity of grassland ecosystems.

(*iii*) *Green gas effect*

Livestock production is the largest methane source emitter in the world and the third largest in the United States. Most of this methane is a result of manure storage and enteric fermentation, which is methane produced in the digestive tract of an animal. Currently in the United States, agriculture accounts for seven percent of the total GHG emitted.Carbon dioxide from livestock production is a result of fuel use from equipment and changes in the carbon content of soil, such as, crops, deforestation and direct land use by animals (Hermansen et al., 2011). The source of nitrous oxide in livestock production is the application of manure and artificial fertilizers on fields and from ammonia losses during and after the growing season (Hermansen et al., 2011).

(*iv*) *Animals Effect on Water Quality:* Water is a scarce and valuable resource essential to human and animal life. Water for livestock production is used for drinking, irrigation to grow crops/pasture and for different animal services such as cleaning. The water needed to produce feed is the major factor behind the water footprint of animal products (Hoekstra, 2012). Animals can negatively affect water quality by having free access to water sources where they are able to deposit waste and cause the water to become cloudy from stirring up mud. Waste from animals can be dangerous because it carries harmful bacteria which people may drink. Water contamination can occur in many different ways. In extensive systems, livestock often have access to bodies of water where they are able to deposit waste. This waste travels downstream and has direct contact with humans. In intensive production systems, bacteria can enter water sources during heavy rainfalls that might result in an overflow of the manure catchment basin or from manure that has been put on fields as fertilizer (McAllister et al., 2012).

Lost genetic diversity: The replacement of traditional and local crops and farm animals with more genetically uniform, modern varieties has caused the genetic erosion of crops and livestock species around the world. The widespread use of genetically uniform modern crop varieties has caused agricultural crops to lose about 75% of their genetic diversity in the last century. Today, just 30 crops account for 90% of calories consumed by people, while 14 animal species account for 90% of all livestock production. This lost genetic diversity reduces the potential for modern crops to adapt to, or be bred for, changing conditions – and so directly threatens long-term food security.

Pollution: The use of pesticides, fertilizers and other agrochemicals has increased hugely since the 1950s. For example, the amount of pesticide sprayed on fields has increased 26-fold over the past 50 years. These chemicals don't just stay on the fields they are applied to. Some application methods – such as pesticide spraying by aeroplane – lead to pollution of adjacent land, rivers or wetlands. Due to inappropriate water management and irrigation technology, fertilizers and pesticides also commonly run-off from fields to adjacent rivers and lakes and contaminate groundwater sources. These chemicals eventually end up in the marine environment too.

Pesticides often don't just kill the target pest. Beneficial insects in and around the fields can be poisoned or killed, as can other animals eating poisoned insects. Pestcides can also kill soil microorganisms. Pesticide pollution of rivers, lakes and wetlands also directly poisons freshwater species, as well as people. Some pesticides are suspected of disrupting the hormone messaging systems of wildlife and people, and many can remain in the environment for generations.

Unlike pesticides, fertilizers are not directly toxic. However, their presence in freshwater and marine areas alters the nutrient system, and in consequence the species composition of specific ecosystems. Their most dramatic effect is eutrophication – resulting in an explosive growth of algae due to excess nutrients. This depletes water of dissolved oxygen, which in turn can kill fish and other aquatic life.

LEACHING OF NUTRIENTS AND EUTROPHICATION OF WATERS

Loading of waters is caused by crop and grassland production and livestock production. Phosphorus and nitrogen leach to rivers, lakes and the sea from arable land causingeutrophication. Eutrophication is a condition in an aquatic ecosystem where high nutrient concentrations stimulate growth of algae, since nitrogen and phosphorus are among the main growth limiting nutrients in aquatic environments. This leads to imbalanced functioning of the aquatic system causing intense algal growth (excess of filamentous algae and phytoplankton blooms), production of excess organic matter, increased oxygen consumption and consequent oxygen depletion. The gross nutrient balance for nitrogen provides an indication of potential water pollution (eutrophication driver, OECD 2001).

WATERBORNE ZOONOTIC DISEASES

Animal farms can also have a major negative impact on our environment and the health ofhumans. The protection of water that has been affected by farming helps to reduce the risk ofwater-borne diseases to both humans and animals. They become water borne when the excrement of the diseased animals gets into a water system. The runoff from animal farms compromises the quality of surface water by seeping into water systems either directly from livestock excrement or precipitation runoff. Some of the strains of protozoa that are of concern in waterborne zoonotic diseases are *Cryptosporidium parvum* and *Giardia duodenalis*.

The feces of farm animals are of greater concern than other animals because farm animals are kept in masses. Since there are so many livestock, they have a greater amount of feces trapped in lagoons. Bacteria are another form of pathogens that plague contaminated water. The main bacteria species we are dealing with is known as *Campylobacter*. The main food borne bacteria that cause complications in human health are the pathogens *Salmonella* and *E. coli*.They are mostly prevalent among livestock and can lead to severe intestinal dysfunction in humans. Animal farms are common, and all animals produce waste. Depending on the quality of waste management, the chances of excrement seeping into groundwater or making its way into our water system are good or bad. Some farms may not put enough effort or money into waste management, greatly increasing the chances of parasites from faeces contaminating water, and in turn, causing disease or infection in humans.

Climate Change: Climate change is one of the key factors affecting the agro-food production and agricultural practices in Africa, Europe and worldwide. Farming practices, livestock, and clearing of land for agriculture are significant contributors to the build-up of greenhouse gases in the atmosphere.

Animal agriculture is responsible for 18% of the total release of greenhouse gases world-wide (this is more than all the cars, trucks, planes, and ships in the world combined). Livestock account for an estimated 9% of global CO2 (Carbon Dioxide) emissions, estimated 35-40% of global CH4 (Methane) emissions and 65% of NO2 (Nitrous Oxide) emissions.

Sources include fertilizers, livestock, wetland rice cultivation, manure management, burning of savanna and agricultural residues, and ploughing. For example, rice production is in Ndop, North West region, Cameroon and Abakelike, Ebonyi State, Nigeria, are one of largest producers of methane. The UN Food and Agriculture Organization (FAO) recently stated that the livestock sector alone is responsible for 18% of all greenhouse gas production. In addition, the conversion of forests to agriculture – particularly in tropical Asia – accounts for a roughly similar percentage of greenhouse gas emissions as agriculture itself. The problems surrounding livestock production cannot be considered in isolation, nor are they limited to the environmental impact. The most abundant GHG are water vapor, carbon dioxide, methane, nitrous oxide and ozone. This is not just a problem that impacts our planet, it's a humanitarian crisis. Our demand for animal based products is diverting precious resources like land, water and fossil fuels to produce farmed animals instead of feeding the estimated billion + people that are malnourished in the world.

Energy consumption and greenhouse gas emissions: Animals can provide a useful source of draught power to farmers in the developing world. The indirect effects contributing to this percentage include emissions associated with production of feed consumed by livestock and carbon dioxide emission from deforestation in Central and South America, attributed to livestock production. Because a large fraction of GHG emissions attributed to livestock production involves methane (from enteric fermentation and manure management), care is appropriate in considering contributions of these emissions to global warming.

In this context, energy use includes energy from fossil, nuclear, hydroelectric, biomass, geothermal, technological solar, and wind sources. (It excludes solar energy captured by photosynthesis, used in hay drying, etc.) The estimated energy use in agricultural production includes embodied energy in purchased inputs. Intensification and other changes in the livestock industries influence energy use, emissions and other environmental effects of meat production.

GREENHOUSE GAS EMISSIONS TO THE AIR

Agriculture is an important contributor to global emissions of greenhouse gases (GHG), in particular for methane (CH_4) and nitrous oxide (N_2O). Emissions from farms with a stock of ruminant animals are particularly high due to CH4 emissions from digestion and manure handling, and due to the intensive nitrogen cycle. Most of the greenhouse gas emissions from agriculture are caused by the decomposition of organic matter in the soil, the digestion of bovines and the decomposition of manure. Other minor emission sources include nitrogen fertilization, liming of arable land and use of fossil energy in agriculture. One common feature in emissions from agriculture is that it is difficult to reduce them without directly influencing the volume of agricultural production (Niemi and Ahlstedt, 2006).

Today, the main source of carbon dioxide emissions is fossil fuel usage; nonetheless, the second largest cause of increased carbon dioxide emissions is due to land conversion for agriculture. This is so because the conversion of land for agriculture involves the destruction of plant life which leads to the release of carbon dioxide into the air. Agriculture adds carbon dioxide to the atmosphere through the burning of biomass by processes such as deforestation. These activities increase decomposition rates of organic carbon in soil. The burning of plants releases the carbon stored in the biomass and allows oxidation to occur,creating carbon dioxide.

METHANE AS A GREENHOUSE GAS

Methane is a more potent greenhouse gas than carbon dioxide, with a global warming potential 21 times greater than carbon dioxide. However, due to its shorter atmospheric lifetime (of 12 years) it is estimated that global emissions would only need to be reduced by about 8% from current levels to stabilize methane concentrations at today's levels (IPCC, 1996). This is a much smaller percentage reduction than those required to stabilize atmospheric concentrations of the other major greenhouse gases, carbon dioxide (CO_2) and nitrous oxide (N_2O).

Enteric fermentation is the anaerobic fermentation of polysaccharides and other feed components in the gut of animals. Methane is produced as a waste product of this fermentation process. In ruminant animals such as cows and sheep, plant polymers in the feed cannot be digested by host enzymes alone. Instead, ruminant animals have an expanded gut (retrculorumen, generally termed the rumen) in which food is broken down by fermentation prior to gastric digestion in the abomasum. In an adult ruminant, the rumen represents about 85% of the total stomach capacity and contains digesta equal to about 10% to 20% of the animal's weight. Food enters the rumen where it is fermented to volatile fatty acids (VFA), carbon dioxide and methane. The VFAs pass through the rumen wall into the circulatory system and are oxidized in the liver, supplying a major part of the energy needs of the host; they may also be directly utilized by the host as building blocks for synthesis of cell material. The gaseous waste products of the fermentation, carbon monoxide and methane, are mainly removed from the rumen by eructation.

Animal waste (Manure): Manure is organic matter used as organic fertilizer in agriculture. Manurescontribute to the fertility of the soil by adding organic matter and nutrients, such as nitrogen, that are trapped by bacteria in the soil. Higher organisms then feed on the fungi and bacteria in a chain of life that comprises the soil food web. It is also a product obtained after decomposition of organic matter like cow-dung which replenishes the soil with essential elements and adds humus to the soil.

Manure can be a large source of GHG especially from methane and nitrous oxide.

1. Animal manures contain organic compounds such as carbohydrates and proteins. Theserelatively complex compounds are broken down naturally by bacteria. In the presence ofoxygen, the action of aerobic bacteria results in the carbon being converted to carbon dioxideand, in the absence of oxygen, anaerobic bacteria transform the carbon to methane. Wherecarbon dioxide is evolved this is part of the natural cycling of carbon in the environment andresults in no overall increase in atmospheric carbon dioxide; the carbon dioxide, originally absorbed from the atmosphere through photosynthesis by the plants which formed the livestockfeed, is simply being released.

   In an anaerobic reaction however the carbon dioxide which wasabsorbed is being converted into and released as methane, and as methane has a higher globalwarming potential than carbon dioxide, this results in an overall contribution to the greenhouseeffect. When livestock are in fields and their manure ends up being spread thinly on the ground,aerobic decomposition usually predominates. However with modern intensive livestockpractices, where animals are often housed or kept in confined spaces for at least part of the year,manure concentrations will be higher and manure will often be stored in tanks or lagoonswhere anaerobic conditions generally predominate and methane will be evolved. There istherefore a need to adopt measures which avoid the evolution of methane or convert evolvedmethane to carbon dioxide.

2. Animal manures contain nitrogen in the form of various complex compounds. If manures are applied to land, then this nitrogen enters the nitrogen cycle, as various bacteria in the soil break down these nitrogen containing compounds. Under the right conditions this can lead to the evolution of nitrous oxide which has an even higher global warming potential than methane. therefore, any measures to reduce methane releases to atmosphere resulting from animalmanures, should attempt to avoid creating conditions which increase nitrous oxide releases.Nitrous oxide emissions are influenced by nitrogen availability, soil moisture content andtemperature. Of these, nitrogen availability is the most important and themost readily controlled.

Unless well managed, manure and other substances from livestock operations may cause water contamination. With good management, manure has environmental benefits. Manure deposited on pastures by grazing animals themselves is applied efficiently for maintaining soil fertility. Animal manures are also commonly collected from barns and concentrated feeding areas for efficient re-use of many nutrients in crop production, sometimes after composting. For many areas with high livestock density, manure application substantially replaces application of synthetic fertilizers on surrounding cropland.

ENVIRONMENTAL IMPACT OF MEAT PRODUCTION

The environmental impact of meat production varies because of the wide variety of agricultural practices employed around the world. All agriculture practices have been found to have a variety of effects on the environment. Some of the environmental effects that have been associated with meat production are pollution through fossil fuel usage, and water and land consumption. Meat is obtained through a variety of methods, including organic farming, free range farming, intensive livestock production, subsistence agriculture, hunting and fishing.

Grazing and land use: In comparison with grazing, intensive livestock production requires large quantities of harvested feed. The growing of cereals for feed in turn requires substantial areas of land. However, where grain is fed, less feed is required for meat production. This is due not only to the higher concentration of metabolizable energy in grain than in roughages, but also to the higher ratio of net energy of gain to net energy of maintenance where metabolizable energy intake is higher. A pound of beef (live weight) requires about seven pounds of feed, compared to more than three pounds for a pound of pork and less than two pounds for a pound of chicken. However, assumptions about feed quality are implicit in such generalizations.

EFFECTS ON WILDLIFE

Grazing (especially, overgrazing) may detrimentally affect certain wildlife species, e.g. by altering cover and food supplies. However, habitat modification by livestock grazing can also benefit some wildlife species. mixed effects suggest that wildlife diversity may be enhanced and maintained by grazing livestock in some places while excluding livestock in some places. The kind of grazing system employed (e.g. rest-rotation, deferred grazing, HILF grazing) is often important in achieving grazing benefits for particular wildlife species.

BENEFICIAL ENVIRONMENTAL EFFECTS

Among other environmental benefits of meat production is conversion of materials that might otherwise be wasted, to produce high-protein food. For example, Elferink et al. stated that "Currently, 70% of the feedstock used in the Dutch feed industry originates from the food processing industry." US examples of "waste" conversion with regard to grain include. Much soy meal used as livestock feed is produced from material left after extraction of the soybean oil used in foods and in production of biodiesel, soaps and industrial fatty acids.There are environmental benefits of meat-producing small ruminants for control of specific invasive or noxious weeds (such as spotted knapweed, tansy ragwort, leafy spurge, yellow starthistle, tall larkspur, etc.) on rangeland. Small ruminants are also useful for vegetation management in forest plantations, and for clearing brush on rights-of-way.

POSSIBLE SOLUTIONS TO THE EFFECT OF AGRICULTURE ON THE ENVIRONMENT

The FAO report recommends a range of measures to mitigate livestock's threats to the environment:

1. *Land degradation:* Restore damaged land through soil conservation, silvopastoralism, better management of grazing systems and protection of sensitive areas.
2. *Greenhouse gas emissions:* Sustainable intensification of livestock and feed crop production to reduce carbon dioxide emissions from deforestation and pasture degradation, improved animal nutrition and manure management to cut methane and nitrogen emissions.
3. *Water pollution:* Better management of animal waste in industrial production units, better diets to improve nutrient absorption, improved manure management and better use of processed manure on croplands.
4. *Biodiversity loss:* As well as implementing the measures above, improve protection of wild areas, maintain connectivity among protected areas, and integrate livestock production and producers into landscape management.

5. *Precision Feed Management:* Farmers are now using a process called Precision Feed Management which allows the farmer to feed his animals a more precise amount of nutrients so there is greater feed use and less waste in the form of uneaten food and animal manure. When animals are better able to use the food they eat, fewer nutrients are released into the environment.
6. The use of biogas or methane digesters on farms not only serves as a source of energy for the farm, thereby decreasing the amount of fossil fuels, but also allows a reduction in methane, CH_4, and nitrous oxide, N_2O, and a decrease in the use of synthetic fertilizers (Hermansen et al., 2011). When manure is stored in a digester, it is covered, which prevents much of the odor from escaping into the air.

   When farmers put manure on their fields as a form of fertilizer, they can use several different methods to reduce odor and better use the nutrients in manure. By using a drag hose and injection to spread manure, odor-causing compounds are integrated into the soil and cannot escape into the environment. This helps to reduce the amount of nitrous oxide and ammonia that is released (Wright et al., 2011). An Odor Management Plan (OMP) helps farmers assess odor issues on their farm and discover how best to alleviate the issues.
7. Mitigation options for reducing methane emission from ruminant enteric fermentation include genetic selection, immunization, rumen defaunation, diet modification and grazing management, among others. The principal mitigation strategies identified for reduction of agricultural nitrous oxide emission are avoiding over-application of nitrogen fertilizers and adopting suitable manure management practices.
8. Mitigation strategies for reducing carbon dioxide emissions in the livestock sector include adopting more efficient production practices to reduce agricultural pressure for deforestation (notably in Latin America), reducing fossil fuel consumption, and increasing carbon sequestration in soils.At a national level, livestock represents up to half of New Zealand's greenhouse gas emissions.
9. One solution is for countries to adopt policies that provide incentives for better management practices that focus on land conservation and more efficient water and fertilizer use.
10. People in developed countries to eat less meat and to consider how and where the meat that they do eat is produced. At the same time, people in certain regions of the world, such as Nigeria, Cameroon and southern Africa, are suffering from a deficiency of animal protein, and the means to enrich their diets is needed.

10. *Fossil Fuels:* More than a third of all raw materials and fossil fuels consumed in the United States are used in animal production. The production of one calorie of animal protein requires more than ten times the fossil fuel input as a calorie of plant protein (*The American Journal of Clinical Nutrition*). Producing a single hamburger uses enough fuel to drive 20 miles and causes the loss of five times its weight in topsoil.
11. *Air:* The massive amounts of excrement produced by livestock farms emit toxic gases such as hydrogen sulfide and ammonia into the air. Roughly 80% of ammonia emissions in the U.S. come from animal waste (*The U.S. Environmental Protection Agency*).When the cesspools holding tons of urine and feces get full, factory farms will frequently get around water pollution limits by spraying liquid manure into the air, creating mists that are carried away by the wind.Air pollutants generated by animal farms can cause respiratory illness, lung inflammation, and increase vulnerability to respiratory diseases, such as asthma. Emissions of reactive organics and ammonia from animal farming can play a role in the formation of ozone (smog) and air pollution (*The U.S. Environmental Protection Agency*)

OPTIONS FOR REDUCING METHANE EMISSIONS FROM LIVESTOCK MANURES.

(i) *Impact of reduction of livestock numbers:* A reduction of livestock numbers i will directly reduce the quantity of manure and hence methane emissions from this source. The overall impact would be dependent upon thetypes of livestock whose population diminished, as manure output is directly related to drymatter intake and body size.

(ii) *Impact of increased rumen fermentation efficiency and/or animal productivity*: All methods which improve rumen fermentation efficiency are likely to increase thedigestibility of the diet which in turn means that there is less digestible organic matter in thefaeces for methanogenic activity. For example, increasing the digestibility of a ration by 5%units would decrease the volatile substrate by just over 10% according to IPCC methodology.

MITIGATION OF METHANE EMISSION IN RUMINANT ANIMALS

Ionophores

Although the mode of action of ionophores can vary slightly among compounds, the end result is often similar, a decrease in counts of Gram-positive bacteria in the rumen. Because Grampositive bacteria are for the most part lactate producers, and Gram-negative bacteria are for the most part propionate and succinate producers, the inclusion of ionophores in ruminant diets often leads to a decrease in the acetate to propionate ratio

(A:P). This reduction in A:P has been the hallmark of this category of additives and is believed to be partially responsible for the improved performance observed in feedlot cattle. Added benefits of ionophores include a decrease in ammonia production in the rumen, which in turn, can lead to a more efficient use of dietary protein and a possible reduction in methane production.

Nonionic surfactants: Nonionic surfactants (NIS) have been proposed as a feed additive with the potential to modify ruminal fermentation. The proposed mode of action of NIA is the stimulation of enzyme production by fungi and bacteria, as well as the improvement in the affinity of enzymes to their substrates (Wang et al., 2004; Cong et al., 2009). When polyoxyethylenesorbitanmonooleate was added to in vitro incubations in combination with monensin, a synergistic enhancement in the reduction of A:P was observed along with an increased enzymatic activity, and increased in vitro digestibility of the substrates (Wang et al., 2004).

Fatty acids and organic acids: Fumaric acid has been proposed as a potential feed additive in methane mitigation as it provides an alternative electron sink and is a metabolic precursor of propionate. The stoichiometry of fumarate metabolism in ruminal fermentations indicates potentially promising results (Ungerfeld et al., 2007), however fumarate has not been consistently effective at decreasing methane productionin vivo (McGinn et al., 2004; Beauchemin and McGinn, 2006).

Hexose partitioning: During rumen fermentation, feedstuffs are converted into short-chain volatile fatty acids (VFAs), ammonia, methane, carbon dioxide, cell material and heat.

Propionate precursors: Within the rumen, hydrogen produced by the fermentation process may react to produce eithermethane or propionate. By increasing the presence of propionate precursors such as the organicacids, malate or fumarate, more of the hydrogen is used to produce propionate, and methaneproduction is reduced.

Acetogens: Acetogens are bacteria that produce acetic acid by the reduction of carbon dioxide withhydrogen, thus reducing the hydrogen available for reaction to produce methane. This would not only decrease methane production, but would also increase the efficiency of ruminant production.

Methane oxidizers: Methane oxidisers could also be introduced as direct-fed microbial preparations. The oxidationreaction would compete with the production of methane, which is a strictly anaerobic process.Methane oxidisers from gut and non-gut sources could be screened for their activity in rumenfluid *in vitro* and then selected methane oxidisers could be introduced into the rumen on a dailybasis in a manner analogous with current feed supplements.

Probiotics: The most widely used microbial feed additives (live cells and growth medium) are based on*Saccharomyces cerevisiae*(SC) and *Aspergillusoryzae*(AO). Their effect on rumen fermentation and animal productivity are wide ranging and this has been reviewed recently by several authors (Martin and Nisbet, 1992; Newbold, 1992). There is very limited information on their effect on methane production and all of this is *in vitro*. AO has been seen to reduce methane by 50% which was directly related to a reduction in the protozoal population 45%). Probiotics are already widely available in the EU to improve animal productivity but theimplications of this on methane production are unclear. If research proved probiotics to beeffective at reducing methane output, existing users would continue with their use, but furtheruptake would require incentives, as many producers are already apparently sceptical about thebenefits of probiotics.

Aerobic treatments: Aerobic treatments can be applied to liquid manures through aeration and to solid manures bycomposting. Aeration involves dissolving sufficient oxygen in the liquid manure to allowbacteria to oxidise the organic carbon. Systems for aeration involve mechanical methods forpassing air through the liquid, usually driven by electric motors. When considering methanereduction using this technique, emissions of greenhouse gases from electricity generation shouldbe deducted from any saving. Solid manures can be aerobically treated by composting. This may require de-watering of liquid manures or addition of other dry organic materials to increase porosity and penetration of air. Also organic material may have to be added to increase the carbon:nitrogen ratio to levels suitable for composting. As with aeration, composting requires energy input to turn the compost ensuring good mixing and air penetration. Greenhouse gas emission attributable to this energy input should again be deducted from any savings in methane emissions.

Anaerobic digestion: Anaerobic digestion (AD) is the bacterial fermentation of organic material under controlledconditions in a closed vessel. The process produces biogas which is typically made up of 65%methane and 35% carbon dioxide with traces of nitrogen, sulphur compounds, volatile organiccompounds and ammonia. This biogas has a typical calorific value of 17 to 25 MJ/m3 and canbe combusted directly in modified gas boilers, used to run an internal combustion engine orsimply flared.

Applying this process to animal manures ensures that most of the carbon is ultimately convertedto carbon dioxide before being released to atmosphere. Typically, between 40% and 60% of theorganic matter present is converted to biogas. The remainder consists of a relatively odour freeresidue with an appearance similar to peat, which has some value as a soil conditioner and also,with some systems, a liquid residue which has potential as a fertiliser.According to IPCC (IPCC 1997), AD releases 5% of the manure's total methane potential. Thisrelease is largely due to further decomposition of the digested material on removal from the digester. These emissions can be minimised through covered storage with gas collection or byreducing storage times. An additional benefit of utilising biogas from AD plants to produce heatand electricity is that this will offset greenhouse gas emissions resulting from fossil fuel energysources and this should be accounted for when considering the contribution of AD to widergreenhouse gas reduction.

Forage type and supplementation: Supplementing forages whether of low or high quality, with energy and protein supplements, isa well documented method of increasing microbial growth efficiency and digestibility, and thusincreasing milk and meat productivity. The direct effect on methanogenesis is variable andunclear.Research has shown that increasing the level of non-structural carbohydrate in the diet (by25%) would reduce methane production by as much as 20%, but this may result in detrimentalhealth effects e.g. acidosis, fertility problems (Moss, 1994). Also with the implementation ofquotas for milk production in the EU, many producers are optimising milk production fromhome-grown forages in order to reduce feed costs. Supplementing poor quality forages andchemically upgrading them may be a good option for increasing productivity and in turnreducing methane emissions per unit product.Feeding of ruminants to optimise rumen and animal efficiency is a developing area and theefficient deployment of appropriate nutritional information to all livestock producers wouldbenefit the environment in terms of both methane and nitrogen emissions.

HIGH GENETIC MERIT DAIRY COWS

Improving the genetic merit of dairy cows has escalated in the last decade with the import of Holstein genetic material from US and Canada for use on the EU native dairy breeds. As a result, average national yields have increased. One of the major improvements is the ability of the cow to partition nutrients into milk preferentially to maintenance and/or growth. This has undoubtedly resulted in increased efficiency. This could reduce methane emissions by 20 to 30% through reduced numbers.

REFERENCES

Beauchemin, K.A., and S.M. McGinn. 2006. Methane Emissions from Beef Cattle: Effects of Fumaric Acid, Essential Oil, and Canola Oil. J. Anim. Sci. 84: 1489-1496.

Cong, Z.H., S.X. Tang, Z.L. Tan, Z.H. Sun, C.S. Zhou, X.F. Han, M. Wang, and G.P. Ren. 2009. Effects of Different Nonionic Surfactants on *in vitro* Fermentation Characteristics of Cereal Straws. J. Anim. Sci. 87: 1085-1096.

D. Atkinson and C.A. Watson (1996). The Environmental Impact of Intensive Systems of Animal Production in the Lowlands. Animal Science, 63, pp. 353-361. doi:10.1017/S135772980001523X.

De-Chavez and Tauli-Corpus (2008). Guide to Climate Change. Available on Line at www.tebtebba.org Retrived on 1st February 2014. Facts on Animal Farming and the Environment. http://www.onegreenplanet.org/animalsandnature/facts-on-animal-farming-and-the-environment/

IPCC, (1996) IPCC Guidelines for National Greenhouse Gas Inventories, (Revised Guidelines 1996).

McGinn, S.M., K.A. Beauchemin, T. Coates, and D. Colombatto. 2004. Methane Emissions from Beef Cattle: Effects of Monensin, Sunflower Oil, Enzymes, Yeast, and Furmaric Acid. J. Anim. Sci. 82: 3346-3356.

Moss A R (1994) Methane Production by Ruminants - Literature Review of I. Dietary Manipulation to Reduce Methane Production and II. Laboratory Procedures for Estimating Methane Potential of Diets. Nutrition Abstracts and Reviews (Series B) 64 (N°12): 786-806.

"Neighbours of Vast Hog Farms Say Foul Air Endangers Their Health," by Jennifer Lee , The New York Times 11 May 2003) The Global Benefits of Eating Less Meat by Mark Gold and Jonathon Porritt.

Niemi J. &Ahlstedt, J. 2006. Finnish Agriculture and rural industries 2006. Agrifood Research Finland.Economic Research.Publications 106a.

Ozor, N. (2009). Implication of Climate Change for National Development. The Way Forward. Debating Policy Options for National development. www.aiaenigeria.org/publication.

Ungerfeld, E.M., R.A. Kohn, R.J. Wallace, and C.J. Newbold. 2007. A meta-analysis Offumarate Effects on Methane Production in Ruminal Batch Cultures. J. Anim. Sci. 85: 2556-2563.

Wang, Y., T.W. Alexander, and T.A. McAllister. 2004. *In vitro* Effects of Monensin and Tween 80 on Ruminal Fermentation of Barley Grain: Barley Silage-based Diets for Beef Cattle. Anim. Feed Sci. Technol. 116: 197-209.

Pages: 105-151

SEED TECHNOLOGY, PLANT GROWTH AND CROPPING SYSTEM

Edited by: Dr. Pawan Kumar Tyagi; Dr. Pawan Kumar 'Bharti'

ISBN: 978-93-5056-738-8

Edition: 2015

Published by: Discovery Publishing House Pvt. Ltd., New Delhi (India)

Traditional Rice of West Bengal
Diversity, Conservation and Agronomic Characterization

Anjan Kumar Sinha

ABSTRACT

West Bengal state is a home land of thousands of traditional rice varieties from time immemorial. In the year 1975 more than five thousand of traditional rice varieties had been available in the agricultural fields of this state but after the large scale introduction of HYVs this number has been drastically fall down and merely 5 to 8 hundred varieties are only available now a days. We may lose these varieties also in near future if proper conservation strategy should not be taken immediately. Small and marginal farmers of this state is the main keepers of these varieties and they cultivated these varieties into their fields were conventional varieties failed to produced.

But unfortunate aspect is that these farmers also switch over to the traditional varieties to the HYVs for the high yield and the number of the folk rice varieties decreasing day by day. Landraces are treasure of genetic variation and consist

Department of Botany, Bankura Sammilani College, Bankura - 722 102, West Bengal. (India).

of numerous important gene pools which my utilized for the future crop improvements programme because the present HYVs are fail to perform better in present changing environmental condition. Thus for the maintaining agro-biodiversity and sustainable agriculture conservation of traditional varieties is top most important.

INTRODUCTION

West Bengal, the third largest economy in India consists of 19 districts with an area of 88752 Km^2, with a population of over 90 Million. West Bengal is the fourth most populous state in India, and ranks second in terms of population density. In West Bengal about 70% of the population is based on agriculture. State of West Bengal is divided into 13 livelihood zones considering several important factors such as climate, population, agriculture, poverty, and water related issues etc. Different zones and districts fall under the various livelihood zones are given in table 6.1 and figure 6.1.

Table 6.1: Different Zones and Districts Fall Under the Various Livelihood Zones of W.B.

Sl. No.	Zones	District Falling Under the Various Zone
1.	Zone 1	Darjeeling
2.	Zone 2	Jalpaiguri
3.	Zone 2a	Koch Bihar
4.	Zone 3	Uttar Dinajpur, Dakshin Dinajpur and Maldah
5.	Zone 4:	Maldah
6.	Zone 5:	Maldah, Murshidabad
7.	Zone 6:	Birbhum, Bardhman
8.	Zone 7	Birbhum, Bardhman, Nadia, Hugli, Haora, East Midnapur, West Midnapur, Bankura, North 24 Parganas
9.	Zone 7a	Birbhum, Bardhman
10.	Zone 8:	Purulia, Bankura, West Midnapur
11.	Zone 9:	Purulia
12.	Zone 10:	Kolkata, Nadia, Haora, North and South 24 Parganas
13.	Zone 11:	South 24 Parganas
14.	Zone 12:	South 24 Parganas, East Midnapur
15.	Zone 13:	South 24 Parganas

Source: IWMI (2010). West Bengal Situation Analysis: 1-4.

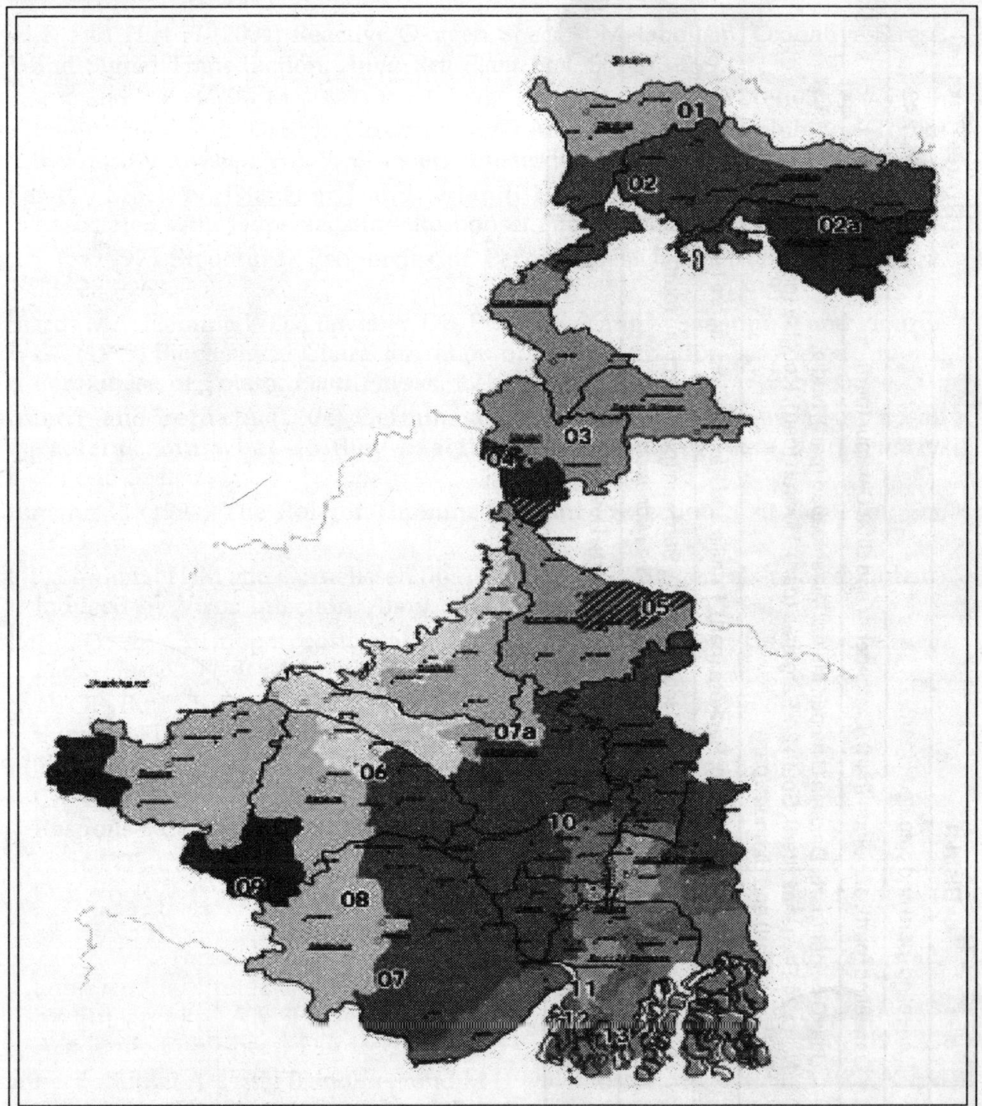

Fig. 6.1: Different Livelihood Zones of West Bengal

Based on different agro-climatic condition like, rainfall, temperature, soil types and topography of land, West Bengal has been broadly divided into six agro-climatic zones. Various agro-climatic zones and districts fall under the different zone are given in table 6.2. Out of six zones, Gangetic Alluvial and Vindhya Alluvial Zones are very fertile with higher percentages of irrigated land (Anonymous, 2009).

Table 6.2: Different Agro-climatic Zones and Districts Fall within the Various Zone and Area

Sl. No.	Zones	District	Area (Lakh ha)
1.	Northern Hill Zone	Darjeeling (part) and Jalpaiguri (part)	2.43
2.	Terai- Teesta Alluvial Zone	Darjeeling (part), Jalpaiguri (part), Coochbehar and Uttar Dinajpur (part)	12.15
3.	Gangetic Alluvial Zone	Uttar Dinajpur (part), Dakshin Dinajpur, Malda, Murshidabad (part), Nadia, North 24-Parganas (part), South 24-Parganas (part), Howrah (part), Hooghly (part), Burdwan (part) and Birbhum (part)	15.3
4.	Red and Laterite Zone	Burdwan (part), Birbhum (part), Bankura (part), Purulia and Paschim Midnapore (part)	24.8
5.	Alluvial Zone	Murshidabad (part), Howrah (part), Hooghly (part), Burdwan (part), Birbhum (part), Bankura (part), Paschim Midnapore (part) and Purba Midnapore (part)	17.5
6.	Coastal Saline Zone	North 24-Parganas (part), South 24- Parganas (part), Howrah (part) and Purba Midnapore (part)	14.6

Rice is the staple food grain of West Bengal. West Bengal state of India is known as bowl of rice because it constitutes major food item and is being cultivated in major portion of agricultural fields. West Bengal in India is richest reservoir of rice biodiversity; many types of rice cultivars like wild races, landraces and many other varieties were widely available in this state from century past to the present date and ecotypes of rice spontaneously evolved in the state are so diverse and different that scientists at one time coined them as *Oryza sativa* var. *benghalensis* (Chatterjee *et al*, 2008). According to an estimate West Bengal possess vast genetic diversity of rice in recent past. In the year 1975, 5556 rice varieties were recorded in West Bengal (Guevarra, 2000). The unfortunate aspect is that out of over five thousand landraces of rice more than 90% of the total number of traditional varieties have disappeared from the rice fields of Bengal and out of the existing landraces none is being cultivated in organized way. More than 90% of cultivation of the rice growing parts of the West Bengal is done using high yielding varieties only.

Landraces of rice is the main genetic resources for crop improvement programme. So many important genes are integrated in the large number of gene pool of landraces. There is a vice-versa relation in between the crop improvement and the depletion of the crop varieties. There is a negative consequence of the green revolution; scientific breeding is responsible for the genetic erosion of the germplasm from agricultural field (Paddock 1970). Frankel (1973) on his first report on “Survey of crop genetic resources and their centres of diversity” pointed out that scientific breeding was responsible for the gradual erosion of the natural resources like germplasm or genetic resources in terms of number of crop species as well as genetic diversity expressed by the amount of genetic variation within a species. On the one way green revolution has considerably improved production of food grains in our country (Srivastava and Jaffe 1993) but on the other side high yielding varieties which are the back bone of green revolution has indirectly stimulated erosion of landraces and wild varieties of rice from the agricultural fields (Fowler and Moony 1990). Presently more than 90% of rice cultivation of West Bengal is being done using high yielding varieties only. Due to larger amount of High Yielding Varieties were introduced into the agricultural fields, landraces were disappearing fast (Holden *et al,* 1993), (Durning, 1990) (Matson *et al,* 1997). Importance of landraces can never be denied in agriculture system because improvement in existing varieties depends upon desirable genes which are possibly present in landraces and wild varieties only (Shiva, 1991). Landraces of rice offer a valuable gene pool for future breeding programme (Richharia 1979), (Patra 2000). Ex-situ conservation in gene bank is one of the means to maintaining genetic diversity (Lipton and Longhurst, 1989). In this work we tried to investigate present status of rice diversity in West Bengal, their conservation and characterization of existing varieties.

MATERIALS AND METHODS

Indigenous rice landraces were collected from the indigenous farmers of 12 districts of West Bengal in the year 2010, 2011 & 2012 during the kharif season for *in-situ* conservation. These varieties have been propagated in a small farm at village-Ranbahal, District-Bankura, West Bengal, which is situated at an elevation of 78 m above mean sea level with commanding red and lateritic condition. The annual rainfall of the area is 284.225 mm during last five years in the month of June and July. Nearly 90 percent of the total precipitation is received during the crop season. As of date this farm consists of more than 150 traditional varieties of rice and has been repeatedly grown form the last 5 years.

Field Evaluation of the Experimental Material

The materials were grown using completely randomized block design with three replications. Each variety was transplanted (45 day's old seedling) in a plot of 6m^2 with a spacing of 25cm. between rows and 20cm. between plants in a row. A random sample of five competitive plants ware used for observations on different traits under study. No synthetic nutrients were applied. During the crop period the water depth of the field was 40-50cm.

Observations Recorded

Five plants per replication were taken randomly and tagged to record data on the following traits, except for 50% flowering, maturity days which were recorded on plot basis. Two major types of parameter were taken for field evaluation of landraces of rice - (1) Morphological traits and (2) Agronomic traits.

Standard Evaluation System for Collected and Cultivated Landraces of Rice

Various morphological and agronomic data were collected and evaluated according to the IBPGR-IRRI (1980) and Guidelines for the conduct of test for Distinctiveness, Uniformity and Stability on rice (DUS Test) by PPV & FRA (Shoba Rani *et al.* 2004). The major parameters measured were as outlined as follows:

Agro-Morphological Traits

Out of the 150 traditional varieties important morphological, agronomical and physiological characters of 54 important and rare traditional rice cultivars of West Bengal has been describing below. Morphological characters like basal leaf sheath colour, stem length, leaf length width ratio, colour of stigma, awning characteristics, exertion of panicles, decorticated grain SHAPE, DECORTICATED GRAIN COLOUR etc; physiological characters like time of heading (50% flowering of plants) and maturity duration etc; agronomic characters like panicle number, number of grains per panicle, decorticated grain length width ratio, 1000 grains weight, and yield potential; physicochemical characters like presence of aroma, presence of carbohydrate into the endosperm of the kernel etc. are used for the characterization of the varieties.

RESULTS AND DISCUSSION

Different agromorphic characters of these selected important 54 traditional varieties are summarized below.

Name of Landrace: ***Agniban***

Characters	Salient Features
01. Basal leaf: Sheath colour	Green
02. Time of heading (50% of plants with panicle)	68 days
03. Stem: length	123.5cm
04. Decorticated grain: Shape	Short bold
05. Decorticated grain: Colour	Red
06. Endosperm: content of Carbohydrate	21.7gm/100gm.
07. Decorticated grain: Aroma	Absent
08. Leaf length width ratio	40.76
09. Stigma colour	White
10. Awning	Absent
11. Panicle number	24
12. Panicle exertion	Exerted
13. No of grain/panicle	203
14. Lemma and palea colour	Straw
15. Grain: length width ratio	3.07
16. Decorticated grain: LXW ratio	2.40
17. Maturity duration (seed to seed)	127 days
18. 1000 grains weight	20.8gm
19 Yield	54.04 q/ha

Special agronomic feature: Red rice, Drought resistant.End use: For daily cooking.

Name of Landrace: ***Bachi***

Characters	Salient Features
01. Basal leaf: Sheath colour	Green
02. Time of heading (50% of plants with panicle)	73 days
03. Stem: length	139cm
04. Decorticated grain: Shape	Short bold
05. Decorticated grain: Colour	Yellowish white
06. Endosperm: content of Carbohydrate	21.6gm/100gm
07. Decorticated grain: Aroma	Absent

(Contd...)

08. Leaf length width ratio	43.21
09. Stigma colour	White
10. Awning	Absent
11. Panicle number/plant	15
12. Panicle exertion	Partly exerted
13. No of grain/panicle	211
14. Lemma and palea colour	Brown furrows on straw
15. Grain: length width ratio	2.22
16. Decorticated grain: LXW ratio	1.83
17. Maturity duration (seed to seed)	99 days
18. 1000 grains weight	23.3gm
19. Yield	46.6 q/ha

Special agronomic feature: Long stem, medium land, drought resistant varietyEnd use: For daily cooking.

Name of Landrace: ***Badshabhog***

Characters	Salient Features
01. Basal leaf: Sheath colour	Colourless
02. Time of heading (50% of plants with panicle)	111 days
03. Stem: length	158cm
04. Decorticated grain: Shape	Short bold
05. Decorticated grain: Colour	White
06. Endosperm: content of Carbohydrate	22.8gm/100gm
07. Decorticated grain: Aroma	Present
08. Leaf length width ratio	50.55
09. Stigma colour	White
10. Awning	Absent
11. Panicle number	13
12. Panicle exertion	Well exerted
13. No of grain/panicle	268
14. Lemma and palea colour	Background brown spot on straw
15. Grain: length width ratio	2.81
16. Decorticated grain: LXW ratio	2.2
17. Maturity duration (seed to seed)	126 days
18. 1000 grains weight	11.6gm
19. Yield	26.94 q/ha

Special agronomic feature: Long stem, aromatic.End use: For making 'Kheer'(Sweet rice), ritual cuisine.

Name of Landrace: ***Badamsaru***

Characters	Salient Features
01. Basal leaf: Sheath colour	Colourless
02. Time of heading (50% of plants with panicle)	114 days
03. Stem: length	168cm
04. Decorticated grain: Shape	Long slender
05. Decorticated grain: Colour	White
06. Endosperm: content of Carbohydrate	20.9gm/100gm
07. Decorticated grain: Aroma	Absent
08. Leaf length width ratio	52.48
09. Stigma colour	White
10. Awning	Absent
11. Panicle number	20
12. Panicle exertion	Exerted
13. No of grain/panicle	218
14. Lemma and palea colour	Straw
15. Grain: length width ratio	3.95
16. Decorticated grain: LXW ratio	3.15
17. Maturity duration (seed to seed)	168 days
18. 1000 grains weight	19.1gm
19. Yield	42.56 q/ha

Special agronomic feature: Slender rice.End use: For daily cooking.

Name of Landrace: ***Bahurupi***

Characters	Salient Features
01. Basal leaf: Sheath colour	Green
02. Time of heading (50% of plants with panicle)	76 days
03. Stem: length	126cm
04. Decorticated grain: Shape	9.02mm
05. Decorticated grain: Colour	White
06. Endosperm: content of Carbohydrate	20.3gm/100gm
07. Decorticated grain: Aroma	Absent
08. Leaf length width ratio	35.17
09. Stigma colour	White
10. Awning	Absent
11. Panicle number	21
12. Panicle exertion	Exerted
13. No of grain/panicle	170
14. Lemma and palea colour	Background brown spot on straw

(Contd...)

15. Grain: length width ratio	3.39
16. Decorticated grain: LXW ratio	2.80
17. Maturity duration (seed to seed)	120 days
18. 1000 grains weight	25.7gm
19. Yield	53.82 q/ha

Special agronomic feature: Drought resistant, medium slender grain.End use: For daily cooking.

Name of Landrace: ***Baskamini***

Characters	Salient Features
01. Basal leaf: Sheath colour	Green
02. Time of heading (50% of plants with panicle)	89 days
03. Stem: length	114cm
04. Decorticated grain: Shape	Short bold
05. Decorticated grain: Colour	White
06. Endosperm: content of Carbohydrate	23.4gm/100gm
07. Decorticated grain: Aroma	Present
08. Leaf length width ratio	49.52
09. Stigma colour	White
10. Awning	Absent
11. Panicle number	20
12. Panicle exertion	Well exerted
13. No of grain/panicle	231
14. Lemma and palea colour	Straw
15. Grain: length width ratio	2.43
16. Decorticated grain: LXW ratio	2.15
17. Maturity duration (seed to seed)	99 days
18. 1000 grains weight	14.9gm
19. Yield	37.31 q/ha

Special agronomic feature: Aromatic.End use: For making 'Kheer'(Sweet rice), ritual cuisine.

Name of Landrace: ***Bhadoi***

Characters	Salient Features
01. Basal leaf: Sheath colour	Light purple
02. Time of heading (50% of plants with panicle)	65 days
03. Stem: length	72.5cm
04. Decorticated grain: Shape	Medium slender
05. Decorticated grain: Colour	Variegated brown

(Contd...)

06. Endosperm: content of Carbohydrate	23.2gm/100gm
07. Decorticated grain: Aroma	Absent
08. Leaf length width ratio	42.81
09. Stigma colour	White
10. Awning	Absent
11. Panicle number	5
12. Panicle exertion	Well exerted
13. No of grain/panicle	73
14. Lemma and palea colour	Gold and gold furrows on straw
15. Grain: length width ratio	2.98
16. Decorticated grain: LXW ratio	2.51
17. Maturity duration (seed to seed)	98 days
18. 1000 grains weight	24.1gm
19. Yield	7.87 q/ha

Special agronomic feature: Short maturity duration, drought resistantEnd use: For daily cooking.

Name of Landrace: ***Bhuri***

Characters	Salient Features
01. Basal leaf: Sheath colour	Green
02. Time of heading (50% of plants with panicle)	114 days
03. Stem: length	145cm
04. Decorticated grain: Shape	Short bold
05. Decorticated grain: Colour	Red
06. Endosperm: content of Carbohydrate	21.1gm/100gm
07. Decorticated grain: Aroma	Absent
08. Leaf length width ratio	46.11
09. Stigma colour	White
10. Awning	Absent
11. Panicle number	9
12. Panicle exertion	Exerted
13. No of grain/panicle	146
14. Lemma and palea colour	Brown furrows on straw
15. Grain: length width ratio	2.52
16. Decorticated grain: LXW ratio	2.14
17. Maturity duration (seed to seed)	152 days
18. 1000 grains weight	28.5gm
19. Yield	37.24 q/ha

Special agronomic feature: Salt resistant.End use: For daily cooking.

Name of Landrace: ***Byamajhupi***

Characters	Salient Features
01. Basal leaf: Sheath colour	Purple
02. Time of heading (50% of plants with panicle)	112 days
03. Stem: length	148cm
04. Decorticated grain: Shape	Long slender
05. Decorticated grain: Colour	White
06. Endosperm: content of Carbohydrate	21.9gm/100gm
07. Decorticated grain: Aroma	Absent
08. Leaf length width ratio	37.18
09. Stigma colour	Purple
10. Awning	Absent
11. Panicle number	15
12. Panicle exertion	Partly exerted
13. No of grain/panicle	285
14. Lemma and palea colour	Straw
15. Grain: length width ratio	3.77
16. Decorticated grain: LXW ratio	3.03
17. Maturity duration (seed to seed)	107 days
18. 1000 grains weight	20.6gm
19. Yield	56.65 q/ha

Special agronomic feature: Medium land variety, presence of awn.End use: For daily cooking.

Name of Landrace: ***Barani***

Characters	Salient Features
01. Basal leaf: Sheath colour	Purple line
02. Time of heading (50% of plants with panicle)	77 days
03. Stem: length	125cm
04. Decorticated grain: Shape	Short bold
05. Decorticated grain: Colour	White
06. Endosperm: content of Carbohydrate	22.7gm/100gm
07. Decorticated grain: Aroma	Absent
08. Leaf length width ratio	42.44
09. Stigma colour	White
10. Awning	Absent
11. Panicle number	20
12. Panicle exertion	Exerted
13. No of grain/panicle	261
14. Lemma and palea colour	Brown

(Contd...)

15. Grain: length width ratio	3.08
16. Decorticated grain: LXW ratio	2.43
17. Maturity duration (seed to seed)	99 days
18. 1000 grains weight	20.7gm
19. Yield	48.49 q/ha

Special agronomic feature: Medium land type, brown lemma palea colour.End use: For daily cooking..

Name of Landrace: ***Chandrakanta***

Characters	Salient Features
01. Basal leaf: Sheath colour	Light purple
02. Time of heading (50% of plants with panicle)	72 days
03. Stem: length	158cm
04. Decorticated grain: Shape	Short bold
05. Decorticated grain: Colour	Light Red
06. Endosperm: content of Carbohydrate	21.3gm/100gm
07. Decorticated grain: Aroma	Absent
08. Leaf length width ratio	82.77
09. Stigma colour	Light green
10. Awning	Absent
11. Panicle number	23
12. Panicle exertion	Exerted
13. No of grain/panicle	305
14. Lemma and palea colour	Straw
15. Grain: length width ratio	3.30
16. Decorticated grain: LXW ratio	2.28
17. Maturity duration (seed to seed)	99 days
18. 1000 grains weight	23.0gm
10. Yield	47.84 q/ha

Special agronomic feature:Red rice, drought resistant.End use: For daily cooking.

Name of Landrace: ***Chotodidi***

Characters	Salient Features
01. Basal leaf: Sheath colour	Green
02. Time of heading (50% of plants with panicle)	108 days
03. Stem: length	167cm
04. Decorticated grain: Shape	Short bold
05. Decorticated grain: Colour	Variegated brown
06. Endosperm: content of Carbohydrate	23.4gm/100gm
07. Decorticated grain: Aroma	Absent
08. Leaf length width ratio	30.30

(Contd...)

09. Stigma colour	White
10. Awning	Absent
11. Panicle number	18
12. Panicle exertion	Partly exerted
13. No of grain/panicle	149
14. Lemma and palea colour	Straw
15. Grain: length width ratio	2.57
16. Decorticated grain: LXW ratio	1.99
17. Maturity duration (seed to seed)	150 days
18. 1000 grains weight	31.9gm
19. Yield	41.38 q/ha

Special agronomic feature: Red riceEnd use: For daily cooking.

Name of Landrace: ***Daharlagra***

Characters	Salient Features
01. Basal leaf: Sheath colour	Green
02. Time of heading (50% of plants with panicle)	50 days
03. Stem: length	92.25cm
04. Decorticated grain: Shape	Basmati type
05. Decorticated grain: Colour	White
06. Endosperm: content of Carbohydrate	20.9gm/100gm
07. Decorticated grain: Aroma	Absent
08. Leaf length width ratio	35.71
09. Stigma colour	White
10. Awning	Absent
11. Panicle number	18
12. Panicle exertion	Exerted
13. No of grain/panicle	230
14. Lemma and palea colour	Straw
15. Grain: length width ratio	4.45
16. Decorticated grain: LXW ratio	4.11
17. Maturity duration (seed to seed)	74 days
18. 1000 grains weight	19.1gm
19. Yield	47.37 q/ha

Special agronomic feature: photosensitive, short duration, fine grain.End use: For daily cooking, making 'moori'(rice bubble).

Name of Landrace: ***Danarguri***

Characters	Salient Features
01. Basal leaf: Sheath colour	Green
02. Time of heading (50% of plants with panicle)	72 days
03. Stem: length	142cm
04. Decorticated grain: Shape	Short bold
05. Decorticated grain: Colour	White
06. Endosperm: content of Carbohydrate	23.2gm/100gm
07. Decorticated grain: Aroma	Present
08. Leaf length width ratio	70
09. Stigma colour	Light green
10. Awning	Absent
11. Panicle number	14
12. Panicle exertion	Well exerted
13. No of grain/panicle	204
14. Lemma and palea colour	Straw
15. Grain: length width ratio	3
16. Decorticated grain: LXW ratio	1.84
17. Maturity duration (seed to seed)	150 days
18. 1000 grains weight	11.0gm
19. Yield	26.04 q/ha

Special agronomic feature: Aromatic.End use: For making 'Kheer'(Sweet rice), ritual cuisine.

Name of Landrace: ***Dharansal***

Characters	Salient Features
01. Basal leaf: Sheath colour	Green
02. Time of heading (50% of plants with panicle)	118 days
03. Stem: length	161cm
04. Decorticated grain: Shape	Long bold
05. Decorticated grain: Colour	White
06. Endosperm: content of Carbohydrate	20.9gm/100gm
07. Decorticated grain: Aroma	Absent
08. Leaf length width ratio	52.72
09. Stigma colour	White
10. Awning	Absent
11. Panicle number	21
12. Panicle exertion	Exerted
13. No of grain/panicle	161
14. Lemma and palea colour	Straw

(Contd...)

15. Grain: length width ratio	3.37
16. Decorticated grain: LXW ratio	2.77
17. Maturity duration (seed to seed)	150 days
18. 1000 grains weight	22.4gm
19. Yield	31.56 q/ha

Special agronomic feature: Photosensitive, drought resistant.End use: For daily cooking.

Name of Landrace: ***Dudherswar***

Characters	Salient Features
01. Basal leaf: Sheath colour	Green
02. Time of heading (50% of plants with panicle)	114 days
03. Stem: length	180.5cm
04. Decorticated grain: Shape	Long slender
05. Decorticated grain: Colour	White
06. Endosperm: content of Carbohydrate	20.9gm/100gm
07. Decorticated grain: Aroma	Absent
08. Leaf length width ratio	58.99
09. Stigma colour	White
10. Awning	Absent
11. Panicle number	8
12. Panicle exertion	Exerted
13. No of grain/panicle	234
14. Lemma and palea colour	Straw
15. Grain: length width ratio	3.81
16. Decorticated grain: LXW ratio	3.44
17. Maturity duration (seed to seed)	149 days
18. 1000 grains weight	23.0gm
19. Yield	27.47 q/ha

Special agronomic feature: Fine grain, salt tolerant.End use: For daily cooking.

Name of Landrace: ***Fulkhar***

Characters	Salient Features
01. Basal leaf: Sheath colour	Green
02. Time of heading (50% of plants with panicle)	110 days
03. Stem: length	112cm
04. Decorticated grain: Shape	Long bold
05. Decorticated grain: Colour	White
06. Endosperm: content of Carbohydrate	21.8gm/100gm
07. Decorticated grain: Aroma	Absent

(Contd…)

08. Leaf length width ratio	30.3
09. Stigma colour	White
10. Awning	Absent
11. Panicle number	11
12. Panicle exertion	Exerted
13. No of grain/panicle	159
14. Lemma and palea colour	Straw
15. Grain: length width ratio	3.82
16. Decorticated grain: LXW ratio	2.95
17. Maturity duration (seed to seed)	158 days
18. 1000 grains weight	22.10gm
19. Yield	24.14 q/ha

Special agronomic feature: Drought resistant, photoresistnat.End use: For daily cooking.

Name of Landrace: ***Fulpagri***

Characters	Salient Features
01. Basal leaf: Sheath colour	Green
02. Time of heading (50% of plants with panicle)	113 days
03. Stem: length	139cm
04. Decorticated grain: Shape	Medium slender
05. Decorticated grain: Colour	White
06. Endosperm: content of Carbohydrate	24.3gm/100gm
07. Decorticated grain: Aroma	Absent
08. Leaf length width ratio	63.03
09. Stigma colour	White
10. Awning	Absent
11. Panicle number	11
12. Panicle exertion	Exerted
13. No of grain/panicle	127
14. Lemma and palea colour	Purple spot on straw
15. Grain: length width ratio	3.50
16. Decorticated grain: LXW ratio	2.77
17. Maturity duration (seed to seed)	142 days
18. 1000 grains weight	16.9gm
19. Yield	14.5 q/ha

Special agronomic feature: medium land type, photosensitive.End use: For daily cooking.

Name of Landrace: ***Gangajali***

Characters	Salient Features
01. Basal leaf: Sheath colour	Green
02. Time of heading (50% of plants with panicle)	117 days
03. Stem: length	152cm
04. Decorticated grain: Shape	Long slender
05. Decorticated grain: Colour	White
06. Endosperm: content of Carbohydrate	22.7gm/100gm
07. Decorticated grain: Aroma	Present
08. Leaf length width ratio	58.06
09. Stigma colour	White
10. Awning	Present
11. Panicle number	10
12. Panicle exertion	Well exerted
13. No of grain/panicle	132
14. Lemma and palea colour	Gold and gold furrows on straw
15. Grain: length width ratio	3.81
16. Decorticated grain: LXW ratio	3.44
17. Maturity duration (seed to seed)	158 days
18. 1000 grains weight	19.6gm
19. Yield	15.94 q/ha

Special agronomic feature: Photosensitive, awning, aromatic End use: For making 'Kheer'(Sweet rice), ritual cuisine.

Name of Landrace: ***Jamainadu***

Characters	Salient Features
01. Basal leaf: Sheath colour	Green
02. Time of heading (50% of plants with panicle)	113 days
03. Stem: length	146cm
04. Decorticated grain: Shape	Long bold
05. Decorticated grain: Colour	White
06. Endosperm: content of Carbohydrate	22.2gm/100gm
07. Decorticated grain: Aroma	Absent
08. Leaf length width ratio	56.81
09. Stigma colour	Purple
10. Awning	Absent

(Contd...)

11. Panicle number	9
12. Panicle exertion	Exerted
13. No of grain/panicle	166
14. Lemma and palea colour	Brown
15. Grain: length width ratio	2.86
16. Decorticated grain: LXW ratio	2.86
17. Maturity duration (seed to seed)	149 days
18. 1000 grains weight	23.5gm
19. Yield	35.09 q/ha

Special agronomic feature: Photosensitive, medium land type.End use: For daily cooking.

Name of Landrace: ***Kaksal***

Characters	Salient Features
01. Basal leaf: Sheath colour	Green
02. Time of heading (50% of plants with panicle)	70 days
03. Stem: length	137cm
04. Decorticated grain: Shape	Long bold
05. Decorticated grain: Colour	Light red
06. Endosperm: content of Carbohydrate	23.3gm/100gm
07. Decorticated grain: Aroma	Absent
08. Leaf length width ratio	39.81
09. Stigma colour	Light green
10. Awning	Absent
11. Panicle number	21
12. Panicle exertion	Exerted
13. No of grain/panicle	141
14. Lemma and palea colour	Brown (tawny)
15. Grain: length width ratio	2.91
16. Decorticated grain: LXW ratio	2.43
17. Maturity duration (seed to seed)	98 days
18. 1000 grains weight	30.3gm
19. Yield	51.26 q/ha

Special agronomic feature: Red rice, photosensitive.End use: For daily cooking.

Name of Landrace: ***Kakua***

Characters	Salient Features
01. Basal leaf: Sheath colour	Green
02. Time of heading (50% of plants with panicle)	118 days
03. Stem: length	173cm
04. Decorticated grain: Shape	Short bold
05. Decorticated grain: Colour	Light brown
06. Endosperm: content of Carbohydrate	20.8gm/100gm
07. Decorticated grain: Aroma	Absent
08. Leaf length width ratio	55.8
09. Stigma colour	White
10. Awning	Present
11. Panicle number	13
12. Panicle exertion	Exerted
13. No of grain/panicle	109
14. Lemma and palea colour	Brown furrows on straw
15. Grain: length width ratio	2.51
16. Decorticated grain: LXW ratio	2.24
17. Maturity duration (seed to seed)	153 days
18. 1000 grains weight	28.7gm
19. Yield	24.87 q/ha

Special agronomic feature: Red rice, grains with long awn.End use: For daily cooking.

Name of Landrace: ***Kalamkati***

Characters	Salient Features
01. Basal leaf: Sheath colour	Green
02. Time of heading (50% of plants with panicle)	103 days
03. Stem: length	126cm
04. Decorticated grain: Shape	Long slender
05. Decorticated grain: Colour	White
06. Endosperm: content of Carbohydrate	21.3gm/100gm
07. Decorticated grain: Aroma	Absent
08. Leaf length width ratio	41.83
09. Stigma colour	Light green
10. Awning	Absent
11. Panicle number	21

(Contd...)

12. Panicle exertion	Exerted
13. No of grain/panicle	119
14. Lemma and palea colour	Straw
15. Grain: length width ratio	3.91
16. Decorticated grain: LXW ratio	3.18
17. Maturity duration (seed to seed)	150
18. 1000 grains weight	22.5cm
19. Yield	29.43 q/ha

Special agronomic feature: Fine grain, drought resistant. End use: For daily cooking.

Name of Landrace: ***Kalobayar***

Characters	Salient Features
01. Basal leaf: Sheath colour	Purple line
02. Time of heading (50% of plants with panicle)	136 days
03. Stem: length	194cm
04. Decorticated grain: Shape	Short bold
05. Decorticated grain: Colour	Light brown
06. Endosperm: content of Carbohydrate	22.3gm/100gm
07. Decorticated grain: Aroma	absent
08. Leaf length width ratio	26.1
09. Stigma colour	Purple
10. Awning	Absent
11. Panicle number	9
12. Panicle exertion	Exerted
13. No of grain/panicle	157
14. Lemma and palea colour	Black
15. Grain: length width ratio	2.40
16. Decorticated grain: LXW ratio	1.96
17. Maturity duration (seed to seed)	162 days
18. 1000 grains weight	20.5gm
19. Yield	20.09 q/ha

Special agronomic feature: Long maturity, many node, lodging tendency, photosensitive. End use: For daily cooking.

Name of Landrace: ***Kalobhat***

Characters	Salient Features
01. Basal leaf: Sheath colour	Green
02. Time of heading (50% of plants with panicle)	84 days
03. Stem: length	150cm
04. Decorticated grain: Shape	Long bold
05. Decorticated grain: Colour	Black
06. Endosperm: Content of Carbohydrate	22.3gm/100gm
07. Decorticated grain: Aroma	Present
08. Leaf length width ratio	32.37
09. Stigma colour	White
10. Awning	Absent
11. Panicle number	17
12. Panicle exertion	Exerted
13. No of grain/panicle	139
14. Lemma and palea colour	Straw
15. Grain: length width ratio	3.12
16. Decorticated grain: LXW ratio	2.59
17. Maturity duration (seed to seed)	134
18. 1000 grains weight	27.0cm
19. Yield	39.47 q/ha

Special agronomic feature: Black kernel End use: For daily cooking.

Name of Landrace: ***Kalojira***

Characters	Salient Features
01. Basal leaf: Sheath colour	Green
02. Time of heading (50% of plants with panicle)	80 days
03. Stem: length	145cm
04. Decorticated grain: Shape	Short bold
05. Decorticated grain: Colour	White
06. Endosperm: content of Carbohydrate	21.6gm/100gm
07. Decorticated grain: Aroma	Present
08. Leaf length width ratio	33.38
09. Stigma colour	White?

(Contd...)

10. Awning	Absent
11. Panicle number	20
12. Panicle exertion	Well exerted
13. No of grain/panicle	236
14. Lemma and palea colour	Black
15. Grain: length width ratio	2.86
16. Decorticated grain: LXW ratio	2.15
17. Maturity duration (seed to seed)	128
18. 1000 grains weight	12.6gm
19. Yield	37.96 q/ha

Special agronomic feature: Aromatic. End use: For making 'Kheer'(Sweet rice), ritual cuisine.

Name of Landrace: ***Kanakchur***

Characters	Salient Features
01. Basal leaf: Sheath colour	Green
02. Time of heading (50% of plants with panicle)	134 days
03. Stem: length	149cm
04. Decorticated grain: Shape	Short bold
05. Decorticated grain: Colour	White
06. Endosperm: Content of Carbohydrate	22.6gm/100gm
07. Decorticated grain: Aroma	Present
08. Leaf length width ratio	48.41
09. Stigma colour	Green
10. Awning	Present
11. Panicle number	12
12. Panicle exertion	Well exerted
13. No of grain/panicle	167
14. Lemma and palea colour	Brown furrows on straw
15. Grain: length width ratio	2.53
16. Decorticated grain: LXW ratio	2.42
17. Maturity duration (seed to seed)	158 days
18. 1000 grains weight	19.5gm
19. Yield	24.49 q/ha

Special agronomic feature: Aromatic, grains with long awn. End use: For making 'Kheer'(Sweet rice).

Name of Landrace: ***Kartiksal***

Characters	Salient Features
01. Basal leaf: Sheath colour	Green
02. Time of heading (50% of plants with panicle)	61 days
03. Stem: length	138cm
04. Decorticated grain: Shape	Short bold
05. Decorticated grain: Colour	White
06. Endosperm: content of Carbohydrate	20.8gm/100gm
07. Decorticated grain: Aroma	Absent
08. Leaf length width ratio	42.17
09. Stigma colour	White
10. Awning	Absent
11. Panicle number	20
12. Panicle exertion	Exerted
13. No of grain/panicle	301
14. Lemma and palea colour	Straw
15. Grain: length width ratio	3.09
16. Decorticated grain: LXW ratio	2.39
17. Maturity duration (seed to seed)	103 days
18. 1000 grains weight	19.9gm
19. Yield	37.81 q/ha

Special agronomic feature: Medium maturation, photosensitive. End use: For daily cooking, Making of 'Chireh' (beaten rice).

Name of Landrace: ***Kelesh***

Characters	Salient Features
01. Basal leaf: Sheath colour	Purple line
02. Time of heading (50% of plants with panicle)	85 days
03. Stem: length	91cm
04. Decorticated grain: Shape	Short bold
05. Decorticated grain: Colour	Light brown
06. Endosperm: content of Carbohydrate	21.6gm/100gm
07. Decorticated grain: Aroma	Absent
08. Leaf length width ratio	45.25
09. Stigma colour	Purple

(Contd...)

10. Awning	Absent
11. Panicle number	09
12. Panicle exertion	Well exerted
13. No of grain/panicle	72
14. Lemma and palea colour	Black
15. Grain: length width ratio	2.80
16. Decorticated grain: LXW ratio	2.20
17. Maturity duration (seed to seed)	102 days
18. 1000 grains weight	19.7gm
19. Yield	9.39 q/ha

Special agronomic feature: Drought resistant, short maturity duration.End use: For daily cooking.

Name of Landrace: ***Kheuch***

Characters	Salient Features
01. Basal leaf: Sheath colour	Green
02. Time of heading (50% of plants with panicle)	134 days
03. Stem: length	120cm
04. Decorticated grain: Shape	Short bold
05. Decorticated grain: Colour	White
06. Endosperm: content of Carbohydrate	23.1gm/100gm
07. Decorticated grain: Aroma	Absent
08. Leaf length width ratio	60.5
09. Stigma colour	White
10. Awning	Absent
11. Panicle number	9
12. Panicle exertion	Well exerted
13. No of grain/panicle	134
14. Lemma and palea colour	Brown furrows on straw with straw on base and apex
15. Grain: length width ratio	2.51
16. Decorticated grain: LXW ratio	2.01
17. Maturity duration (seed to seed)	158 days
18. 1000 grains weight	27.1gm
19. Yield	46.53 q/ha

Special agronomic feature: Long maturity duration.End use: For daily cooking, Making of 'Chireh' (beaten rice).

Name of Landrace: ***Kataribhog***

Characters	Salient Features
01. Basal leaf: Sheath colour	Green
02. Time of heading (50% of plants with panicle)	119 days
03. Stem: length	150cm
04. Decorticated grain: Shape	Short slender
05. Decorticated grain: Colour	White
06. Endosperm: content of Carbohydrate	22.9gm/100gm
07. Decorticated grain: Aroma	Present
08. Leaf length width ratio	59.11
09. Stigma colour	Light green
10. Awning	Absent
11. Panicle number	18
12. Panicle exertion	Well exerted
13. No of grain/panicle	206
14. Lemma and palea colour	Straw
15. Grain: length width ratio	4.33
16. Decorticated grain: LXW ratio	3.62
17. Maturity duration (seed to seed)	132 days
18. 1000 grains weight	14.0gm
19. Yield	32.76 q/ha

Special agronomic feature: Fine grain, aromatic. End use: For making 'Kheer'(Sweet rice), ritual cuisine.

Name of Landrace: ***Lal-badshabhog***

Characters	Salient Features
01. Basal leaf: Sheath colour	Green
02. Time of heading (50% of plants with panicle)	67 days
03. Stem: length	130cm
04. Decorticated grain: Shape	Short bold
05. Decorticated grain: Colour	White
06. Endosperm: content of Carbohydrate	20.4gm/100gm
07. Decorticated grain: Aroma	Present
08. Leaf length width ratio	52.53

(Contd...)

09. Stigma colour	White
10. Awning	Absent
11. Panicle number	16
12. Panicle exertion	Well exerted
13. No of grain/panicle	314
14. Lemma and palea colour	Red
15. Grain: length width ratio	2.92
16. Decorticated grain: LXW ratio	2.21
17. Maturity duration (seed to seed)	124 days
18. 1000 grains weight	10.7gm
19. Yield	32.10 q/ha

Special agronomic feature: Aromatic, red lemma palea colour. End use: For making 'Kheer'(Sweet rice), ritual cuisine.

Name of Landrace: ***Laltipa***

Characters	Salient Features
01. Basal leaf: Sheath colour	Green
02. Time of heading (50% of plants with panicle)	107 days
03. Stem: length	165cm
04. Decorticated grain: Shape	Short bold
05. Decorticated grain: Colour	Light brown
06. Endosperm: content of Carbohydrate	23.1gm/100gm
07. Decorticated grain: Aroma	Absent
08. Leaf length width ratio	42.17
09. Stigma colour	Purple
10. Awning	Absent
11. Panicle number	15
12. Panicle exertion	Exerted
13. No of grain/panicle	193
14. Lemma and palea colour	Brown furrows on straw
15. Grain: length width ratio	2.56
16. Decorticated grain: LXW ratio	2.03
17. Maturity duration (seed to seed)	145 days
18. 1000 grains weight	27.6gm
19. Yield	50.5 q/ha

Special agronomic feature: Red rice, drought resistant. Red rice, long bold kernel, photosensitiveEnd use: For daily cooking.

Name of Landrace: ***Langalmura***

Characters	Salient Features
01. Basal leaf: Sheath colour	Green
02. Time of heading (50% of plants with panicle)	117 days
03. Stem: length	167cm
04. Decorticated grain: Shape	Long bold
05. Decorticated grain: Colour	Red
06. Endosperm: content of Carbohydrate	22.1gm/100gm
07. Decorticated grain: Aroma	Absent
08. Leaf length width ratio	34.16
09. Stigma colour	Purple
10. Awning	Absent
11. Panicle number	12
12. Panicle exertion	Exerted
13. No of grain/panicle	169
14. Lemma and palea colour	Straw
15. Grain: length width ratio	2.15
16. Decorticated grain: LXW ratio	2.33
17. Maturity duration (seed to seed)	154 days
18. 1000 grains weight	30gm
19. Yield	38.16 q/ha

Special agronomic feature: Red rice, drought resistant. Red rice, long bold kernel, photosensitive End use: For daily cooking, Making of 'Chireh' (beaten rice).

Name of Landrace: ***Malabati***

Characters	Salient Features
01. Basal leaf: Sheath colour	Green
02. Time of heading (50% of plants with panicle)	122 days
03. Stem: length	136cm
04. Decorticated grain: Shape	Long bold
05. Decorticated grain: Colour	Light brown
06. Endosperm: content of Carbohydrate	22.9gm/100gm
07. Decorticated grain: Aroma	Absent
08. Leaf length width ratio	45.9
09. Stigma colour	Purple
10. Awning	Absent

(Contd...)

11. Panicle number	12
12. Panicle exertion	Exerted
13. No of grain/panicle	170
14. Lemma and palea colour	Brown furrows on straw
15. Grain: length width ratio	2.83
16. Decorticated grain: LXW ratio	2.46
17. Maturity duration (seed to seed)	160 days
18. 1000 grains weight	26.7gm
19. Yield	34.17 q/ha

Special agronomic feature: long bold kernel, photosensitive, salt tolerant.End use: For daily cooking.

Name of Landrace: ***Malsira***

Characters	Salient Features
01. Basal leaf: Sheath colour	Green
02. Time of heading (50% of plants with panicle)	110 days
03. Stem: length	126cm
04. Decorticated grain: Shape	Medium slender
05. Decorticated grain: Colour	White
06. Endosperm: content of Carbohydrate	23.0gm/100gm
07. Decorticated grain: Aroma	Absent
08. Leaf length width ratio	65.03
09. Stigma colour	White
10. Awning	Absent
11. Panicle number	13
12. Panicle exertion	Exerted
13. No of grain/panicle	284
14. Lemma and palea colour	Purple
15. Grain: length width ratio	3.3
16. Decorticated grain: LXW ratio	2.67
17. Maturity duration (seed to seed)	147 days
18. 1000 grains weight	20gm
19. Yield	19.06 q/ha

Special agronomic feature: PhotosensitiveEnd use: For daily cooking, Making of 'Chireh' (beaten rice).

Name of Landrace: ***Marichsal***

Characters	Salient Features
01. Basal leaf: Sheath colour	Green
02. Time of heading (50% of plants with panicle)	128 days
03. Stem: length	152cm
04. Decorticated grain: Shape	Short bold
05. Decorticated grain: Colour	White
06. Endosperm: content of Carbohydrate	20.6gm/100gm
07. Decorticated grain: Aroma	Absent
08. Leaf length width ratio	43.75
09. Stigma colour	Purple
10. Awning	Absent
11. Panicle number	9
12. Panicle exertion	Well exerted
13. No of grain/panicle	173
14. Lemma and palea colour	Gold and gold furrows on straw
15. Grain: length width ratio	2.2
16. Decorticated grain: LXW ratio	1.56
17. Maturity duration (seed to seed)	159day
18. 1000 grains weight	21.3gm
19. Yield	32.4 q/ha

Special agronomic feature: Long maturity, short bold grain, long straw.End use: For daily cooking.

Name of Landrace: ***Nagrasal***

Characters	Salient Features
01. Basal leaf: Sheath colour	Green
02. Time of heading (50% of plants with panicle)	115 days
03. Stem: length	114cm
04. Decorticated grain: Shape	Short bold
05. Decorticated grain: Colour	Light brown
06. Endosperm: content of Carbohydrate	21.2gm/100gm
07. Decorticated grain: Aroma	Absent
08. Leaf length width ratio	42.5
09. Stigma colour	Light green

(Contd...)

10. Awning	Absent
11. Panicle number	11
12. Panicle exertion	Exerted
13. No of grain/panicle	188
14. Lemma and palea colour	Gold and gold furrows on straw
15. Grain: length width ratio	3.13
16. Decorticated grain: LXW ratio	2.02
17. Maturity duration (seed to seed)	155 days
18. 1000 grains weight	33.6gm
19. Yield	43.85 q/ha

Special agronomic feature: Red rice, drought resistant. End use: For daily cooking, Making of 'Chireh' (beaten rice).

Name of Landrace: ***Narkeljhopa***

Characters	Salient Features
01. Basal leaf: Sheath colour	Green
02. Time of heading (50% of plants with panicle)	75 days
03. Stem: length	109cm
04. Decorticated grain: Shape	Short bold
05. Decorticated grain: Colour	White
06. Endosperm: content of Carbohydrate	20.9gm/100gm
07. Decorticated grain: Aroma	Absent
08. Leaf length width ratio	22.30
09. Stigma colour	White
10. Awning	Absent
11. Panicle number	20
12. Panicle exertion	Exerted
13. No of grain/panicle	185
14. Lemma and palea colour	Straw
15. Grain: length width ratio	3.42
16. Decorticated grain: LXW ratio	2.35
17. Maturity duration (seed to seed)	130 days
18. 1000 grains weight	18.4gm
19. Yield	42.93 q/ha

Special agronomic feature: Photosensitive.End use: For daily cooking, Making of 'Chireh' (beaten rice).

Name of Landrace: ***Neta***

Characters	Salient Features
01. Basal leaf: Sheath colour	Light purple
02. Time of heading (50% of plants with panicle)	93 days
03. Stem: length	98cm
04. Decorticated grain: Shape	Long bold
05. Decorticated grain: Colour	Red
06. Endosperm: content of Carbohydrate	22.7gm/100gm
07. Decorticated grain: Aroma	Absent
08. Leaf length width ratio	39.16
09. Stigma colour	Purple
10. Awning	Present
11. Panicle number	15
12. Panicle exertion	Exerted
13. No of grain/panicle	98
14. Lemma and palea colour	Gold and gold furrows on straw
15. Grain: length width ratio	3.15
16. Decorticated grain: LXW ratio	2.55
17. Maturity duration (seed to seed)	115 days
18. 1000 grains weight	20.5gh
19. Yield	19.47 q/ha

Special agronomic feature: Short maturity, long awn, drought resistant.End use: Making of 'Chireh' (beaten rice).

Name of Landrace: ***Nikunja***

Characters	Salient Features
01. Basal leaf: Sheath colour	Green
02. Time of heading (50% of plants with panicle)	112 days
03. Stem: length	137cm
04. Decorticated grain: Shape	Long bold
05. Decorticated grain: Colour	Light brown
06. Endosperm: content of Carbohydrate	20.2gm/100gm
07. Decorticated grain: Aroma	Absent
08. Leaf length width ratio	60.81
09. Stigma colour	White

(Contd...)

10. Awning	Present
11. Panicle number	10
12. Panicle exertion	Exerted
13. No of grain/panicle	215
14. Lemma and palea colour	Brown with tip and base straw
15. Grain: length width ratio	3.38
16. Decorticated grain: LXW ratio	2.56
17. Maturity duration (seed to seed)	147 days
18. 1000 grains weight	21.3gm
19. Yield	29.11 q/ha

Special agronomic feature: Photosensitive.End use: For daily cooking.

Name of Landrace: ***Nonabogra***

Characters	Salient Features
01. Basal leaf: Sheath colour	Green
02. Time of heading (50% of plants with panicle)	108 days
03. Stem: length	94cm
04. Decorticated grain: Shape	Short bold
05. Decorticated grain: Colour	Red
06. Endosperm: content of Carbohydrate	21.6gm/100gm
07. Decorticated grain: Aroma	Absent
08. Leaf length width ratio	25.81
09. Stigma colour	White
10. Awning	Absent
11. Panicle number	11
12. Panicle exertion	Exerted
13. No of grain/panicle	166
14. Lemma and palea colour	Straw
15. Grain: length width ratio	2.82
16. Decorticated grain: LXW ratio	2.13
17. Maturity duration (seed to seed)	142 days
18. 1000 grains weight	29.3gm
19. Yield	33.3 q/ha

Special agronomic feature: Salt tolerant, photosensitive. End use: For daily cooking, for preparation of moori (Rice bubbles).

Name of Landrace: ***Nugembaro***

Characters	Salient Features
01. Basal leaf: Sheath colour	Green
02. Time of heading (50% of plants with panicle)	134 days
03. Stem: length	146cm
04. Decorticated grain: Shape	Short bold
05. Decorticated grain: Colour	White
06. Endosperm: content of Carbohydrate	23.6gm/100gm
07. Decorticated grain: Aroma	Absent
08. Leaf length width ratio	40.83
09. Stigma colour	Light green
10. Awning	Absent
11. Panicle number	13
12. Panicle exertion	Exerted
13. No of grain/panicle	161
14. Lemma and palea colour	Straw
15. Grain: length width ratio	2.33
16. Decorticated grain: LXW ratio	1.93
17. Maturity duration (seed to seed)	163 days
18. 1000 grains weight	26.1gm
19. Yield	35.51 q/ha

Special agronomic feature: photosensitive. Short bold grain, long straw. End use: For daily cooking, for preparation of moori (Rice bubbles).

Name of Landrace: ***Patnai-23***

Characters	Salient Features
01. Basal leaf: Sheath colour	Green
02. Time of heading (50% of plants with panicle)	117 days
03. Stem: length	156cm
04. Decorticated grain: Shape	Extra long slender
05. Decorticated grain: Colour	White
06. Endosperm: content of Carbohydrate	Medium
07. Decorticated grain: Aroma	Absent
08. Leaf length width ratio	44.6
09. Stigma colour	Green

(Contd...)

10. Awning	Absent
11. Panicle number	14
12. Panicle exertion	Exerted
13. No of grain/panicle	130
14. Lemma and palea colour	Straw
15. Grain: length width ratio	4
16. Decorticated grain: LXW ratio	3.77
17. Maturity duration (seed to seed)	152 days
18. 1000 grains weight	27.6gm
19. Yield	30.91 q/ha

Special agronomic feature: Extra long slender grain.End use: For daily cooking.

Name of Landrace: ***Radhatilak***

Characters	Salient Features
01. Basal leaf: Sheath colour	Green
02. Time of heading (50% of plants with panicle)	82 days
03. Stem: length	124cm
04. Decorticated grain: Shape	Short bold
05. Decorticated grain: Colour	White
06. Endosperm: content of Carbohydrate	21.4gm/100gm
07. Decorticated grain: Aroma	Present
08. Leaf length width ratio	55.18
09. Stigma colour	White
10. Awning	Absent
11. Panicle number	28
12. Panicle exertion	Well exerted
13. No of grain/panicle	284
14. Lemma and palea colour	Straw
15. Grain: length width ratio	3.02
16. Decorticated grain: LXW ratio	2.37
17. Maturity duration (seed to seed)	133 days
18. 1000 grains weight	12.0gm
19. Yield	30.24 q/ha

Special agronomic feature: Aromatic.End use: For making ‘Kheer’(Sweet rice), ritual cuisine.

Name of Landrace: ***Raghusal***

Characters	Salient Features
01. Basal leaf: Sheath colour	Green
02. Time of heading (50% of plants with panicle)	110 days
03. Stem: length	126cm
04. Decorticated grain: Shape	Long slender
05. Decorticated grain: Colour	Red
06. Endosperm: content of Carbohydrate	20.6gm/100gm
07. Decorticated grain: Aroma	Absent
08. Leaf length width ratio	54.03
09. Stigma colour	White
10. Awning	Absent
11. Panicle number	20
12. Panicle exertion	Exerted
13. No of grain/panicle	194
14. Lemma and palea colour	Straw
15. Grain: length width ratio	3.5
16. Decorticated grain: LXW ratio	3.1
17. Maturity duration (seed to seed)	152 days
18. 1000 grains weight	24.5gm
19. Yield	57.1 q/ha

Special agronomic feature: Drought resistant, red rice.End use: For daily cooking, making of 'Chireh' (beaten rice).

Name of Landrace: ***Rupsal***

Characters	Salient Features
01. Basal leaf: Sheath colour	Green
02. Time of heading (50% of plants with panicle)	114 days
03. Stem: length	161cm
04. Decorticated grain: Shape	Long slender
05. Decorticated grain: Colour	Red
06. Endosperm: content of Carbohydrate	22.9gm/100gm
07. Decorticated grain: Aroma	Absent
08. Leaf length width ratio	51.05
09. Stigma colour	White
10. Awning	Present

(Contd...)

11. Panicle number	12
12. Panicle exertion	Exerted
13. No of grain/panicle	137
14. Lemma and palea colour	Gold and gold furrows on straw
15. Grain: length width ratio	3.87
16. Decorticated grain: LXW ratio	3.2
17. Maturity duration (seed to seed)	152 days
18. 1000 grains weight	22.7gm
19. Yield	28.82 q/ha

Special agronomic feature: Drought resistant.End use: For daily cooking.

Name of Landraces: ***Sindurmukhi***

Characters	Salient Features
01. Basal leaf: Sheath colour	Green
02. Time of heading (50% of plants with panicle)	117 days
03. Stem: length	123cm
04. Decorticated grain: Shape	Long bold
05. Decorticated grain: Colour	Light brown
06. Endosperm: content of Carbohydrate	21.6gm/100gm
07. Decorticated grain: Aroma	Absent
08. Leaf length width ratio	43.9
09. Stigma colour	Purple
10. Awning	Absent
11. Panicle number	13
12. Panicle exertion	Exerted
13. No of grain/panicle	128
14. Lemma and palea colour	Brown furrows on straw
15. Grain: length width ratio	3.42
16. Decorticated grain: LXW ratio	2.83
17. Maturity duration (seed to seed)	154 days
18. 1000 grains weight	26.2gm
19. Yield	25.15 q/ha

Special agronomic feature: Drought resistant, photosensitive. End use: For daily cooking, for preparation of moori (Rice bubbles).

Name of Landrace: ***Sitasal***

Characters	Salient Features
01. Basal leaf: Sheath colour	Purple line
02. Time of heading (50% of plants with panicle)	110 days
03. Stem: length	145cm
04. Decorticated grain: Shape	Short bold
05. Decorticated grain: Colour	White
06. Endosperm: content of Carbohydrate	21.1gm/100gm
07. Decorticated grain: Aroma	Absent
08. Leaf length width ratio	51.8
09. Stigma colour	White
10. Awning	Present
11. Panicle number	15
12. Panicle exertion	Exerted
13. No of grain/panicle	157
14. Lemma and palea colour	Reddish to light purple
15. Grain: length width ratio	3.6
16. Decorticated grain: LXW ratio	2.04
17. Maturity duration (seed to seed)	140 days
18. 1000 grains weight	15.9gm
19. Yield	23.69 q/ha

Special agronomic feature: Drought resistant, photosensitive.End use: For daily cooking.

Name of Landrace: ***Suakalma***

Characters	Salient Features
01. Basal leaf: Sheath colour	Green
02. Time of heading (50% of plants with panicle)	114 days
03. Stem: length	178cm
04. Decorticated grain: Shape	Basmati type
05. Decorticated grain: Colour	White
06. Endosperm: content of Carbohydrate	22.2gm/100gm
07. Decorticated grain: Aroma	Absent
08. Leaf length width ratio	42.93
09. Stigma colour	Light green
10. Awning	Present

(Contd...)

11. Panicle number	10
12. Panicle exertion	Exerted
13. No of grain/panicle	284
14. Lemma and palea colour	Straw
15. Grain: length width ratio	3.88
16. Decorticated grain: LXW ratio	3.22
17. Maturity duration (seed to seed)	150 days
18. 1000 grains weight	25.3 gm
19. Yield	46.55 q/ha

Special agronomic feature: Drought resistant, photosensitive, grains with awn.End use: For daily cooking.

Name of Landrace: ***Talmugurdhan***

Characters	Salient Features
01. Basal leaf: Sheath colour	Green
02. Time of heading (50% of plants with panicle)	115 days
03. Stem: length	172cm
04. Decorticated grain: Shape	Long bold
05. Decorticated grain: Colour	Variegated brown
06. Endosperm: content of Carbohydrate	20.6 gm/100 gm
07. Decorticated grain: Aroma	Absent
08. Leaf length width ratio	38.66
09. Stigma colour	White
10. Awning	Absent
11. Panicle number	16
12. Panicle exertion	Exerted
13. No of grain/panicle	172
14. Lemma and palea colour	Straw
15. Grain: length width ratio	2.72
16. Decorticated grain: LXW ratio	2.86
17. Maturity duration (seed to seed)	145 days
18. 1000 grains weight	32.5gm
19. Yield	56.16 q/ha

Special agronomic feature: Drought resistant, photosensitive.End use: For daily cooking.

Name of Landrace: ***Tulsibhog***

Characters	Salient Features
01. Basal leaf: Sheath colour	Green
02. Time of heading (50% of plants with panicle)	118 days
03. Stem: length	145cm
04. Decorticated grain: Shape	Short bold
05. Decorticated grain: Colour	White
06. Endosperm: content of Carbohydrate	20.8gm/100gm
07. Decorticated grain: Aroma	Present
08. Leaf length width ratio	66.05
09. Stigma colour	Yellow
10. Awning	Absent
11. Panicle number	9
12. Panicle exertion	Well exerted
13. No of grain/panicle	343
14. Lemma and palea colour	Black
15. Grain: length width ratio	2.79
16. Decorticated grain: LXW ratio	2.05
17. Maturity duration (seed to seed)	156 days
18. 1000 grains weight	10.1gm
19. Yield	19.99 q/ha

Special agronomic feature: Aromatic.End use: For making 'Kheer'(Sweet rice), ritual cuisine.

Name of Landrace: ***Valki***

Characters	Salient Features
01. Basal leaf: Sheath colour	Green
02. Time of heading (50% of plants with panicle)	118 days
03. Stem: length	94cm
04. Decorticated grain: Shape	Short bold
05. Decorticated grain: Colour	Variegated brown
06. Endosperm: content of Carbohydrate	22.2gm/100gm
07. Decorticated grain: Aroma	Absent
08. Leaf length width ratio	40.58
09. Stigma colour	White
10. Awning	Absent

(Contd...)

11. Panicle number	9
12. Panicle exertion	Partly exerted
13. No of grain/panicle	141
14. Lemma and palea colour	Purple furrows on straw
15. Grain: length width ratio	2.48
16. Decorticated grain: LXW ratio	2.05
17. Maturity duration (seed to seed)	150 days
18. 1000 grains weight	27.1gm
19. Yield	26.03 q/ha

Special agronomic feature: Drought resistant, photosensitive.End use: For daily cooking.

Name of Landrace: ***Vutmuri***

Characters	Salient Features
01. Basal leaf: Sheath colour	Light purple
02. Time of heading (50% of plants with panicle)	78 days
03. Stem: length	73cm
04. Decorticated grain: Shape	Medium slender
05. Decorticated grain: Colour	Light brown
06. Endosperm: content of Carbohydrate	22.7gm/100gm
07. Decorticated grain: Aroma	Absent
08. Leaf length width ratio	53.74
09. Stigma colour	Purple
10. Awning	Present
11. Panicle number	25
12. Paniclo oxortion	Well exerted
13. No of grain/panicle	81
14. Lemma and palea colour	Black
15. Grain: length width ratio	2.81
16. Decorticated grain: LXW ratio	2.56
17. Maturity duration (seed to seed)	105 days
18. 1000 grains weight	20.4gm
19. Yield	25.5 q/ha

Special agronomic feature: Drought resistant, photosensitive, short duration.End use: For preparation of moori (Rice bubbles).

DISCUSSION

Agronomic evaluation and agromorphic characterization is an important prerequisite for the development of rice cultivars with high yield potentiality for the fulfilment of the growing demand for food of the World because rice is a staple food grain of more than half of the World population. So many unexploited landraces varieties still exists in various agricultural fields, whose gene pool may be utilized for the production of more improved high yielding varieties. In this study extensive survey was conducted to checkout present scenario of the available landraces of various district of West Bengal; there collection, cultivation at study farm in in-situ condition and morpho-agronomic characterization and evaluation.

The study of 50 important landraces presently available in West Bengal revealed a significant amount of information for various morphological and agronomic characters and their importance in hybridization programme which are summarized below.

From the morphological study of these 54 landraces of rice it was revealed that various important agronomic features were present among these varieties. Landraces varieties possess highly polymorphic characters within population and high variable in appearance in contrast with the present HYVs which are genetically pure. From the morphological point of view high polymorphism was found on some qualitative character like Basal leaf sheath colour, Pubescence of Blade surface, Flag leaf attitude (early observation), Flag leaf attitude (late observation), Anthocyanin colouration of keel, Lemma: Anthocyanin colouration of below apex, Lemma: Anthocyanin colouration of apex, Panicle curvature, Spikelet: colour of tip of lemma , Panicle attitude of branching, Sterile lemma colour, Kernel (Decorticated grain) shape, Kernel colour and on quantitative morphological characters like Stem length etc. Wide genetic variability was reported in the landraces for the physiological character like Time of heading and Time of Maturity. There was wide genetic variability in the rice landraces for agronomic characters like 1000 grain weight, Panicle length, Grain length, Grain width and on Number of spikelet's/panicle etc.

Low morphological variability were observed from the qualitative characters like Coleoptile colour, Intensity of green colour, Leaf auricle, Shape of ligule, Colour of ligule, Culm attitude, Spikelet: density of pubescence of lemma, Colour of Stigma, Anthocyanin colouration of node of stem, Anthocyanin colouration of Internodes, Awning, Panicle secondary branching, Panicle exertion, Leaf senescence and Decorticated grain aroma etc. Low variation was also observed on agronomic characters panicle number, tillers per plant and weight of 5 panicles.

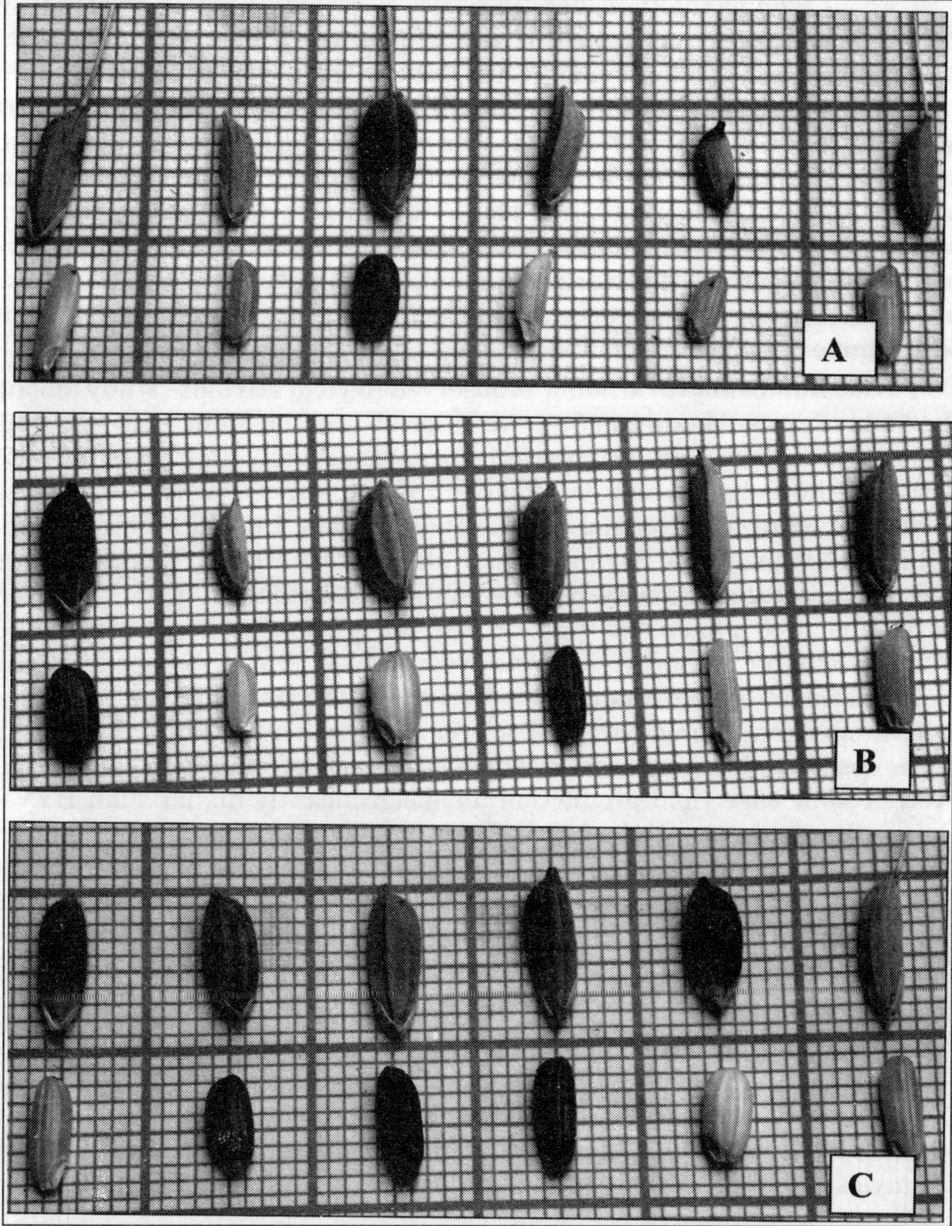

Anthocyanin colouration of Rice Hull and Seed Coat of different landraces of rice.

A. (Left to Right) Suakalma, Kataribhog, Kakua, Dhuderswar, Badshabhog, Gangajali.

B. (Left to Right) Malabati, Danarguri, Nugembaro, Chandrakanta, Daharlagra, Dharansal.

C. (Left to Right) Bahurupi, Bhuri, Kalobhat, Sindurmukhi, Bachi, Byamajhupi.

About 62% of the landraces varieties possessed white kernel colour, 24% of the varieties consists of fine aroma, 95% found with long leaf length, 87% showed medium leaf blade width, 29% with long stem length and 6% variety possess very long stem length, 56% variety showed medium panicle length, 82% of the variety consist of medium panicle number per plant, 56% with short grain length, 36% with medium grain width, 49% varieties possess medium weight of 5 panicle, 57% of the variety showed medium number of spikelet's per panicle, 82% of the varieties with medium tillers per plant, and 56% of the varieties showed late maturity duration. These important phenotypic characters could be utilized for the rice improvement programme.

Wide number of variation was observed in yield attribute study among the 54 landraces. Maximum 33% varieties showed medium yield and 24% varieties with low yield. 16% varieties was moderately high yielding, 14% varieties showed very high yield potential and only 2% varieties possess very low yielding potential. Landraces variety like Agniban, Bachi, Bahurupi, Byamajhupi, Barani, Chandrakanta, Daharlagra, Kaksal, Khuch and Talmugurdhan variety possess high yield potential. They produced 54.04 q/ha, 46.6 q/ha, 53.82 q/ha, 56.65 q/ha, 48.49 q/ha, 47.84 q/ha, 51.26 q/ha, 46.53 q/ha and 56.16 q/ha rice respectively and if we compare this yield potential of these landraces variety to the presently most widely cultivated high yielding variety Mtu 7029 or any other presently used HYVs it was observed that a landraces varieties were possess same yield potential, even in some case yield production have significantly higher than HYVs. Generally yield potential of Mtu 7029 is near about 48.93 q/ha but in Agniban, Bahurupi, Byamajhupi, Khuch and Talmugurdhan product much more yield than the HYVs, and they produced 54.04 q/ha, 53.82 q/ha, 56.65 q/ha, 51.26 q/ha, 56.16 q/ha yield respectively in control condition. Traditional and marginal farmers could select high yielding or very high yielding varieties for their traditional agricultural practice.

From the physico-chemical analysis of 54 landraces of rice in was observed that, variety Fulpagri consist of maximum carbohydrate content (24gm/100gm) and variety Bahurupi possesses minimum carbohydrate content (20.3gm/100gm). All the 55 varieties consist of minimum quantity of amylose content in their kernel endosperm and it varied from 0.9% to 1.5%.

Among these 54 varieties 10 varieties namely- Badshabhog, Baskamini, Danarguri, Gangajali, Radhatilak, Kalojira, Kanakchur , Kataribhog, Lalbadshabhog and Tulsibhog variety consist of fine Aroma. Variety Bhadoi have minimum maturity periods and Nugen baro, Khuch, Geush have maximum maturity duration. Variety Kalobhat consist of black coloured kernel and medium aroma.

CONCLUSION

Green revolution of India has introduced number of High Yielding Variety (HYV) into the farmer's field and unfortunately after the introduction of HYV landraces have been gradually decreasing from the agricultural field. Due to the consequence of overpopulation, urbanization and encroaching of the agricultural field, yield production from these landraces are becoming insufficient for the growing demands of food. To overcome the growing demands of the food grains farmers switch over from the landraces to the HYVs. As a result the number of traditional varieties has drastically fallen down from the agricultural fields of of West Bengal. This situation is true for not only this state rather it is true for the whole country as well as the whole World.

Another important aspect is sustainable agriculture. Introduction of the HYVs into the agricultural fields has a diverse effect; on the one side it fulfils the growing demand of food and on the other side it is responsible for the gradual erosion of landraces of Rice. In present changing environmental condition HYVs are facing some difficulties. The major problem of current HYVs is non-sustainable yield production. Due to the adverse effect of present changing climatic condition the yield production are becoming very unstable and these varieties are easily susceptible to the pathogenic attack. But on the other side it was observed that yield production of the traditional varieties was unaltered even in adverse climatic situation and these varieties were more resistant to the pathogenic attack.

If we look at the present socio-economic demand of food grain, the present HYVs will be unable to mange future food crisis. To compete with this food crisis we have to improve our present HYVs (more yield stable, resistant to pathogenic attack etc.) taking the help of rice landraces which is the gift of nature, possibly consisting of numerous unexploited gene pool, which may be utilized for the production of drought resistant, pathogonic resistant, yield stabilized, high yielding varieties in future but conservation of these traditional varieties is topmost priority for this purpose.

Needless to mention, the landraces are disappearing fast from the rice field of this state. Proper conservation is necessary otherwise we may lose these naturally growing varieties. These varieties are valuable as they possess treasure of genetic material which may prove valuable in future crop development and improvement programmes. As most of the landraces are in informal agriculture sectors, our information about them is incomplete and out of date. Future of productivity of rice solely depends upon conservation of these landraces. Sinha and Mishra (2002, 2003) have done remarkable efforts on conservation and cultivation of rice landraces of Bankura district of West Bengal, the present study adds a new dimension confining itself to the 13 district of West Bengal. Importance of these varieties is immense keeping their gene pool in mind. In present era when much stress is being laid to conservation of landraces, we cannot afford to lose landraces of rice varieties. Another important issue is sustainable agriculture in present situation where climate change is adversely affecting agricultural productivity. Beyond any doubt, local varieties which are sustained in particular climatic condition since thousands of years back are better suited as compared to HYVs. So, proper solution of climate change as well as agriculture may successfully rest on conserving landraces of rice.

REFERENCES

Anonymous, (2009): Annual Report, 2005-06, Department of Agriculture, Government of West Bengal, Writers' Buildings, Kolkata - 700 001, pp. 174.

Chatterjee, S.D., Adhikari, B., Ghosh, A., Ahmed, J., Neogi, S. B. and Pandey, N. (2008): The Rice Bio-diversity in West Bengal. Department of Agriculture, Govt. of West Bengal, pp. 50.

Durning, A.B. (1990): Crop Evolution, Adaption and Yield. Cambridge University Press, Cambridge.

Frankel, O.H. (1973): Survey of Crop Genetic Resources in Their Centres of Diversity. First Report. FAO/IBP, Rome.

Fowler, C., Mooney, P. (1990): Shattering: Food, Politics and Loss of Genetic Diversity. University of Arizona Press, Tucson.

Guevarra, E. (2000): Folk Rice Variety of West Bengal. Genetic Resources Centre, IRRI, Manila.

Holden, J., Peacock, J. and Williams, T. (1993): Genes, Crops and the Environment. Cambridge University Press. Cambridge.

IWMI. (2010): West Bengal Situation Analysis. Rajarhat PRASARI, Kolkata (India) In Consultation with Food and Agriculture Organization of the United Nations, Rome (Italy), pp. 1-4.

IBPGR-IRRI – Rice Advisory Committee (1980): Descriptors for Rice. IRRI, Los Banos, Phillipines, pp. 21.

Lipton, M., and Longhurst, R. (1989): New Seeds and Poor People. Johns Hopkins University Press. Baltimore.

Matson, A.P., Parton, W.J., Power, A.G., Swift, M.J. (1997): "Agricultural Intensification and Ecosystem Properties." *Science*, 277: 504-509.

Paddock, W.C. (1970): How Green is the Green Revolution? *Bio Science*, 20: 897-902.

Patra, B.C. (2000): Collection and Characterization of Rice Genetic Resources from Keonjhar District of Orissa. *Oryza*, 34: 324-326.

Richharia, R.H. (1979): An Aspect of Genetic Diversity in Rice. *Oryza*, 16: 1-31.

Shiva, V. (1991): The Violence of the Green Revolution. Third World Network. Penang.

Srivastava, J.P., Jaffe, S. (1993): Best Practices for Moving Seed Technology: New Approaches to doing Business. World Bank Technical Paper No. 213. The World Bank. Washington, DC.

Shobha Rani N, Shobha Rao LV, Viraktamath BC, Mishra B. (2004): National Guidelines for the Conduct of Tests for Distinctiveness, Uniformity and Stability. Directorate of Rice Research, pp. 6-13.

Sinha, A.K., Mishra, P.K. (2012): Agronomic Evaluation of Landraces of Rice (*Oryza sativa* L.) of Bankura District of West Bengal. *Columban Journal of Life Science*, 13(1 & 2): 35-38.

Sinha, A.K., Mishra, P.K. (2012): Rice Diversity of Bankura District of West Bengal (INDIA). *Bioscience Discovery*, 3(3): 284-287.

Sinha, Anjan Kumar, Mishra, P.K. (2013): Selected Agronomic Traits of Indigenous Rice (*Oryza sativa* L.) Variety of Lateritic Region of West Bengal. *Environment & Ecology*, 31(2c): 1011-1017.

Sinha, A.K., Mishra, P.K. (2013): Agro-morphological Characterization of Rice Landraces Variety (*Oryza sative* L.) of Bankura District of West Bengal. *Research in Plant Biology*, 3(5): 28-36.

Sinha, A.K., Mishra, P.K. (2013): Agromorphological Characterization and Morphology Based Genetic Diversity Analysis of Landraces of Rice Variety (*Oryza sativa* L.) of Bankura District of West Bengal. *International Journal of Current Research*, 5(10): 2764-2769.

Sinha, A.K., Mishra, P.K. (2013): Morphology Based Multivariate Analysis of Phenotypic Diversity of Landraces of Rice (*Oryza sativa* L.) of Bankura District of West Bengal. *Journal of Crop and Weed*, 9(2): 115-121.

Pages: **152-159**

SEED TECHNOLOGY, PLANT GROWTH AND CROPPING SYSTEM

Edited by: **Dr. Pawan Kumar Tyagi; Dr. Pawan Kumar 'Bharti'**

ISBN: 978-93-5056-738-8

Edition: **2015**

Published by: **Discovery Publishing House Pvt. Ltd., New Delhi (India)**

A New Record of Multi-branching in Date Palm (*Phoenix sylvestris* L.) in India

Pawan Kumar 'Bharti'

ABSTRACT

Generally, date palm doesn't show branching phenomenon in trunk. Even the healthy plant can become dead after cutting its stem. But sometimes, branching can be observed in date palm tree.

This article is an evidence of branching in date palm in India. A date palm is observed with seven branches on its crown segment. This is indeed first time observed event and unrecorded phenomenon of multi-branching in date palm (*Phoenix sylvestris* L.) in Indian circumstances. Author wants to register this record in some appropriate and suitable periodicals as one of his small discoveries.

Key words: Date Palm, Branching event, first record, Indian circumstances.

Society for Environment, Health, Awareness of Nutrition & Toxicology (SEHAT-India), 20, Jamaalpur Maan, Raja Ka Tajpur, Bijnore (UP) - 246 735, India

INTRODUCTION

In Indian agricultural landscape, the palms grow on field edges; individuals or clusters are occasionally present, sometimes close to the houses. They form hedges, together with shrubs such as acacias, *Calotropis procera* and henna[1]. Whether wild or cultivated, this palm is used for other purposes as well. The fruit is sweet and edible, although the seed is large compared to the amount of flesh. It is used both as food and as fodder for domestic animals. The stem is widely used as building material – beams in houses and half-pipes to conduct water – and the leaves for matting and basketry. The palm is also planted as an ornamental along roadsides and in gardens. Additionally, many parts of the plant are used for their medicinal properties[1].

Date palm is the tallest of the Phoenix species and the non-branching trunk can grow, under some conditions, taller than 30 M. the plant has one terminal shoot apex that ensures the growth lengthwise[2]. Belonging to the Angiosperms-Monocotyledones, *Palmaceae* is a family of about 200 genera and 1500 species[3]. Phoenix (*Coryphoideae Phoeniceae*) is one of the genera, which contains more than a dozen species, all native to the tropical or subtropical regions of Africa or Southern Asia, including *Phoenix dactylifera* and *P. sylvestris*[4].

Phoenix dactylifera L. and *P. sylvestris:*

The distinction between *P. sylvestris* and *P. dactylifera* was not always clear. *Phoenix dactylifera* L. is a palm in the genus Phoenix, cultivated for edible sweet fruits in Arabian and Asian countries and frequently grows in wasteland and roadside in India. It's probably originated from lands around Iraq. *Phoenix dactylifera* grows 70-75 feet in height, growing singly or forming a clump with several stems from a single root system[5].

Phoenix sylvestris Roxb., together with 13 other species, forms the genus *Phoenix*. In a phylogenetic study combining morphological, anatomical and genetic data, it appears close to the date palm (*Phoenix dactylifera* L.) and to *Phoenix theophrasti*[6]. The phylogeny of the genus itself remains to be elucidated. *Phoenix sylvestris* is widely distributed in South Asia, from Pakistan to Myanmar, across India, Nepal, Bhutan and Bangladesh[6]. This palm produces edible fruits but it is generally called "wild date palm" to distinguish it from the closely related *Phoenix dactylifera*, which is known as "date palm" and is cultivated agriculturally as the commercial source of edible dates. This palm is a major source of sugar in India, and the sap is sometimes fermented into a drink called "toddy," which explains the names "sugar date palm" and "toddy palm." In present-day India, it is commonly found on low ground in the sub-Himalayan tract, along riverbanks on the Deccan Plateau (south-central India), in forests up to elevations of 1350 m in Himachal Pradesh, and especially on lower hill slopes in Haryana (northwestern India). It survives in disturbed areas, such as wastelands or seasonally inundated areas[1]. Apart from its distribution in a "wild" state, *P. sylvestris* is also cultivated in parts of South Asia, mostly in its eastern and southeastern Parts.

In English, it is called date-sugar palm, Indian wine palm, sugar palm or wild date palm. Its local names in South Asia are numerous, according to the different regions and languages spoken: *sendhi, kejur, khajur, khaji, salma, thalma, thakil* (Hindi-Urdu); *kajar, kejur* (Bengali, Bengal); *khejuri* (Oriya, Orissa, W. Bengal); *khajur* (Kolami, Andhra Pradesh, Maharashtra); *khijur* (Santali); *sindi* (Gondi); *khajur, khaji* (Punjabi); *seindi* (Berar); *inta kattinta* (Kerala); *sendi, khajura, khajuri* (Bambaiya, Mumbai, Mahashashtra); *boichand, sendri, shindi* (Marathi, Maharashtra); *kharak* (Gujarati, Gujarat); *sandole-ka-nar* (Dakhini, Deccan); *itchumpannay, periaitcham, itcham-nar, ichal, ithal pannay* (Tamil, Tamilnadu); *ita, pedda-ita, itanara, ishan-chedi* (Telugu, Andhra Pradesh); *ichal, kullu, ichalu mara* (Kannada, Karnataka); *andadayichali, sunindu* (Karnataka); *khurjjuri, kharjura, madhukshir* (Sanskrit)[7].

There are complex relationships between *P. sylvestris* and *P. dactylifera*[1]. Morphologically, *P. sylvestris* is close to the date palm, but several characters allow their differentiation. *Phoenix sylvestris* is a strictly solitary palm, also distinguished by its dense spherical crown composed of relatively short leaves with small leaf bases forming a characteristic dense and regular pattern of small diamond-shaped leaf scars on the trunk of old specimens. Leaf segments are grayish, not very rigid and sometimes twisted. Basal acanthophylls are long, deeply channeled adaxially, grouped by two and the transition with foliar segments is progressive. *Phoenix dactylifera* is considerably less homogeneous morphologically than *P. sylvestris*. Barrow[6] distinguished *P. sylvestris* by having channeled acanthophylls, but this characteristic is also common in *P. dactylifera*. In both species, leaf segments are clustered and disposed on various planes. The fruits of *P. sylvestris* are smaller (15-25 × 12 mm) than those of the date palm (40-70 × 20–30 mm)[6]. Because of this morphological proximity, *P. sylvestris* has long been considered as the wild progenitor of the cultivated date palm. However, a genetic study challenged this hypothesis and with the discovery of truly wild date palm (*Phoenix dactylifera*) populations, it is now completely rejected. Nevertheless, the two species are inter-fertile, and their relationship remains to be investigated[1].

DATE PALM TRUNK

The date palm trunk, also called stem or stipe is vertical, cylindrical and columnar of the same girth all the way up. The girth does not increase once the canopy of fronds has fully developed. It is brown in colour, lignified and without any ramification. Its average circumference is about 1 to 1.10 m. The trunk is composed of tough, fibrous vascular bundles cemented together in a matrix of cellular tissue, which is much lignified near the outer part of the trunk. Being a monocotyledon, date palm does not have a cambium layer. The trunk is covered for several years with the bases of the old dry fronds, making it rough, but with age these bases weather and the trunk becomes smoother with visible cicatrices of these bases. Vertical growth of date palm is ensured by its terminal bud, called phyllophore, and its height could reach more than 20 metres[8].

Sometimes date palms show a branching phenomenon which was studied by Zaid[9] and found to be attributed to several causes. Branching in date palm is a result of dichotomy, axillary bud development, polyembryony or attack by a disease. Branched date palms are fertile and can produce as much fruit as a single headed palm. There is a need of a further analysis of the vascular system of branched date palm. This anatomical study is necessary to show the continuity of growth from the single to the divided state of the stem. It is necessary to study *in vitro* the regenerating capacity of divided portions of the apical meristem and axillary buds of these specimens in the hope of establishing a rapid mass propagation technique for date palm[8]. Branching abnormality in date palm trees has been observed and recorded in two different locations in Egypt. Frequently, this phenomenon occurs naturally. Sometimes, farmers decapitate or wound the terminal bud of the tree in order to extract a sweet drink (coined as 'Lagby'). Generally, the axillary buds around the wounded area: of the apical region are dormant. Decapitation or wounding this apical dome enhances and accelerates the outgrowth of these buds to form new branches.

BRANCHING IN DATE PALM

The causes of such abnormal growth like branching may be due to different internal as well as external reasons. Zaid[9] and Fisher[10] have cited some examples of the true dichotomous branching in angiosperms especially in Palmaceae. In survey and observations, researchers[11] found a specimen of branched palm in Rosetta (Rashid) region (Northwest Delta in Egypt). Zaid[9] found the same phenotype in one specimen after three years of survey in Moroccan date plantations. Another system of dichotomous branching was noticed in one specimen in Siwa Oasis[12]. The growth system of this tree differed drastically from that in Rashid region. It is important to suggest that these two cases of dichotomous branching were produced from natural seeds germination[12]. This may suggest that both of them are genetic seggregants. Therefore, different genetic factors may control such phenotypes, one responsible for elongated branching and the other for compact branching[12].

In addition to the internal causes of the stem branching in date palm and or the genetic effect on abnormality of the branching, there are external effects may cause such phenomenon. Zaid[9] and Dijerbi[13] reported that the two minor diseases in date palm (Black Scorch and Belaat diseases) were responsible for the destruction of the terminal bud. Some attacked palms could recover or revert by developing one or several lateral buds. Another interesting cause of abnormal branching or outgrowth of new axillary buds in date palm is the artificial decapitation or wounding the apical dome by the farmers. In most cases, this procedure leads to complete damage of the whole apical dome and subsequently death of the tree and hence the survival chances are very less in this process. It is not always that the outgrowth of new branches is produced from activation of dormant axillary bud but also there is a chance to initiate adventitious buds[14].

The physiological events of releasing the new formed axillary buds after apical decapitation in mature trees could be explained on the basis of the production of cytokinin and auxins & development of axillary buds[15].

Table 7.1: Geographical Position of Observed Multi-branched Indian Date Palm

Sl.No.	Particulars	Details
1.	Latitude	29° 07' 54.38" N
2.	Longitude	78° 21' 51.91" E
3.	Altitude	748 Ft

In Indian conditions, many joint date palm trees are observed with a common complex root system, but the true branching in date plant has still not been documented except those reported in *Phoenix dactilifera* (L.) Roxb. by some Indian researchers[16]. But branching in *Phoenix sylvestris* has so far not been documented in India. This date plant has a nodule like bund on the upper portion of stem (as seen in Fig. 7.1), which gives platform to seven secondary stems (branches). The base of these seven branches is a mysterious nodule and might have some good events as well as evidences for further studies in this regard. Author wants to register this record in some appropriate and suitable periodicals as one of his small discoveries.

Geographical position of observed multi-branched Indian Date Palm is given in Table 7.1. The specimen is situated on a road side near Village Dhoondly Tabibpur, Bijnore (UP), India. This multi-branched specimen of Indian date plant (*Phoenix sylvestris* L.) presented in this study (given in Fig. 7.1) is a first record of branching or even multi-branching in Indian circumstances. Height of this tree is about 24 feet and circumference of 3.5 ft. Hence, it may be:

1. A new variant or
2. Deformity in the individual part or
3. A degree of adaptation or
4. Starting of new evolution.

Further, investigations are needed to ascertain factors that lead to branching in this phenotype.

Photos by: Dr. Pawan Kumar 'Bharti'

Fig. 7.1 (A-B): First Multi-branching Event in Indian Date Palm (*Phoenix sylvestris* L.)

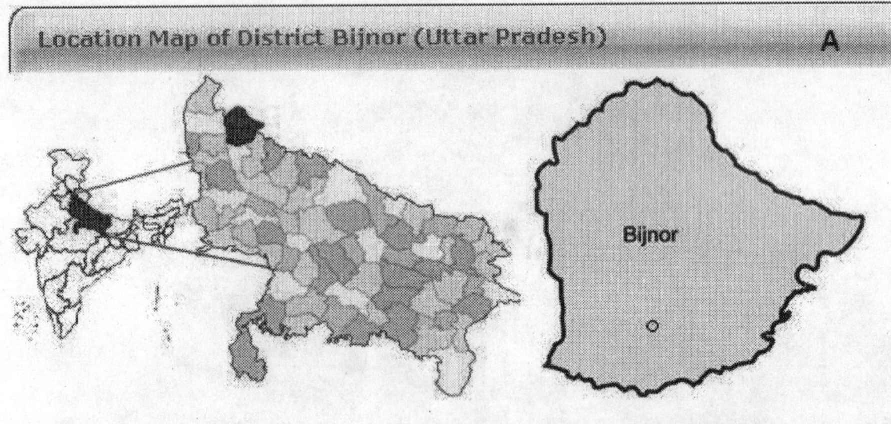

A

Fig. 7.2 (A-B): Map Showing the Location of Date Plant in India

REFERENCES

1. Newton, C., Gros-Balthazard, M., Ivorra, S., Paradis, L. Pintaud, J and Terral, J. *Phoenix dactilifera* and *P. sylvestris* in Northwestern India: A Glimpse of Their Complex Relationships. *PALMS* 57(1), 37-50 (2013).
2. Jain, Shri Mohan; Jameel M. Al-Khayri and Dennis V. Johnson. Date Palm Biotechnology, *Springer*, 741 (2011).

3. Dowson, V.H.W. Date Production and Protection. *FAO Plant Production and Protection Paper No. 35. Food and Agriculture Organization of the United Nations.* (1982).
4. Munier, P. Le Palmeir-dattier, *Paris: Maisonneuve et Larose*, pp: 221(1973).
5. Morton, J. Date. In: Fruits of Warm Climates. (Eds. Julia F. Morton and Miami, FL.) Purdue University. Center for New Crops and Plants Products, 5-11 (1987).
6. Barrow, S.A Revision of *Phoenix* L. (Palmae: Coryphoideae). *Kew Bulletin* 53, 513-575 (1998).
7. Parmar, C. and Kaushal, M.K. *Phoenix sylvestris*, In: Wild Fruits of Sub-Himalayan Region (eds. Parmar, C. and Kaushal, M.K.) *Kalyani Publishers, New Delhi, India*, 58-61 (1982).
8. http://www.pubhort.org/datepalm/datepalm1/datepalm1_46.pdf as Accessed on 08 May 2014.
9. Zaid, A. Branching Phenomenon in Date Palm. *Date Palm Journal* 5 (1), 48-58 (1987).
10. Fisher, J.B. Axillary and Dichotomous Branching in Palm Chamaedorea. *Amer. J. Bot.* 61 (10), 1046-1056 (1974).
11. Harhash, M.M. and H.E. El-Wakil. Branching Abnormality and Axillary Buds Outgrowth After Apical Dome Decapitation of Date Palm (*Phoenix dactilifera* L.). The First International Conference on Date Palms. Al-Ain, United Arab Emirates, March 8-10, 572-582 (1998).
12. FAO. Date Palm Cultivation, Plant Production and Protection, Paper 156, Rev. 1 *Food and Agricultural Organization of the United Nations*, (ISBN: 92-5-104863-0). http://www.fao.org/docrep/006/y4360e/y4360e05.htm, (2002).
13. Djerbi, M. Diseases of Date palm (*Phoenix dactylifera* L.). Regional Project for Palm and Date Research Center in the Near East and North Africa, Baghdad, Iraq, 114 (1983).
14. Goodwin, P.B. Phytohormones and Growth and Development of Organs of the Vegetative Plants: A Comprehensive Treatise. In: (eds. D.S. Letham, P.B. Goodwin and S.T. Higgins). *El-Sevier/North-Holland and Biomedical Press* 11, 31-173 (1978).
15. Abo El-Nil, M.M. and A.S.AI-Ghamdi. Stimulation of Growth and Tissue Culture of Date Palm Axillary Buds by Injection of Offshoot with a Cytokinin. In: *Proceeding of 2nd Symposium of the Date Palm in Saudi Arabia.* Vol. II, 43-49 (1986).
16. Harikrishnan, B. and Shriramamurthy, K. Report on Tricotomous Branching in *Phoenix dactilifera* (L.) Roxb. *The Indian Forester* 131(4), 597-597 (2005).

Pages: **160-178**

SEED TECHNOLOGY, PLANT GROWTH AND CROPPING SYSTEM

Edited by: **Dr. Pawan Kumar Tyagi; Dr. Pawan Kumar 'Bharti'**

ISBN: 978-93-5056-738-8

Edition: **2015**

Published by: **Discovery Publishing House Pvt. Ltd., New Delhi (India)**

Effect of Straw Management in Nitrogen Scheduling on Rice – Wheat Cropping System

Ram Swaroop[1], Prafull Kumar[2], Avadhesh Kumar Koshal[3]

ABSTRACT

The field experiment was "Performance of rice crop as affected by wheat straw management and nitrogen scheduling in rice-wheat cropping system" conducted at Crop Research Centre, Sardar Vallabhbhai Patel University of Agriculture and Technology, Meerut during Kharif 2007. Six different treatments comprising wheat straw management and nitrogen scheduling were tested in a randomized block design with four replication. Among the nitrogen scheduling two split applications was found better than three split application. Nutrients removal was higher in the treatments of wheat straw incorporation followed by burning and straw removal. Available nutrients estimated at different stages were higher in the treatments of wheat straw incorporation followed by burning and removal. The soil of experimental site was low in organic carbon and available nitrogen,

1 Sardar Vallabhbhai Patel University of Agriculture and Technology, Meerut - 250 110, U.P., (India).

2 Chandra Shekhar Azad University of Agriculture and Technology, Kanpur - 208 002, U.P., (India).

3 Project Directorate for Farming Systems Research, Modipuram, Meerut - 250110, U.P., (India).

medium in available phosphorous and potassium having 8.02 pH and sandy loam texture. Wheat straw management affected the organic carbon content of soil significantly. Bulk density also decline with the incorporation or burning of wheat straw.

Results reveal that growth parameter, yield attributing character and yields were affected significantly by different treatment and were higher in the treatment of wheat straw incorporation.

Key words: Nitrogen scheduling, Cropping system, DAT & RWS.

INTRODUCTION

Rice (*Oryza sativa*) is a staple food of India and it occupies about 43.81 million hectare area in India. Rice-wheat cropping system is one of the most important cropping systems occupying 10.5 million hectare land in India (Rajkhowa and Borah 2008). 19.6 million tonnes of rice straw is burnt as a surplus farm waste in combine harvested area of northern India which results in loss of organic matter and 100, 20.1, 19.8 and 80.2% of NPK and S respectively, beside causing environmental pollution (Thind, 2003 and Mishra *et al.* 2001).Area under rice which was 37.76 million hectare, during 1971-72 with production of 43.07 million tonnes and productivity of 1141 kg ha^{-1} increased to 43.81 million hectare, with total production of 93.35 million tonnes and productivity 2131 kg ha^{-1} during 2006-07 (Anonymous 2007-08).

The recycling of nutrients through crop residue management is gaining renewed importance for maintaining soil fertility and crop productivity. Wheat straw in combine harvesting is often burnt from the field after harvest despite its roll in soil productivity if returned to the soil (Tanaka 1978). Crop residue management and its impact on soil organic matter and nutrient recycling is gaining importance with the current renewed focus on agricultural sustainability. Burning of crop residue results in emission of trace gases and particulate matter, loss of plant nutrients, and thus adversely affects the pedology. It has been estimated that for the year 2000 the emission of CH_4, CO, N_2O and NO_x was 110, 2306, 2 and 84 Gg respectively from the field burning of rice and wheat straw in India (Gupta *et al.* 2004).

In 2000, the total agriculture residue production in India was 347 million tonnes, of which rice and wheat straw accounted for more than 200 million tonnes. For every 4 tonnes rice or wheat grain, about 6 tonnes of straw is produced. Large amount of crop residue is produced from rice-wheat cropping system (RWS) in India from major involved states viz. UP, MP, Punjab, Bihar, Maharashtra, Haryana, Gujrat and HP (Thakur 2003). Crop residue is one of major sources of organic matter and plant nutrient if it is managed properly. Recycling of such crop residue also reduce soil erosion, vis-a-vis nutrient loss and improve the physico-chemical and biological properties of the soil. Incorporation of residues as a means of nutrient recycling in the soil-plant ecosystem is an essential component of sustainable productivity in nutrient exhaustive rice-wheat cropping system, as it alters the soil environment which in turn influences the microbial population and activity in the soil and subsequent nutrient transformation (Kumar and Goh 2000).

Incorporation of crop residues preserved plant nutrients as well as improve physical, chemical and biological properties of soil, however this practice result in immobilization of plant nutrient particularly nitrogen (Mikkelson and Rao 1976). High C: N ratio of added crop residues may lead to immobilization of basal applied nitrogen at initial stage due to poor nitrogen supply. Therefore application of some nitrogen prior to rice transplanting may bring down the C: N ratio of added residue which will reduce the immobilization rate and supply of sufficient nitrogen at the early stage of crop.

Keeping in view the present investigation on "Performance of rice (*Oryza sativa*) crop as affected by wheat straw management and nitrogen scheduling in rice-wheat cropping system" was conducted with following objectives.

1. Effect of wheat straw management and nitrogen scheduling on growth parameters, yield attributing characters and yield of the rice crop.
2. Effect of wheat straw management and nitrogen scheduling on nutrient content on rice crop.
3. Effect of wheat straw management and nitrogen scheduling on soil properties.

Experimental Site and Location

The field experiment was conducted at Crop Research Centre of Sardar Vallabhbhai Patel University of Agriculture & Technology Modipuram, Meerut during kharif 2007. Meerut is situated on the Delhi- Dehradun highway road. Geographically Meerut is located at 29° 04° N latitude and 77° 42° E longitude at an altitude of 237 meters above the mean sea level (Fig. 8.1).

Meerut is located in subtropical and semi arid climate characterized with hot summer and extremely cold winters. The mean maximum temperature of 43° C to 45° C is not uncommon during summer while very low temperature (3° C) accompanied by frost may be experienced in December & January. The winters are cool and the frost generally occurs to words the end of December and may continue till the end of January. The total rainfall and its distribution in this region is variable. About 80-90% of it is received during July to September and few showers of cyclonic rains are also received during December and January.

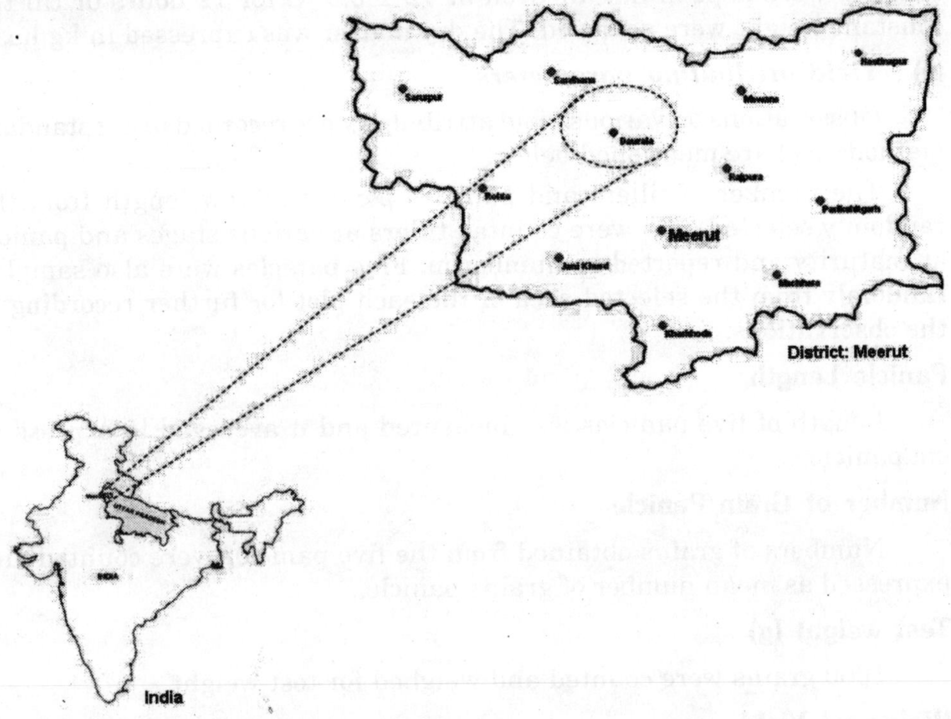

Fig. 8.1: Experimental Site and Location

MATERIAL AND METHODS

(A) Crop Studies

(i) *Growth, yield parameters & biochemical parameters for crop studies*

An area was marked for recording various growth observation of the crop. Growth observations were recorded at 30, 60 DAT and at harvest of the crop yield and yield attributing characters were recorded at harvest. Methodology adopted for recording various parameters was as under: number of effecting tillers falling in per meter row length, panicle length/5 plants, number of grains/panicle.

Plant Height

Five hills were marked in the plot and the height was measured with the help of meter scale from the base of plant to the tip of the tallest leaf up to emergence of spike and thereafter up to the tip of panicle. Average shoot height was computed and expressed in cm.

Dry Matter Accumulation

Five plants from one row of the sampling area were cut close to the ground surface from each plot separately. After initial sun drying, the samples were kept in hot air oven at 72 ± 0.5 °C for 72 hours or till the constant weight were achieved. The dry matter was expressed in kg ha^{-1}.

(ii) *Yield attributing parameters*

Observations on various yield attributes were recorded using standard methods and are mentioned below:

The number of tillers and panicles per meter row length from the randomly selected area were counted tillers at various stages and panicle at maturity and reported in number/m. Five panicles were also sampled randomly from the selected area of the each plot for further recording of the observations.

Panicle Length

Length of five panicles was measured and it averaged to express in cm/panicle.

Number of Grain/Panicle

Numbers of grains obtained from the five panicles were counted and expressed as mean number of grains/panicle.

Test weight (g)

1000 grains were counted and weighed for test weight.

Biological Yield

The weight of total produce obtained from each plot was recorded in kilograms before threshing and finally expressed in q ha^{-1}.

Grain Yield

The weight of grains harvested from the net plot area was recorded in kg and finally expressed in q ha^{-1}.

Straw Yield

The straw yield was computed on difference basis. Grain yield was subtracted from the biological yield of net plot and expressed as kg ha^{-1} and finally expressed in q ha^{-1}.

(iii) *Biochemical analysis*

The plant samples was analyzed for total N and estimated by automatic nitrogen analyzer using 0.2 gram finely powdered plant sample (Jackson, 1973).

(B) Soil Studies

A composite soil sample was collected from a depth of 0-15 cm after harvesting of wheat crop. The experimental soil was sandy loam in texture having, low organic carbon and medium in available phosphorus and potassium. Nursery field was prepared by two harrow ploughing followed by two deep ploughing with tractor drawn cultivator. Before sowing of nursery field was levelled manually and then irrigated for puddling, there after a certified seed of rice Pusa basmati- 1 was sown @ 30 kg/ha on 25.6.2007. After harvesting of wheat crop the wheat straw management practice were adopted as per treatment. The wheat straw chopped in 5-10 cm size was incorporated while simply burning was done in the treatment of burning wheat straw incorporated or burnt was having 0.30% N.

Prior to the field preparation 20% of recommended N was applied and mixed by cultivator using power tiller in all the treatments field was manually puddled and 30 days old rice seedling (two seedling/hill) was transplanted on 25.7.2007 with a plant spacing of 20 x 10 cm. Recommended dose of N P and K (100:50:50) respectively were applied for crop production. Full amount of phosphorus and potassium along with basal dose of nitrogen as per the treatments were applied before puddling of field. Rest amount of nitrogen as per treatment was applied in equal split at 20 and 50 days after transplanting. $ZnSO_4$ was also applied @ 25 kg/ha as basal. Rice crop was irrigated as and when required.

Collection of Soil Sample

Soil samples were collected from 0-15 cm depth from each plots, sample were grounded and processed for various physico-chemical analysis.

Available Nitrogen

The soil samples were analyzed for organic carbon (walkley and Black 1934) and available nitrogen (Subbaih and Asija 1956).

(C) Statistical Analysis

The data recorded during the course of investigation were subjected to statistical analysis using analysis of variance technique (ANOVA) for randomized block design as prescribed by Cochran and Cox (1959). Standard error of mean in each case and the critical difference only for significant cases were computed at 5% levels of probability as under.

(i) *Standard error of mean*

Standard error of mean was calculated as fallow

Standard error of mean = $\sqrt{EMSS/r}$

Where,

SEm± =Standard error of mean

EMSS= Error mean sum of square

r = Number of replications on which the observation is based

(ii) *Critical difference*

The critical difference at 5% level of probability was worked out to compare treatments means wherever 'F' test was significant.

Critical difference = SEm± x √2 x t (at error degree of freedom)

RESULTS AND DISCUSSION

1 Effect of wheat straw management and nitrogen scheduling on growth parameters, yield attributing characters and yield of the rice crop

At harvesting of rice the maximum plant height (85.50cm) was measured in the treatment of wheat straw incorporation where nitrogen was applied in two equal splits (T_4). With exception of T_6, plant height recorded in this treatment was found significantly higher than rest of treatments. Significant variation in plant height was recorded due to scheduling of nitrogen with removal and incorporated practices but in case of burning practice no significant variation was found.

It is evident from the Table 8.1 and Fig. 8.2 that the effect of the wheat straw management and nitrogen scheduling on panicle length of rice was non significant although the highest panicle length 23.50 cm was recorded in T_4 and lowest panicle length 22.50 cm in T_1 and T_5. Higher panicle length was found in two split nitrogen scheduling than three splits schedule with similar wheat straw management practice.

Table 8.1: Effect of Wheat Straw Management and Nitrogen Scheduling on Yield Attributing Characters

Treatment	Panicle Length (cm)	No. of Grain/Panicle	1000 Grains Weight(g)
T_1	22.50	63.00	17.69
T_2	23.00	70.00	16.78
T_3	23.00	70.50	17.62
T_4	23.50	77.25	16.59
T_5	22.50	69.00	17.76
T_6	23.00	73.00	16.83
SEm ±	0.56	0.99	0.37
CD at 5%	NS	3.00	NS

The numbers of grains/panicle were affected significantly due to wheat straw management and nitrogen scheduling. The highest numbers of grains/panicle (77.25) were found in the treatment where nitrogen was applied in two equal splits with wheat straw incorporation (T_4) and were significantly higher than other treatments. Numbers of grains/panicle in T_2, T_3 and T_5 were found statistically at par. Higher grain numbers/panicle were found in the treatments, where nitrogen was applied in two equal splits than three split nitrogen application in all wheat straw management practices.

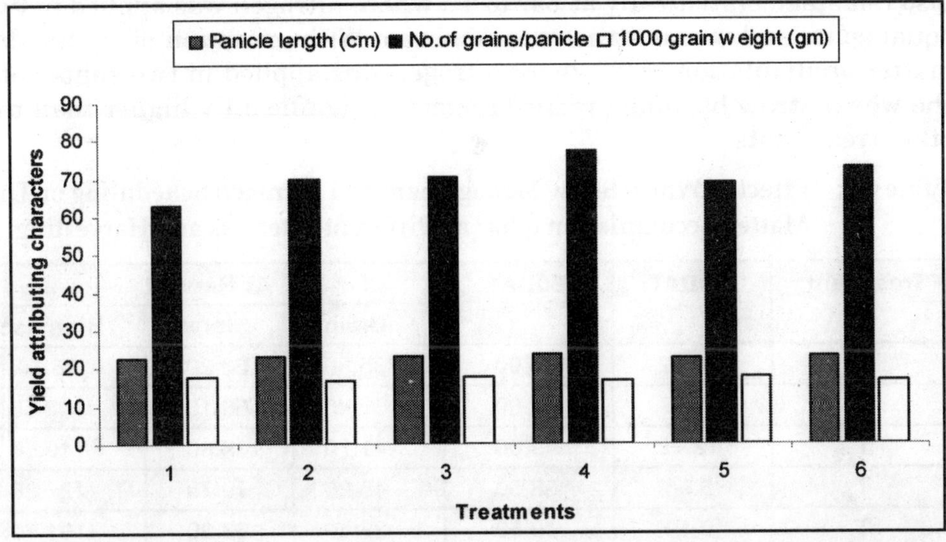

Fig. 8.2: Effect of Wheat Straw Management and Nitrogen Scheduling on Yield Attributing Characters

The 1000 grains weight did not varied significantly due to different wheat straw management practices and nitrogen scheduling although higher values were recorded due to application of nitrogen in three splits rather than two split with every nitrogen management practices.

(a) Dry matter accumulation

It is evident from the data given in Table 8.2 and Fig. 8.3 that dry matter accumulation in rice increased with advancement of growth of the crop. Wheat straw management and nitrogen scheduling influenced the dry matter accumulation significantly at different growth intervals of rice. At 30 DAT of rice, the highest dry matter accumulation 12.42q ha^{-1} was recorded in the treatment wherein 50% nitrogen was applied as basal and rest applied in two equal splits with wheat straw incorporation (T_3) although this treatment was found at par with the treatments of other residue management practices with above said schedule. Dry matter accumulation in T_2, T_4 and T_6 wherein nitrogen application was to be made in two splits with different wheat straw management practices was found statistically at par and significantly lower than the T_3.

At 60 DAT of rice crop the highest dry matter accumulation (58.50 q ha^{-1}) was recorded in the T_4 wherein nitrogen was applied in two equal splits and wheat straw was incorporated and was significantly higher than rest of the treatments. The T_3 and T_5 where 50% nitrogen was applied as basal with incorporated and burnt wheat straw management practices were found statistically at par. Dry matter accumulation in these two treatments also remained statistically at par to T_2, where nitrogen was applied in two equal splits and wheat straw was removed. With exception of T_4, the dry matter accumulation in T_6 where nitrogen was applied in two splits with the wheat straw burning practice remained significantly higher than the other treatments.

Table 8.2: Effect of Wheat Straw Management and Nitrogen Scheduling on Dry Matter Accumulation q ha^{-1} at Different Intervals and Harvesting

Treatment	30DAT	60DAT	At Harvest		
			Grain	Starw	Biomass
T_1	10.52	44.00	35.50	60.20	95.70
T_2	5.55	47.00	39.45	63.10	102.55
T_3	12.42	49.00	41.70	68.80	110.50
T_4	5.96	58.50	48.26	79.70	127.26
T_5	9.10	48.50	38.40	63.30	101.70
T_6	7.40	53.25	41.30	68.10	109.40
SEm ±	1.27	0.93	0.62	0.93	1.12
CD at 5%	3.83	2.79	1.87	2.79	3.38

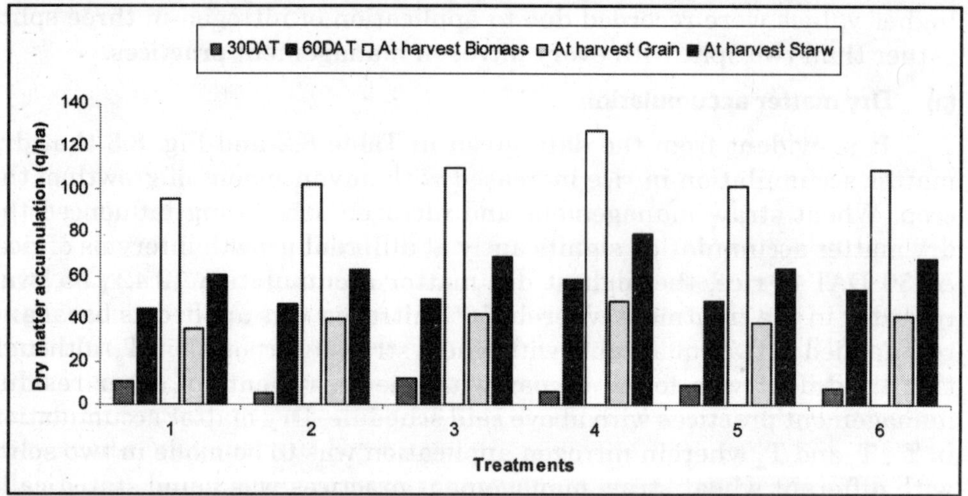

Fig. 8.3: Effect of Wheat Straw Management and Nitrogen Scheduling on Dry Matter Accumulation q ha^{-1} at Different Intervals and Harvesting

At harvest of rice, total dry matter accumulation of biomass (grain + straw) ranged from 95.70 to 127.96 q ha^{-1}. The highest dry matter accumulation was recorded in T_4, which was found significantly higher than the other treatments. No significant difference was found between T_3 and T_6, T_2 and T_5 whereas T_1 accumulated significantly lower dry matter than the other treatments. Biomass accumulation was significantly higher wherein nitrogen was applied in two equal splits (T_2, T_4 and T_6) than the treatments where nitrogen was applied in three splits (T_1, T_3 and T_5) with the corresponding wheat straw management practices.The highest grain yield (48.26 q ha^{-1}) and lowest (35.50 q ha-1) were found in T_4 and T_1. Wheat straw incorporation with nitrogen applied in two equal splits at maximum tillering and PI (T_4) gave significantly higher grain yield as compare to other treatments. Grain yield found in T_6 was statistically at par with T_2 but significantly higher than T_5 and T_1, which were also found significantly different.

The highest (79.70 q ha^{-1}) straw was recorded in T_4, which was significantly higher than the other treatments. Application of nitrogen in three splits with wheat straw incorporation (T_3) was found at par to T_6, where in nitrogen was applied in two equal splits and wheat straw was burnt. Irrespective of wheat straw management practices, the treatments wherein nitrogen was applied in two equal splits (T_2, T_4 and T_6) produced significantly higher straw yield than the treatment where nitrogen was applied in three splits (T_1, T_3 and T_5). At 30 DAT, the higher growth and growth parameter of rice like plant height, number of tillers per meter row length and dry matter accumulation were observed where 50% of nitrogen was applied as basal with wheat straw removal practice. Among the different wheat straw management practices better growth was observed in the order of wheat straw incorporation >wheat straw burning >wheat straw removal. Higher application of basal nitrogen might have narrowed the C: N ratio in all the wheat straw management practice thereby preventing the immobilization of nitrogen.

At 60 DAT and harvest, growth and growth parameter were higher with the application of nitrogen in two splits in all wheat straw management practices. Among the different wheat straw management practices, wheat straw incorporation was found better followed by wheat straw burning and wheat straw removal. Application of nitrogen at maximum tillering and PI stages were found better. Higher value in wheat straw incorporation may be attributed to mineralization of initially immobilized nitrogen in the later stage. The available nutrients in soil were higher with wheat straw incorporation practice therefore higher growth and growth parameters are well expected. Similar observations were also found by Surekha *et al.* (2004). The benefits of wheat straw incorporation than the wheat straw removal were also reported by (Rajput and Warsi 1991), Das *et al.* (2003) and Ma, Liwang *et al.* (1999).

The higher yield attributing characters of rice like effective tillers per meter row length, panicle length and number of grains per panicle were found in the treatment where nitrogen was applied in two splits instead of three splits application in all the wheat straw management practices. Among different management practices the higher yielding characters were found in order of wheat straw incorporation >wheat straw burning >wheat straw removal. These findings fall in accordance with the finding of Surekha *et al.* (2004) and Kachroo and Dixit (2005). Wheat straw incorporation resulted an increase in all yield attributing characters of rice as compared to wheat straw removal treatments. This effect may be attributed to the subsequent decomposition of wheat straw and release plant nutrients slowly throughout the crop growth period causing better uptake of nutrients by rice crop as reported by (Kachroo and Dixit 2005, Rajput and Warsi 1991, Sharma and Mitra 1990, and Regar *et al* 2005).

Results obtained from this study show that wheat straw incorporation produced higher grain yield than wheat straw burning or wheat straw removal. Similarly wheat straw incorporation yielded higher straw and biomass yield over wheat straw burnt and wheat straw removal. These results fall in line with those of (Yadhuvansi and Sharma 2005; Kharub *et al.,* 2004). Higher grain, straw and biomass yield with wheat straw incorporation may be expected due to the decomposition of wheat straw and subsequent release of plant nutrients in slow manner through out the growth period as reported by (Das *et al.,* 2002, 2003, Surekha *et al.,* 2004, Kachroo and Dixit 2005). Wheat straw burning treatment gave more grain, straw and biomass yield than wheat straw removal, which may be explained due to substantial nutrient contribution through ash as most of the elements will be left in the ash due to incomplete burning as the temperature necessary to cause complete burning (>800° C) may not be achieved during burning of cereal wheat straw/grass/legume pasture. This finding gets support from the result of (Kumar and Goh, 2002).

2. Effect of wheat straw management and nitrogen scheduling on nutrient content and uptake by rice crop

The data regarding the nitrogen content of rice plant at different interval of sampling as affected by wheat straw management and nitrogen scheduling are given in Table 8.3 and shown in Fig. 8.4. It is evident from the data that with the advancement in growth, nitrogen content of the rice crop decreased. The nitrogen content of rice was affected by wheat straw management and nitrogen scheduling at 30, 60 DAT and at harvest.

At 30 DAT of rice plant, the highest nitrogen content (2.13%) was recorded where nitrogen was applied 50% as basal and remaining 50% nitrogen was to be applied in two equal split with wheat straw incorporation (T_3) and it was found at par with the treatment having both nitrogen schedule with wheat straw removal T_1 &T_2 and T_6 where nitrogen was to be applied in two equal split with wheat straw burning. There was no significant variation in nitrogen content of rice either in wheat straw removal or burnt with both the schedule of nitrogen. At 60 DAT, the highest nitrogen content (1.40%) recorded in T_6 where nitrogen was applied in two equal split with wheat straw burning was found at par with T_1, T_2 and T_4 and significantly higher than the rest of treatments. It was also observed that the nitrogen applied in two equal split (T_6, T_4 & T_2) gave higher nitrogen content than application of nitrogen in three splits (T_1, T_3 & T_5) with different wheat straw management practices.

Table 8.3: Effect of Wheat Straw Management and Nitrogen Scheduling on Nitrogen Content (%) at Different Intervals and Harvesting

Treatment	30DAT	60DAT	At Harvest		
			Grain	Starw	Biomass
T_1	2.00	1.32	1.22	0.43	0.76
T_2	2.01	1.34	1.24	0.52	0.80
T_3	2.13	1.26	1.37	0.48	0.81
T_4	1.81	1.36	1.42	0.54	0.83
T_5	1.91	1.23	1.25	0.47	0.77
T_6	2.06	1.40	1.27	0.50	0.79
SEm ±	0.05	0.04	0.07	0.03	0.03
CD at 5%	0.15	0.13	NS	NS	NS

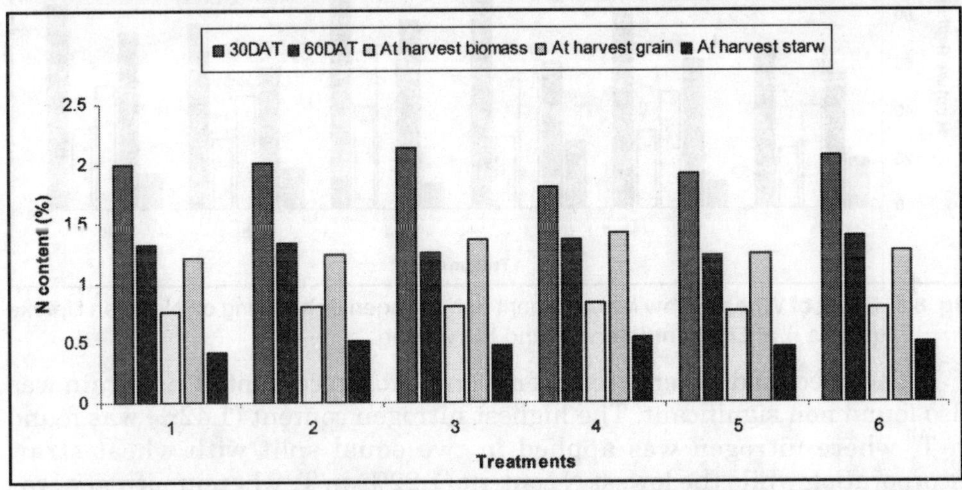

Fig. 8.4 Effect of Wheat Straw Management and Nitrogen Scheduling on Nitrogen Content (%) at Different Intervals and Harvesting

At harvest, the effect of different treatment on nitrogen content of rice biomass was found non significant. It is evident from Table 8.4 and figure 8.5 that the nitrogen content ranged from 0.76 to 0.83 percent. The highest 0.83% nitrogen content was found in T_4 where nitrogen was applied in two equal split with wheat straw incorporation whereas lowest inT_1 where nitrogen was applied in three splits with wheat straw removal.

Table 8.4: Effect of Wheat Straw Management and Nitrogen Scheduling on Nitrogen Uptake (Kg ha⁻¹) at Different Intervals and Harvesting

Treatment	30DAT	60DAT	At Harvest		
			Grain	Starw	Biomass
T_1	21.27	57.90	43.27	25.53	68.80
T_2	11.14	62.96	49.07	32.82	81.89
T_3	27.88	61.71	57.15	33.01	90.17
T_4	10.77	79.34	68.58	43.24	111.82
T_5	17.27	59.39	48.04	29.72	77.76
T_6	15.19	74.52	52.45	34.23	86.69
SEm ±	2.76	2.36	2.44	2.27	3.27
CD at 5%	8.34	7.11	7.38	6.86	9.86

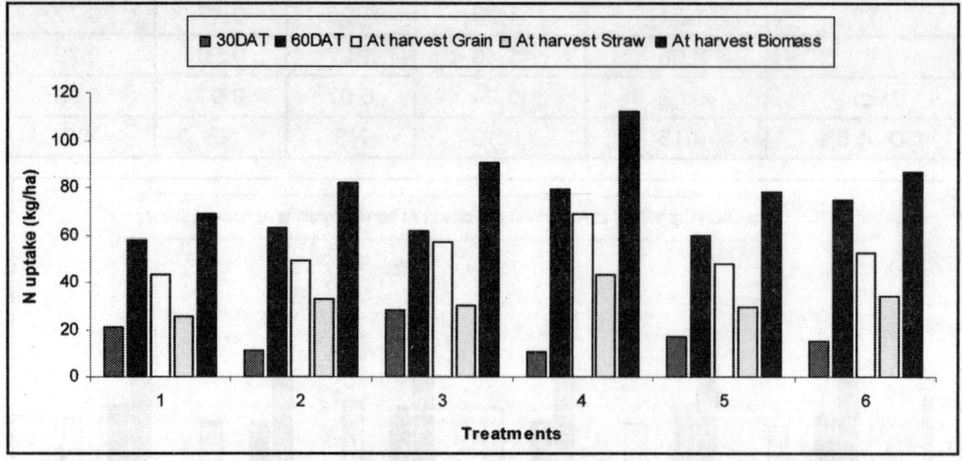

Fig. 8.5 Effect of Wheat Straw Management and Nitrogen Scheduling on Nitrogen Uptake (Kg ha^{-1}) at Different Intervals and Harvesting

The effect of different treatments on nitrogen content of rice grain was also found non significant. The highest nitrogen content (1.42%) was found in T_4 where nitrogen was applied in two equal split with wheat straw incorporation while the lowest N content (1.22%) in T_1 wherein nitrogen was applied in three splits with wheat straw removal. It was also observed that the application of nitrogen in three split gave lower nitrogen content than when nitrogen was applied in two equal split with all wheat straw management practices. The effect of different treatments on nitrogen content in rice straw at harvest was found non significant. The highest nitrogen content (0.54%) was found in T_4 where nitrogen was applied in two equal splits with wheat straw incorporation while lowest in T_1, where nitrogen was applied in three splits with wheat straw removal. It was also found that application of nitrogen in two equal splits gave more nitrogen content than three splits nitrogen schedule in same wheat straw management practice.

Nutrient Uptake by Rice

Data shown in Table 8.5 and Fig. 8.6 clearly indicates that nitrogen uptake increases with crop growth of rice. Nitrogen uptake at different intervals was significantly affected in different wheat straw management. At 30 DAT the highest nitrogen uptake 27.88 kgha^{-1} was found in T_3 where wheat straw was incorporated and 50% nitrogen was applied as basal and it was significantly higher than the all other treatments with exception of $T_{1,}$ whereas rest of the treatments were found statistically at par. The higher nitrogen uptake was recorded where 50% nitrogen was applied as basal while lower uptake in the treatment where application was scheduled in two equal splits. At 60 DAT, the nitrogen uptake 79.34 kg ha^{-1} found in T_4 was at par with T_6 where nitrogen was applied in two equal splits with wheat straw burning. These treatments were significantly higher than rest of the treatments. It is also noticed that the irrespective of wheat straw management practice, application of nitrogen in two equal splits gave higher nitrogen uptake than three split nitrogen application. At harvest of rice, the uptake of nitrogen 111.82 kg ha^{-1} by rice biomass (grain + straw) in T_4 where nitrogen applied in two equal splits with wheat straw incorporation was found significantly higher than the rest of the treatments. T_2 was at par with T_5 and T_6. Within the same wheat straw management practice, application of nitrogen in two equal splits gave significantly higher nitrogen uptake than the three split nitrogen application schedule.

Table 8.5: Effect of Wheat Straw Management and Nitrogen Scheduling on Available NPK (kg ha^{-1})

Treatment	N		P		K	
	60 DAT	After Harvest	60 DAT	After Harvest	60 DAT	After Harvest
T_1	154.20	144.20	15.10	12.90	145.80	141.00
T_2	159.00	147.00	16.30	13.70	152.30	147.60
T_3	167.90	158.07	17.20	15.20	165.20	162.70
T_4	172.75	164.93	18.80	15.80	172.30	169.50
T_5	162.00	147.00	15.60	13.50	156.70	151.00
T_6	166.50	153.00	16.80	14.10	161.40	157.30
Initial value	–	143.80	–	12.70	–	138.20
SEm$\pm$	1.32	1.09	0.32	0.34	2.29	1.87
CD at 5%	3.97	3.29	0.98	1.03	6.92	5.62

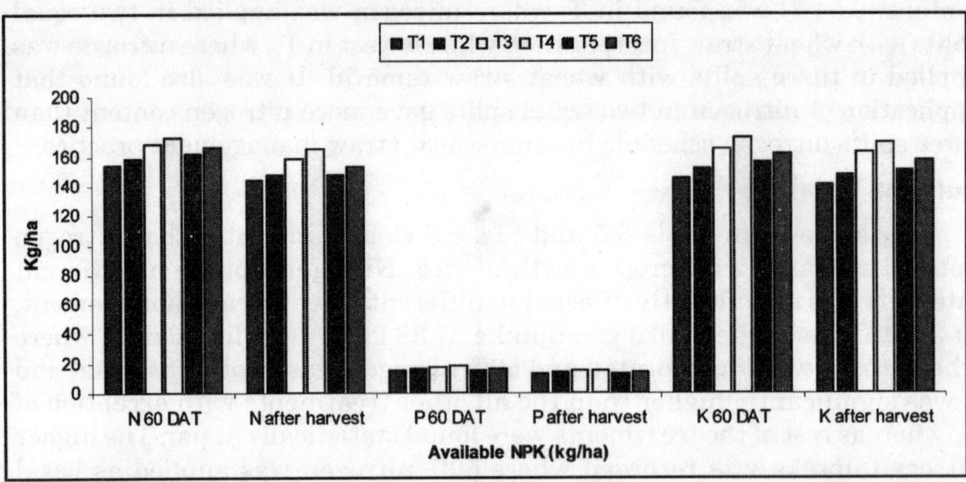

Fig. 8.6: Effect of Wheat Straw Management and Nitrogen Scheduling on Available NPK (kg ha^{-1})

The highest (68.58 kg ha^{-1}) nitrogen uptake by rice grain recorded in T_4 wherein application of nitrogen was made in two equal splits with wheat straw incorporation was significantly higher than rest of the treatments. The T_3 was statistically at par with T_6 and significantly higher than T_1, T_2 & T_5. It was also observed that the treatment having nitrogen application in two equal splits assimilated higher nitrogen than the treatments having nitrogen application in three splits in the same wheat straw management practice.

The highest nitrogen uptake 43.24 kg ha^{-1} by rice straw found in T_4 was significantly higher than the rest of the treatments. T_2 and T_6 assimilated significantly higher nitrogen than T_1 but statistically similar to T_3 and T_6. In general higher nitrogen uptake was recorded wherein application of nitrogen was made in two equal splits than the application of nitrogen in three splits with the same wheat straw management practice. The organic carbon content was influenced by all wheat straw management practices. Increase in organic carbon was in order of wheat straw incorporation followed by wheat straw burning and removal. Similar results were also reported by (Surekha *et al.* 2004 and Kumar *et al* 2004).

3. Effect of wheat straw management and nitrogen scheduling on soil properties

Available Nutrients (Nitrogen)

Data pertaining to the effect of wheat straw management and nitrogen scheduling on the amount of available NPK kg ha^{-1} in the surface soil sample are presented in Table 8.5 and Fig. 8.6.

In comparison to initial available nitrogen value, the estimated value of nitrogen at 60 DAT and after harvest of rice crop increased. A declining trend was notice on available nitrogen after 60 DAT although these values were still higher than initial value.

At 60 DAT of rice, the highest available nitrogen (172.75 kg ha^{-1}) in the soil was found in T_4 where wheat straw was incorporated with application of nitrogen in two equal splits and this was found significantly higher than the other treatments. All the treatments with similar wheat straw management practice varied significantly from each other. It was also observed that available nitrogen was significantly higher wherein nitrogen was applied in two equal splits than the three split application in all wheat straw management practices. In general available nitrogen was higher in wheat straw incorporation followed by burning and removal.

After harvesting of rice crop, the highest available nitrogen 164.93 kg ha^{-1} was found in T_4 where in nitrogen was applied in two equal split with wheat straw incorporation. It was significantly higher than the other treatments. With the exception of T_2 and T_5, the available nitrogen in T_1 was significantly lower than other treatments. Within the wheat straw management practices, the treatment where in nitrogen was applied in two equal split gave higher available nitrogen than application of nitrogen in three split. It was higher in wheat straw incorporation followed by burning and removal.

SUMMARY AND CONCLUSION

The field experiment was "Performance of rice crop as affected by wheat straw management and nitrogen scheduling in rice-wheat cropping system" conducted at Crop Research Centre, Sardar Vallabhbhai Patel University of Agriculture and Technology, Meerut during Kharif 2007. The six treatments in the experiment were tested in randomized block design with four replications.

Plant height of rice increased with the advancement of crop growth up to harvesting of crop. Wheat straw incorporation resulted in taller plant than wheat straw burnt and removal. Taller plants were also found due to application of nitrogen in two equal split instead of three splits. Number of tiller /meter row length increased up to 60 DAT of rice crop and thereafter decreased up to harvest. It was also found that at 30 DAT of rice crop, the number of tillers were more wherein 50 % nitrogen was applied as basal. Thereafter, at 60 DAT and harvest more number of tillers was found wherein nitrogen was applied in two equal split than three split. Wheat straw incorporation produced more number of tillers than wheat straw burning and removal.

Dry matter accumulation of rice at 30 DAT varied from 5.55 to 12.42 q ha^{-1} and it increased with successive growth of rice crop. Wheat straw incorporation with application of nitrogen in three split (50% N as basal and rest in two equal split at maximum tillering and penicle initiation stage) resulted higher dry weight of rice but 60 DAT and at harvest wheat straw incorporation with application of nitrogen in two equal split (50% N at maximum tillering and panicle initiation stage) produced higher dry weight than the wheat straw burnt and removal.

Grain and straw yield of rice in various treatments ranged from 35.50 to 48.26 q ha^{-1} and 60.20 to 79.70 q ha^{-1}, respectively. Wheat straw incorporation with nitrogen application in two equal split produced higher grain and straw yield than the wheat straw burning and removal treatments.

Available nitrogen in surface soil (0-15 cm) ranged from 154.20 to 172.75 kg ha^{-1} at 60 DAT of rice and decreased at harvesting. Available soil nitrogen increased due to incorporation of wheat straw followed by wheat straw burning and removal. Nitrogen scheduling had significant effect on availability of nitrogen as it was also higher when nitrogen was applied in two equal split instead of three split.

From the results obtained in this study it may be concluded that:

1. Incorporation of wheat straw (residue) in rice- wheat cropping system would be a technically sound practice because it recycles considerable amount of the nutrient of the soil.
2. Wheat straw incorporation along with the application of 20% nitrogen 30 day before transplanting and rest in two equal split (50% N at maximum tillering and rest 50% N at PI stage) resulted better crop growth and yield.
3. Wheat straw burning represents a quick disposal method but it results in the loss of nutrients, it should be recycled to the soil. Results of wheat straw burning enhance availability of nutrient in the soil over removal.

REFERENCES

Anonymous (2007-08): *Agriculture Statistics at a Glance.*

Cocharan, W.G. and G.M. Cox (1959): Experimental Design, *Oxford and IBH Publishing Co. Bombay.*

Das, K. Medhi, D. N. and Guha, B. (2002): Recycling Effect of Crop Residue with Chemical Fertilizer on Physico-chemical Properties of Soil and on Wheat Yield. *Annals Agricultural Reserach News Series.* 23(2): 219-222.

Das, K. Medhi, D.N. and Guha, B. (2003): Application of Crop Residues in Combination with Chemical Fertilizers for Sustainable Productivity in Rice (*Oryza sativa*)-wheat (Triticum aestivum). System. *Indian Journalof Agronomy,* 48(1): 8-11.

Gupta P.K., Sahai Shivraj, Singh Nahar, Dixit K.C., Singh D.P., Sharma C., Tiwari M.K., Gupta R.K., Garge S. C. (2004): Residue Burning in Rice-wheat Cropping System Causes Implication. *Current Science,* 87 (12): 1713-1717.

Jackson, M.L. (1973): Soil Chemical Analysis. Prentice Hall Inc. Englewood Cliffs, *New Jersey*, pp: 689.

Kachroo ,D. and Dixit, A.K.(2005): Residue Management Practice Using Fly Ash and Various Crop Residue for Productivity of Rice (*Oryza sativa*) - Wheat (*Tritium aestivum*) Cropping System Under Limited Moisture Condition. *Indian Journal of Agronomy,* 50 (4): 249-252.

Kharub, A.S., Sharma, R.K., Mongia, A.D., Chhokar, R.S. Tripathi, S.C. and Sharma, V.K. (2004): Effect of Rice (*Oryza sativa*) Straw Removal Burning and Incorporation on Soil Properties and Crop Productivity Under Rice-wheat (*Triticum aestvum*) System. *Indian Journal of Agricultural Science,* 76 (6): 255-259.

Kumar, K and Goh, K. M. (2000): Crop Residue and Management Practices: Effect on Soil Quality, Soil Nitrogen Dynamics Crop Yield and Nitrogen Recovery. *Advances in Agronomy*, 68: 197-313.

Kumar, Sandeep, Pandey, D. S. and Rana, N. S.(2004): Effect of Tillage, Rice Residue and Nitrogen Management on Yield of Wheat (*Triticum aestivum*) and Chemical Properties Under Rice *(Oryza sativa*) –Wheat Cropping System. *Indian Journal of Agronomy,* 49 (4): 223-225.

Ma, Liwang, Peterson, Gray, A. Ahuja, Lajpat, R. Sherrod, Lucertia, Shaffer, Marvin, J. and Rojas, Kenneth, W. (1999): Decomposition of Surface Crop Residue in Long Term Studies of Dryland Agrocrocy Systems. *Agronomy Journal,* 91: 401-409.

Mikklesen, D.S. and Rao, D.N. (1976): Effect of Rice Incorporation on Rice Plant Growth and Nutrition. *Agronomy Journal*, 68: 752-755.

Mishra, B., Sharma, P.K. and Bronson, K.F. (2001): Decomposition of Rice Straw and Mineralization of Carbon, Nitrogen, Phosphorus and Potassium in Wheat Field Soil in Western Uttar Pradesh. *Journal of Indian Society of Soil Science*, 49: 419-424.

Rajkhowa, D.J. and Borah, D. (2008): Effect of Eice (*Oryza sativa*) Straw Management on Growth and Yield of Wheat (*Triticum aestivum*) *Indian Journal of Agronomy,* 53(2): 112-115.

Rajput, A.L. and Warsi, A.S. (1991): Conrtribution of Organic Materials to Nitrogen Economy in Rice Production. *Indian Journal Agron*. 36(3) 455-456.

Regar, P.L., Rao, S.S. and Vyas, S.P. (2005): Crop Residue Management for Increased Wheat (*Tricticum aesativum*) Production Under Saline Soils of Arid Fringes. *Indian Journal of Agricultural Science,* 75 (2): 83-86.

Sharma, A.R. and Mitra, B.N. (1990): Response on Rice to Rate and Time of Application of Organic Materials. *Journal of Agricultural Science, Cambridge*, 114: 249-252.

Sharma, A.R. and Mitra, B.N. (1991): Effects of Different Rates of Application of Organic and Nitrogen Fertilizer in Rice Based Cropping System. *Journal of Agricultural Science, Cambridge,* 117: 313-318.

Subbiah, B.V.and Asiji, G. I. (1956): A Rapid Procedure for the Estimation of Available Nitrogen in Soils. *Current Science*, 25: 259-260.

Surekha, K., Reddy, M.; Narayan Rao, K.V. and Cruz, P.C. Sta. (2004): Evaluation of Crop Residue Management Practices for Improving Yields, Nutrient Balance and Soil Health Under Intensive Rice- rice System. *Journal of Indian Society of Soil Science*,. 52 (4):448-453.

Tanaka, A. (1978): Role of Organic Matter. *In Soil and Rice*. International Rice Research Institute (IRRI) Los Bonas, pp: 605-620.

Thakur, T.C. (2003). Crop Residue as Animal Feed. *Addressing Resource Conservation Issues in Rice-Wheat System of South Asia, A Resource Book*. Rice Wheat Consortium for Indo-Genetic Plans (CIMMYT), March 2003.

Thind, A.S. (2003): Don't Burnt that Straw. *The Tribune*, 123: 14.

Walkley, A.J. and Black, I.A. (1934): Estimation of Soil Organic Carbon by Chromic Acid Titration Method. *Soil Science*, 37: 29-38.

Yaduvanshi, N.P.S. and Sharma, D.R. (2007): Use of Wheat Residue and Manures to Entrance Nutrient Availability and Rice-wheat Yields in Sodic Soil Under Sodic Water Irrigation. *Journal of Indian Society of Soil Science*, 55(3): 330-334.

Pages: 179-192

SEED TECHNOLOGY, PLANT GROWTH AND CROPPING SYSTEM

Edited by: Dr. Pawan Kumar Tyagi; Dr. Pawan Kumar 'Bharti'

ISBN: 978-93-5056-738-8

Edition: 2015

Published by: Discovery Publishing House Pvt. Ltd., New Delhi (India)

Role of Biotechnology for Enhancing Productivity of Vegetable Crops

Aakansha Goswami[1] and B. Singh[2]

ABSTRACT

Biotechnology is a rapidly developing area of contemporary science. It can bring new ideas, improved tools and novel approaches to the solution of some persistent, seemingly intractable problems in food crop production. Given the pressing need to enhance and stabilize food production in response to mounting population pressures and increasing poverty, there is an urgent need to explore novel technologies that will break traditional barriers. Agricultural biotechnology is usually defined as any technique that uses living organisms, or substances from those organisms, to make or modify a product, to improve plants, or to develop microorganisms for specific uses". It is comprised of a continuum of technologies, ranging from traditional biotechnology such as plant tissue culture

1 Research Associate, Department of Horticulture, Sardar Vallabhbhai Patel University of Agriculture & Technology, Modipuram, Meerut - 250 110 (UP), India.

2 Associate Professor, Department of Horticulture, Sardar Vallabhbhai Patel University of Agriculture & Technology, Modipuram, Meerut - 250 110 (UP), India.

to modern biotechnology such as genetic engineering of plants and represents the latest front in the ongoing scientific progress of this century.

However, its increasing importance, at least in plant improvement, should not obscure the fact that traditional plant breeding, based on hybridization followed by selection and evaluation of a large population in the field, accounts for over 50% of the global increase in agricultural productivity. Not only have particularly important new genotypes been bred in Asia through the so-called Green Revolution but also, worldwide, new varieties have been bred in response to the changing needs of agriculture.

Key words: Biotechnology, Productivity, Vegetable crop.

INTRODUCTION

Vegetables play a major role in National food security for any nation. Vegetable crops, which occupy 8.0 mh has the production of 129.1 mt. In the last one and half decade, country's vegetable production has almost doubled and gross vegetable productivity of the country by one and half times. Major contribution to vegetables comes from potato, tomato, brinjal, okra, beans and cucurbits. Among the cucurbits besides melon, gourds, cucumber and gherkins are important. Cucurbits like pointed gourd, spine gourd are also gaining importance of commerce, which has much more value for export for its medicinal and therapeutic uses. India needs to produce 225 million tons of vegetable by 2020 with respect to fulfill needs as per population of India by this time. To achieve this target, diversification of vegetable system has adequate agro eco-diversity.

Direct and Indirect Benefits of Agricultural Biotechnology

The long-term beneficial impact of biotechnology on vegetable production will be realized both directly and indirectly. Many of the products will benefit producers and processors by improving the economic efficiency of production. Biotechnology will contribute to environmental quality protection by reducing the frequency of agricultural pesticide applications and by allowing more environmentally compatible materials and alternative methods to be employed (1, 2, 4). For example, plant-based pest resistance in both transgenic and conventionally selected varieties will reduce dependence on broad spectrum pesticides. To enjoy continuing benefits from this approach, producers will need to carefully manage their use of such varieties to prevent or delay the development of resistance in the target organisms. Alternative strategies for reducing herbicide use include introducing color or leaf morphology modifications into seedlings to enhance the use of precision, robotic cultivation.

Biotechnology is also being applied to develop microorganisms for biological control of pests (10,12). For example, an insect-attacking virus (baculovirus) has been modified using rDNA techniques to produce a protein toxin from a gene originally obtained from scorpions. These types of products are much slower to be commercialized as they provoke far more public concern than plant-based pest resistance. On the other hand, DNA-based tools allow the detailed analysis of microbial interactions with plants, with other microbes and with the environment in ways never before possible (8).

Sensory and Nutritional Quality

Biotechnology has been applied to improving the sensory properties and shelf life of vegetables. Some of the innovations, particularly in texture or flavour enhancement, have not been highly publicized as originating from plants modified by methods included in a broad definition of biotechnology. These include carrot, potato, celery, pepper, and melon varieties improved through applications of tissue culture. Public awareness of developments in agricultural biotechnology is primarily associated with genetic engineering, particularly of tomato. In 1994, the first genetically engineered food product reached consumer markets. Calgene's Flavr Savr® tomato received widespread publicity during development and commercial introduction. The targeted benefit, shared by several companies developing new tomato varieties, was to deliver to the market tomatoes with improved flavour and reduced rates of softening or decay.

Flavr Savr® technology utilizes the inhibition of the enzyme polygalacturonase to achieve this goal while DNA Plant Technology Corp. In each case, improved flavour quality was expected from allowing the fruit to remain on the vine until the full, natural sensory potential for acids, sugars, and aromatics was attained. These "vine-ripe" traits, often absent from mass-marketed tomatoes that are picked green, are then realized as ripening continues during distribution. Although production issues have slowed large scale commercialization, these enhanced sensory quality tomatoes were generally well received by consumers in test markets and limited retail distribution. Future products entering the commercial pipeline seek to specifically modify the accumulation and stability of sensory traits by increasing the sweetness and by maintaining the acid balance during maturation and ripening of tomatoes.

Both plant and non-plant genes have been introduced into test tomato varieties to increase sucrose accumulation, increase the conversion of sucrose to fructose in the fruit, and sustain organic acids during ripening of tomatoes. One interesting outcome of the focus on consumer traits by the biotechnology industry has been a resurgence of effort to improve tomato sensory quality by conventional breeding. Capitalizing on the general trend for increased consumption of fruits and vegetables and the value-added traits demonstrated by Flavr Savr® and Endless Summer™, an immediate impact at the marketplace has been enhanced interest and demand among wholesale buyers for higher sensory quality tomatoes. This created an opportunity for seed companies and growers to focus more attention on developing conventionally-bred varieties and handling practices that deliver these value-added traits. The consumer now has greater access to higher quality tomatoes from both field and greenhouse production. Sustained improvements in tomato quality will result from continued expansion of sources of diversity, the precision of gene identification, and the control of trait expression that will be available to breeders.

Low Productivity of the Vegetables in the Country

Productivity of different vegetables is comparatively low as compared to other countries. Nature has bestowed varied agro climatic conditions to our country enabling to grow largest number of vegetables from temperate to humid tropics and from sea level to snow line . The poor productivity of different vegetables in our country is due to several reasons. In developed countries maximum production of vegetables is under controlled conditions and production does not suffer from weather, while in our country under controlled conditions vegetable production till date is negligible. Similarly in the developed countries hybrids occupy maximum area and advanced production and protection technologies have been standardized to realize the maximum productivity in vegetable crops.

While in our country area under hybrid vegetables are 10 per cent of total area under vegetable crops and maximum share in production is contributed by open pollinated varieties with the application of farmers own package of practices and their traditional vision. In recent past, concerted efforts have been made from different angles to boost the vegetable production of the country (17, 18).

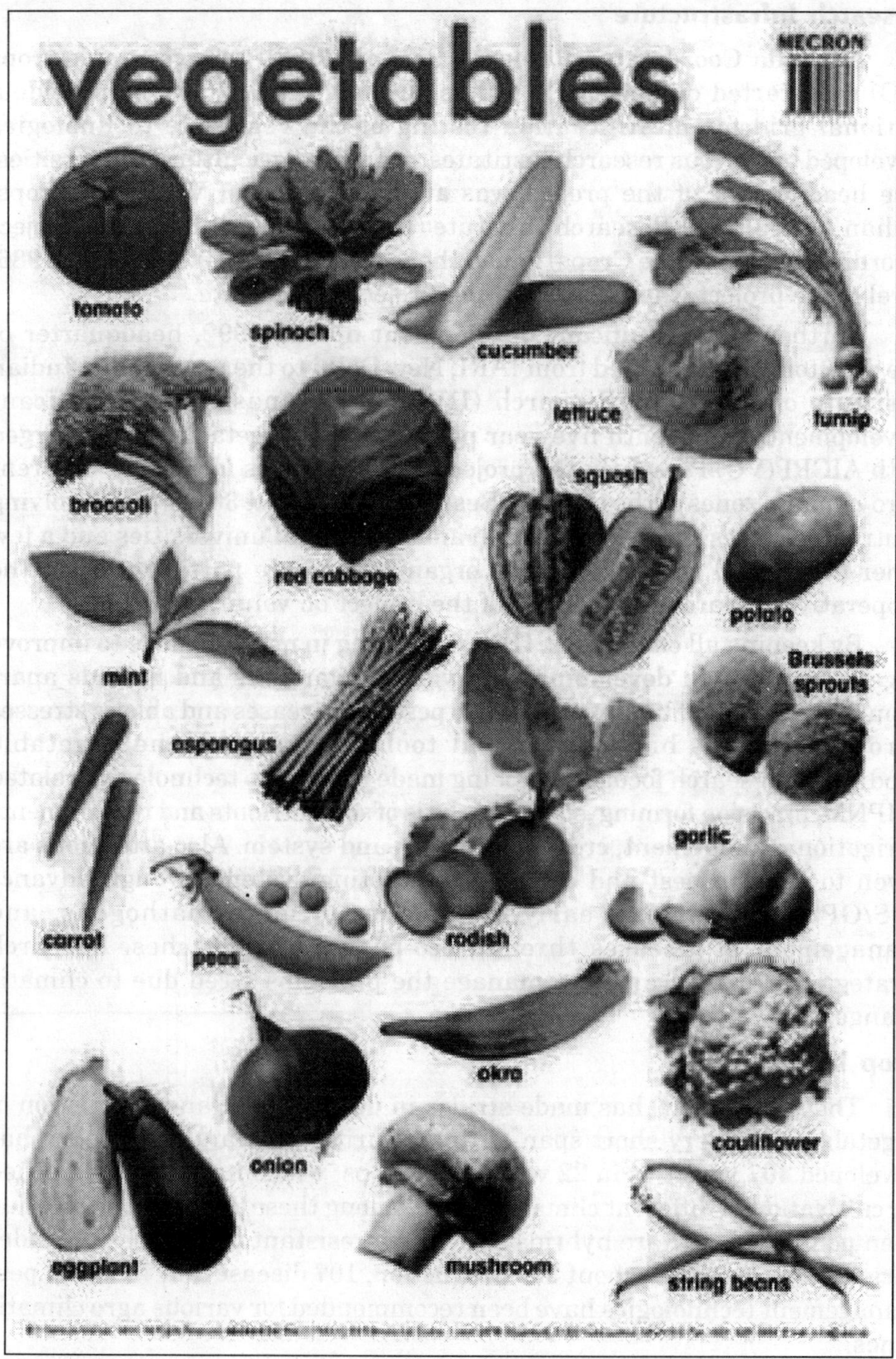
vegetables
NECRON
tomato
spinach
cucumber
lettuce
turnip
broccoli
red cabbage
squash
potato
mint
Brussels sprouts
asparagus
garlic
carrot
peas
radish
okra
cauliflower
onion
eggplant
mushroom
string beans

Research Infrastructure

All India Coordinated Research Project (AICRP) on vegetable crops (VC) was started during the IVth five-year plan in 1970-71, to provide a national grid for multi-location testing of the vegetable technologies developed by various research institutes and state agricultural universities. The headquarter of the project was at the Division of Vegetable Crops, Indian Agricultural Research Institute (IARI), New Delhi and the Project Coordinator (Vegetable Crops) joined the project in July 1971. During 1986, level of the project was elevated to the Project Directorate.

Further, in a significant development during 1992, headquarter of the directorate was shifted from IARI, New Delhi to the present day Indian Institute of Vegetable Research (IIVR) at Varanasi. In a significant development, in eleventh five-year plan the NSP(Vegetables) was merged with AICRP(VC).Presently the project has 29 centres located in different agro-climatic zones of the country. Besides these, about 30 centres involving central institutes, state agricultural and traditional universities and a few other public and private research organizations are participating in the cooperative research programme of the project on voluntary basis.

By keeping all challenges, IIVR is working in mission mode to improve vegetables through developing high yielding varieties and hybrids apart from development of lines resistance to pest and diseases and abiotic stresses through advance biotechnological tools. To improve the vegetable production, research focuses are being made to develop technologies related to IPNM, precision forming ,status analysis of soil nutrients and requirements ,irrigation management, cropping pattern and system. Also attentions are given to develop pest and diseases forecasting system through advance GIS/GPS technologies, early diagnostics of major pathogens, and management of diseases through eco-friendly approaches. Research strategies are also framed to manage the problems faced due to climatic changes.

Crop Improvement

The AICRP (VC) has made strides in development and production of vegetables in a very short span of time. During 39 years, the project has developed 407 varieties in 22 vegetables crops, which have been identified for cultivation in different climatic zones. Among these 246 are high yielding open pollinated, 107 are hybrids and 43 are resistant to diseases. Besides varietal improvement, about 330 production, 107 disease and 70 insect pest management technologies have been recommended for various agro climatic zones.

Table 9.1: High Yielding Open Pollinated Varieties, Hybrids and Varieties Resistant to Diseases of Vegetable Crops

Crop	OP Varieties	Hybrid/Synthetic	Resistant to Diseases	Total
Tomato	37	28	8	73
Brinjal	49	29	7	85
Chilli	22	13	–	35
Garden Pea	25	–	11	36
Cowpea	11	–	–	11
French Bean	10	–	–	10
Dolichos	4	–	–	4
Okra	–	10	14	24
Onion	20	–	–	20
Garlic	10	–	–	10
Cauliflower	14	7	–	21
Cabbage	1	8	–	9
Carrot	3	1	–	4
Muskmelon	9	2	3	14
Water melon	4	1	–	5
Bitter gourd	4	3	–	7
Pumpkin	7	–	–	7
Cucumber	3	3	–	6
Ridge gourd	3	2	–	5
Bottle gourd	7	4	–	11
Spongo gourd	6	–	–	6
Ash gourd	4	–	–	4
Total	**253**	**111**	**43**	**407**

Biotic Stress

Vegetables are highly susceptible to number of diseases. Attempts have been made to develop disease resistant varieties in important vegetable crops. The progress in the development of insect resistance is very limited and so far there are no commercially developed insect resistant varieties. However, the potential sources of resistance of important insect-pests have been identified. Attempts are in progress to transfer such resistance in commercial varieties, Lycopersicon hirsutum F. glabratum is resistant to fruit borer, whitefly and leaf minor. Resistance to shoot and fruit borer in brinjal has been found in Solanum Khasianum and to jassids in Manari

Gota. Cucumis calosus has been identified as a source of resistance to fruitfly in muskmelon. So far, 34 disease resistant varieties in 10 vegetable crops have been identified by AICRP. Some of the promising varieties are mentioned in the table 9.2.

Table 9.2: Vegetable Varieties Resistant/Tolerant to Diseases

Crop	Disease	Variety
Tomato	Bacterial wilt	BT-1, Arka Nidhi, Arka Keshav, Arka Neelkant, Arka Anand, Pusa Purple Cluster
		LE-415
	Verticillium wilt	Pant Bahar
Brinjal	Bacterial wilt	BB-7, 44 & 64, BWR-12
		Pant Rituraj
	Phomopsis blight	Pusa Bhairav
		Pant Samart, Hisar Shyamal
Cabbage	Black rot	Pusa Mukta
		Pusa Shubra
Okra	YVMV	Arka Anamika
		Punjab Padmini
		AB-1
		A_3-2
Cucumber	Powdery mildew	Poinsett
	Downy mildew	-do-
Pea	Powdery mildew	Azad P-2, 4 & 5

Abiotic Stress

Vegetable crops are sensitive to a number of abiotic stress specially temp., humidity, drought and frost etc. Some of the promising resistant varieties are mention here in table 9.3.

Table 9.3: Vegetable Varieties Tolerant to High & Low Temp

Crop	Stress	Variety
Tomato	Low temp.	Pusa Sheetal
	High temp	Pusa Hybrid-1, HS-1
Cauliflower	High temp.	Pusa Early Synthetic
Onion	High temp.& humidity	N-53
Radish	High temp.	Pusa Chetki
	Low temp.	Pusa Deshi
Carrot	Low temp.	Pusa meghali

Hybrids for Present Scenario

When two parents of different genome are crossed, the resulting F_1 progeny shows superiority over its parents. This superiority of F_1 progeny is called hybrid vigour. In vegetables such as tomato, brinjal, sweet pepper, chillies, cabbage, cauliflower, carrot and watermelon hybrids have been developed (19, 20). These hybrids exhibited special features, which gives the following advantages.

1. They posses higher yield potential compared to best variety under cultivation.
2. Mostly the vegetable hybrids are early in nature & fetch high price in the market.
3. The hybrids are also stable in performance.
4. The hybrids are uniform in size.
5. Their quality and appearance are better than the varieties.
6. Better product quality such high TSS in tomato and melons, tenderness in okra.
7. Over and above the hybrids promote the seed industry.

Techniques for Hybrid Seed Production in Vegetables

1. In self pollinated vegetables:
   (a) Use of male sterility
   (b) Manually
   (c) Through vegetative propagation
2. Cross pollinated vegetables:
   (a) Bi-sexual vegetables
   (b) Uni-sexual vegetables
   (c) Monoecy
   (d) Dioecy
3. Micro-propagation
   (a) Tissue culture
   (b) Embryo culture
   (c) Protoplast Fusion Technology

PRODUCTION TECHNOLOGY

The new aspects of vegetable production are described in brief under following heads.

Nursery management: Nursery is the place where young seedlings are raised and nurtured before planting them in to the main field. For raising good crop, it is utmost essential that seedlings should be healthy, vigorous and disease free. Raising the nursery under protected conditions and sowing the individual seed of hybrid in potting plug with artificial culture media is well-established practice in developed countries. However, in our country the most of the nurseries are raised under open conditions and it is one of the main reasons of set back to development of hybrid programme during rainy seasons in the Northern India. Therefore, we have to standardize the nursery raising practice on scientific lines.

Soil Solarization: If anyhow raising nursery is not possible under controlled conditions and there is lack of other facilities like potting plugs, rooting media etc. We need to give proper attention to the selection of site and treatment of seed and nursery soil. Now a days soil solarization has been proved as cheapest and eco-friendly approach for soil disinfection of nursery beds. These are the simple practice, to reduce the population of soil borne pathogens, nematodes, pests and weeds to a substantial level.

Drip Irrigation in Vegetables: Under drip system, water enters the soil and move into the root zones through the combined forces of gravity and capillary action. Thus, the plants withdrawal of moisture from the soils is replenished almost immediately creating a constant and more favorable root zone environment. Consequently the plant does not suffer from stress or shock. This enhances plant growth making it more even, vigorous and optimum.

Micronutrient for vegetable crops: In Vegetables production the micronutrients like Boran, Zinc, Molybdenum and Iron play a very important role.

Fertigation: Fertigation means supplying both water and fertilizer to grow crops through drip irrigation. Fertigation thorough tested on a large number of horticultural crops is ideally suited for hi-tech horticulture production systems. Besides ensuring efficient delivery of two important inputs, it also exploits the synergism of their simultaneous availability to plants.

Plastic Mulching: Covering of soil around the root zone of plant with a plastic film is called plastic mulching. It is an effective practice to restrict weed growth, conserve moisture and reduce the effect of soil borne diseases through soil solarization. Black plastic prevents the germination and growth of weed seeds in contrast to clear plastic. It absorbs more sun energy and retains higher heat underneath the plastic.

Organic Farming: Organic farming is a holistic production management, which promotes and enhances agro eco system health including bio diversity, biological cycles and soil biological activities. International Federation of Organic Agriculture Movement (IFOAM) is an association, which provides help to the farmers in production and certification of organic produce. The nutrient needs are indeed staggering. These are dictated by unrelenting population pressure and the need to procure more per unit land, which is already depleted. The disproportionate use of fertilizer has widened soil imbalance in terms of NPK ratio. A nationwide assessment of nutrient efficiency reveals that:

1. Nitrogen deficiency is universal and will continue to be so.
2. Nearly, 49, 20 and 47 per cent of Indian soils are deficient in phosphorus, potassium and zinc respectively.
3. Potassium deficiency becomes most limiting factor for crop production and iron management.

Management boron and sulphar will also affect the productivity in majority of the Indian soils. Besides it is also estimated that every year nearly 8 million tones of nutrients are depleted. Fortunately, with the vast resources available it should be possible to meet the known nutrient needs through an integrated use of fertilizers, bulky organic, crop residues, human and industrial wastes, compost and bio-fertilizers. Therefore, it is essential that the organic movement is also given a focused attention, through integration of efforts made of scientific line to achieve sustainable production.

Biofertilizers-Vermiculture: Biofertilizers offer an economically attractive and ecologically sound means reducing external inputs and improving the quality and quantity of internal resources. These are inputs containing micro-organisms, which are capable of mobilizing nutrient from non-usable form to usable form through biological processes. They are less expensive, eco-friendly and sustainable. Earthworms have tremendous ability to compost all biodegradable materials. Wastes subjected to earthworm consumption decompose 2-5 times faster than inconventional composting.

Protected cultivation: In our country different climatic conditions in various regions, protected conditions for vegetable production are created locally by using different types of structures. These structures are designed as per climatic requirement of the area for different conditions. Plant protection structures are designed on the basis of temperature, humidity, wind velocity and soil condition etc. Greenhouse, low tunnels, shading net houses, anti-hail nets, bird protection nets, trench (pit type green house), mulch, wind break floating crop cover etc. are some of the common plant protection structures used for raising vegetable crops or their nurseries. A green house is generally covered with a transparent material.

Integrated pests management: In vegetables more than 40% yield loss is caused due to pest attack. As a result, growers face heavy loss due to degradation of quality and marketability. Unlike cereals, the green pods and leaves are mostly used as vegetables, which are more prone to retain the pesticide residue. In recent past, through the world efforts have been made to control the vegetable pest by use of natural enemies, parasite predators besides host specific insect viruses and other entomo-pathogenic microorganisms and to a considerable extent success has been achieved.

Post Harvest Management of Vegetable Crops: Green vegetables due to high moisture content are inherently more liable to deteriorate especially under tropical conditions such as ours. Owing to lack of production, planning and climatic factors, gluts occur frequently leading to distress sale, poor prices to growers and wastage. The post harvest losses estimated to about 20-40 per cent of the total fruit and vegetable production go as waste, costing more than Rs. 30,000 million annually. Thus income of the growers and per capita availability of produce come down. Research in post harvest should probe into screening of vegetable varieties and hybrids for prolonged shelf life and processing character. Standardization of different storage systems including controlled atmosphere system for different vegetable crops, improvement of packaging and transportation system suited to Indian conditions harnessing solar energy for drying as well as storage utilization of wastes for the development of economically viable products and initiating post harvest research specific to improving export potential.

Transgenic for new generation: China was the first country to commercialize transgenic in the early 1990s with the introduction of virus resistant tobacco, which was later followed by a virus resistant tomato. Use of transgenic crops is increasing fast around the world. There were also significant changes in the absolute and relative area occupied by the 7 transgenic crops in 1996 and 1997. Transgenic soybean ranked first in 1997. Among all the vegetables crops the Tomato and Potato crops were used transgenic seeds (3, 2, 9). In India, private companies Mahyco and PGS are conducting field trials on brinjal resistant to fruit and shoot borer and on Cabbage resistant to Diamond back moth.

CONCLUSION

Vegetable production of our country has witnessed commendable progress in past 3 decades. Progress has been made in all respects in vegetable improvement, production and protection technologies. By making the concerted efforts on research and development, we have been able to break the several production barriers. Besides these, there are several other problems from production to post harvest and processing. We have to work hard to tackle these challenges to boost the vegetable production of the country to meet the needs of our growing population and make India more prosperous and healthy nation.

REFERENCES

1. Bradford, K.J. and J.M. Alston. 2004. Diversity of Horticultural Biotech Crops Contributes to Market Hurdles. Calif. Agric. 58(2): 84-85.

2. Clark, D., H. Klee and A. Dandekar. 2004. Despite Benefits, Commercialization of Transgenic Horticultural Crops Lags. Calif. Agric. 58(2): 89-98.

3. European Society for New Methods in Agricultural Research XXXIX Annual Meeting 2009, ESNA Conference: Genomics and Proteomics in Plant and Animal Breeding, Brno, Czech Republic, p. 52.
4. FAO (Food and Agriculture Organization of the United Nations) (2000). Electronic Forum on Biotechnology in Food and Agriculture: Summary of Conference 5 (A Synopsis of the Main Arguments and Concerns Discussed), http://www.fao.org/biotech/logs/c5sum.htm.
5. FAO (Food and Agriculture Organization of the United Nations) (2001a). Ethical Issues in Food and Agriculture. FAO Ethics Series, 1. FAO, Rome, ftp://ftp.fao.org/docrep/fao/003/X9601e/X9601e00.pdf.
6. Gonsalves, D. 2004. Virus-resistant Transgenic Papaya helps Save Hawaiian Industry. Calif. Agric. 58(2): 92-93.
7. Graff, G.D., B.D. Wright, A.B. Bennett and D. Zilberman. 2004. Access to Intellectual Property is a Major Obstacle to Developing Transgenic Horticultural Crops. Calif. Agric. 58(2): 120-126.
8. Huang, J. and S. Rozelle. 2004. China Aggressively Pursuing Horticulture and Plant Biotechnology. Calif. Agric. 58(2): 112-113.
9. Jayaraman K: Bt Brinjal Splits Indian Cabinet. Nat Biotechnol 2010, 28: 296.
10. James, J.S. 2004. Consumer Knowledge and Acceptance of Agricultural Biotechnology Vary. Calif. Agric. 58(2): 99-105.
11. Meléndez-Ortiz, R., Gueye, M.K., Chamay M. (2007): Biotechnology: Eastern African Perspectives on Sustainable Development and Trade Policy, ICTSD and ATPS, 106 pp.
12. Meléndez-Ortiz, R., Sánchez, V. (2005): Trading in Genes: Development Perspectives on Biotechnology, Trade and Sustainability, ICTSD and Earthscan, London, 294 pp.
13. McDougall P: The Cost and Time Involved in the Discovery, Development and Authorization of a New Plant Biotechnology Derived Trait. A Consultancy Study for Crop Life International; Midlothian, Scotland, September: 2011.
14. Miller JK, Herman EM, Jahn M, Bradford KJ: Strategic Research, Education and Policy Goals for Seed Science and Crop Improvement. Plant Sci 2010, 179: 645-652.
15. Rausser, G. and H. Ameden. 2004. Public-private Partnerships Needed in Horticultural Research and Development. Calif. Agric. 58(2): 116-119.
16. Redenbaugh, K. and A. McHughen. 2004. Regulatory Challenges Reduce Opportunities for Horticultural Biotechnology. Calif. Agric. 58(2):106-115.
17. Spielman DJ, Hartwich F, von Grebmer K: Public-private Partnerships in International Research. International Food Policy Research Institute Research Brief No. 9. 2007.
18. Sargsyan, G.J., Vardanyan, I.V., Kirakosyan, D.S., Harutyunyan Z.E. (2008): Application of Biotechnological Methods for Obtaining Initial Material in Selection of Vegetable Crops, International Conference: State-of the-Art Biotechnology in Armenia & ISTC Contribution, Armenia, pp. 236-237.

19. Sargsyan, G.J., Vardanyan, I.V., Kirakosyan, D.S., Harutyunyan Z.E. (2007): Practical Application of *in vitro* Culture in Selection of Vegetable Crops, The Fourth Moscow International Congress: Biotechnology: State of the Art and Prospects of Development, Moscow, Russia, Part 1, p. 315.
20. Sonnino, A., Dhlamini Z., Santucci F.M., Warren P. (2009): Socio-Economic Impacts of Non-Transgenic Biotechnologies in Developing Countries, FAO, Rome, 75 pp.

Index

T

****